Theoretical and Applied Ethics

Hannes Nykänen,
Ole Preben Riis,
Jörg Zeller, eds.

AALBORG UNIVERSITY PRESS

Theoretical and Applied Ethics
Hannes Nykänen, Ole Preben Riis, Jörg Zeller, Eds.

Fifth volume in the series: Applied Philosophy / Anvendt Filosofi
1. edition
© Aalborg University Press, 2013

Painting on frontcover: Jörg Zeller
Layout of cover: akila v/ Kirsten Bach Larsen
Layout: akila v/ Kirsten Bach Larsen

Printed at AKA-PRINT 2013
ISBN: 978-87-7112-116-2
ISSN 2245-313X
Published by:
Aalborg University Press
Skjernvej 4A, 2nd floor
DK – 9220 Aalborg Ø
Phone: +4599407140
aauf@forlag.aau.dk
forlag.aau.dk

This book is published with financial support from Department of Learning and Philosophy, Aalborg University.

All rights reserved. No part of this book may be reprinted or reproduced or utilized in any form or by any electronic, mechanical, or other means, now known or hereafter invented, including photocopying and recording, or in any information storage or retrieval system, without permission in writing from the publishers, except for reviews and short excerpts in scholarly publications.

Contents

Hannes Nykänen, Ole Preben Riis, Jörg Zeller
   Introduction   5

Tito Magri
   First persons   13

Finn Arler
   A five-step model for ethically informed decision-making   39

Mogens Pahuus
   Aspects of morality   65

Michael Kühler
   The phenomenological trouble with moral dilemmas   73

Ole Riis
   Ethical theory and popular ethics   95

Jörg Zeller
   The missing link between theoretical and applied ethics   115

Anne Gerdes
   Ethical Issues in Human Robot interaction   125

Lennart Nørreklit
   Applied ethics and practice ontology   143

Brenda Almond
   Finding a way in tomorrow's world   173

Terje Mesel
   Adverse events as moral challenges in health care   189
Hannes Nykänen
   Morals   205
Patrik Kjærsdam Telléus
   On teaching applied ethics   221
Thessa Jensen
   Designing for relationship   241
Veselin Mitrović
   The human enhancement   257

List of authors   275

Hannes Nykänen, Ole Preben Riis, Jörg Zeller

Introduction
Theoretical and/or applied ethics?

An anthology that presents articles under the title *Theoretical and Applied Ethics* questions – at least indirectly – the difference and correlation between theories of what ethics is or is about, and the application of what it is or is about. Perhaps it even challenges the idea that there exists such a difference. All ethics could be an application of something that has no theoretical foundation – or perhaps it has another kind of foundation? Ethics could ultimately also be a theory about something that is altogether inapplicable. Let's take a brief historical look at the theory-application problem of what we are willing to understand by 'ethics'. Let's begin with a radical Wittgenstein and go back to a deliberate Kant.

Wittgenstein says in *A Lecture on Ethics*:

> …if a man could write a book on Ethics, this book would, with an explosion, destroy all the other books in the world. Our words used as we use them in science, are vessels capable only of containing and conveying meaning and sense, natural meaning and sense. Ethics, if it is anything, is supernatural and our words will only express facts (Wittgenstein, 1993, p. 40).

If we understand facts as things in actual relation to other things, then things can be something only relatively. What we "really" can know about things is what they are or mean in relation to other things. Our knowledge, our theories are relative, not absolute. Things in themselves, independent of whatever else, something that is the case independently

Introduction. Theoretical and/or applied ethics?

of whatever else is the case, i.e., something absolute, can't really be the case because it can't really be related or referred or applied to something else. This implies a dilemma: if ethics is about something absolute – something that is good or valuable in itself – then ethics can't be a science or a theory in the usual sense; theoretical ethics would be impossible, and only applied ethics would be possible. If, on the other hand, ethics is not absolute, it is about something relative – something good or valuable in relation to something else. In the latter case, ethics is possible as a science and theory – for instance about what people under particular circumstances are prepared to regard as good or valuable relative to certain ends. Ethics could then be a part of psychological or sociological studies. In this case, ethics would, according to a famous flock of philosophers, miss the point of what ethics is about intrinsically – the point of the difference between "be" and "ought," "relative" and "absolute." Wittgenstein maintains that ethics is about something supernatural. He concludes his lecture:

> Ethics so far as it springs from the desire to say something about the ultimate meaning of life, the absolute good, the absolute valuable, can be no science. But it is a document of a tendency in the human mind which I personally cannot help respecting deeply and I would not for my life ridicule it (Wittgenstein, 1993, p. 44).

Being a "tendency in the human mind" is, however, not a very clear and satisfying conceptualization of what we should understand by 'ethics'. Let's therefore have a look at the great philosopher Kant to learn how he handles the theory-application dilemma in ethics. As is well known, ethics is, according to Kant, an achievement of reason in its application to practical issues. Reason is the faculty of justification or constitution of something. Practical reason justifies or constitutes, then, apparently actions or practices. The 'or' is decisive here. In contrast to Wittgenstein – in his middle period (1929) between *Tractatus* and *Philosophical Investigations* – ethics is for Kant not the answer to questions such as what is good or valuable in itself, but is the answer to questions about how to act to reach a (desirable) end. To justify one's action means to reach a desirable end by performing that action. The use of 'absolute' and 'relative' is not of absolute or relative being but how to do something with regard to something else or to do it for its own sake. In *Groundwork of the Metaphysics of Morals* Kant 1785 differentiates between three different kinds of practice: craft, wisdom, and morality (or, as I prefer to call it, 'mentality'). The ends of craftsmanship and wisdom are relative: goods and happiness. The end of morality is absolute: to act in a – for every rational being – (necessarily) desirable way – namely, in a way that is capable of constituting a general groundwork for every morally good or right action and practice. We could also say that it is to act in the right spirit of action, the right mentality or, in Greek, to act in a *eudemonian* way. The core of ethics is thus not a theory about what is ethical but a system of rules for how to act ethically. This difference between 'what' and 'how' reminds us again of the difference between 'be' and 'ought'. Some of us (editors) are prone to think the difference in question resembles the difference between 'theory' and 'logic'. Here, 'logic' is understood as the way to think or do something, and 'theory' is understood as the description (conceptualization) or explanation (justification) of something.

In any case, we can see that philosophical ethics finds itself in a curious, permanent tension between theoretical and practical perspectives. Theoretical approaches tend in their abstractness to lose contact with the particular problems that constitute the very meaning of 'moral problem' while approaches that are too particularistic or applied approaches tend to underplay the importance of the fact that it was precisely in a particular situation where the moral problem with its quest for a more perspicuous outlook arose. This curious state of affairs should remind us of the fact that philosophers have not been able to give satisfying accounts either of the theoretical or practical aspects of moral understanding. Whether moral issues are viewed from a purely formal or from an applied point of view, the account will in other words be in some sense flawed; nor will the mere combination of two problematic points of view settle the issue. Contemporary moral philosophy has split into an impenetrable jungle of various approaches, some more theoretical and others more applied. With an eye to the above-mentioned tension between the theoretical and the applied perspectives, it seems reasonable not to settle on any overly one-sided account of morality, except perhaps in order to explore a given perspective. It thus seems that in order not to lose oneself in one way or the other, it is important to stay in contact with both poles of moral inquiry.

Introduction. Theoretical and/or applied ethics?

Given the statements made previously, it might be useful to note that the very notions of theory and application can be misleading. When we speak about moral theory, we seem to take for granted that the notion makes sense, that there is such a thing as moral theory. Similarly, applied ethics gives one the feeling that there is a something that can be applied without too many problems. It could, of course, be said that we have indeed an ethics that we apply in our everyday lives and that theoretical ethics is an attempt to establish universally valid features in our everyday ethics. But is it really the case that moral acting is about applying a certain set of moral beliefs? If so, would moral reasoning have to be about reflecting on what set of beliefs to apply?

Tito Magri asks how one should understand the moral self that is presupposed by ethical reflection. If there is no coherent description of the first-person 'I' of moral agency, this will raise questions about who is supposed to act morally. Magri discusses two different but central ways of accounting for what it is to be a person. Both accounts are in his view necessarily valid in certain ways, but both are also insufficient for an unambiguous account of personhood. Moreover, he argues that it is impossible to unite the accounts into a coherent whole: "The neglect of this duality and the attempts to frame a deeply unitary conception of personhood and of the first person is perhaps an important source of the difficulties which affect both metaphysics and ethics with regard to their understanding and treatment of persons and personal viewpoints".

Finn Arler's article is based on considerations of decisions about environmental policies, where complex factors have to be taken into account and where responsibility is extended beyond the current audience. Arler approaches ethical theories pragmatically and eclectically, as he combines several theories in order to formulate a five-step model that can assist in guiding ethical decisions in practice.

Mogens Pahuus introduces a distinction among four types of moral thinking, each of which corresponds to one of the four main types of normative ethics: utilitarianism, deontological ethics, recognition-ethics, and the ethics of caring. Each type of moral reasoning has its own concepts connected to the kind of relationship that is established in the respective type of reasoning: "When you deal with a certain aspect of action you have to use certain ethical concepts – and therefore a certain ethical theory becomes interesting or adequate" Pahuus believes that the problem with ethical theories is that they usually "have a tendency to establish one universal principle" without realising that in reality all of the four types of reasoning are needed in order to adequately address moral problems

Michael Kühler bases his article on "the view that theoretical ethics and applied ethics should be seen as mutually influential, i.e., that their plausible respective assumptions and conceptions should be harmonized or mutually incorporated in order to reach a coherent overall position". This means especially that so-called "applied worries" raise the question of "whether the familiar rejection of the possibility of 'real' moral dilemmas, featuring prominently in theoretical ethics, really leaves enough conceptual room to incorporate the applied worry of so-called emotional moral remainders, i.e., regret or guilt feelings on the agent's part".

Ole Riis discusses the relationship between popular and theoretical ethics. More particularly, he asks himself whether people's views on different ethical issues might challenge theoretical ethics. Riis reflects on a number of surveys made in the Nordic countries about attitudes to moral issues like abortion, tax-fraud, and moral decision-making. According to Riis, they show that "most people are quite reflexive on ethical problems" and that this fact is relevant for ethical theory. Considering these results could open a way for ethical theory to be more concrete while ethical theory could, in its turn, formulate criticism that is relevant to popular ways of thinking about ethics.

Jörg Zeller's contribution challenges the classic dichotomy between ethical theory and applied ethics. According to Zeller, the ethical challenge concerns how humans can integrate all dimensions of their consciousness and thereby make the factual world a valuable and meaningful reality. Such an integration is expressed by human agency that connects thinking and doing and thereby the issues of free will and responsibility. By focusing on agency, Zeller posits himself closer to Aristotelian phronesis than to Kantian practical reason.

Technological innovation has been a constant source of new ethical dilemmas. Thus, the development of robots with a capacity for intelligent behavior raises ethical questions. Human interaction with such robots does not call for a basic commitment, as robots are without an independent consciousness. It is, however, possible to project a future development, where robots can be installed with a kind of conscious mind. This possibility raises the most fundamental ethical challenge, namely that of a God-like responsibility. This intriguing question is addressed in Anne Gerdes' article.

Introduction. Theoretical and/or applied ethics?

According to Lennart Nørreklit, ethics, if not related to our activities and practice, is only speculation, and thus irrelevant. The only way to connect it to practice, to the things that exist and to what we do, is through ontology. This means that "through ontology, one can apply it." To make ethics relevant and applicable we need guidelines or ontological interpretations to connect it to the practical world. To make these guidelines understandable, ethics needs to be combined also with epistemology.

Brenda Almond addresses some of the fundamental questions concerning applied ethics, namely its methods and stance among ethical theories. She traces important strands of applied ethics in many instances of philosophical ethics from the oldest to the newest. From her perspective on applied ethics as an ethics that "approaches individual issues in their own right," she finds Knud Løgstrup's ethics particularly interesting. Nevertheless, applied ethics cannot, according to Almond, ignore problems that are solely of a general nature; in addressing these problems it must "employ what is sometimes called moral casuistry," that is, find answers to problems of conscience.

The thesis of Terje Mesel's article is that a contextual clarification of the concepts of guilt, shame, and responsibility can facilitate for better coping. First, it is necessary to make a clear distinction between responsibility and guilt. Being responsible implies moral lucidity and a willingness to make clear one's reflection and action in the given situation. However, it does not imply guilt. Second, the question of guilt is complex, especially in health care where so many factors are outside our control. This fact, however, does not diminish our responsibility for what is outside our control. Thirdly, other-oriented feelings of guilt provide a much better ethical bridging than self-oriented feelings of shame. Thus, it is important both to recognize and facilitate for feelings of guilt rather than feelings of shame.

The aim of Hannes Nykänen's article "is to show some aspects of the way ... moral difficulties and violations are repressions." More specifically, they are repressions of what Nykänen thinks to be the fundamental moral relationship, i.e., the I-you relationship. Difficulties with this relationship urge "us to create a kind of secondary morality that I call collective morality or, depending on the context, collective pressure, collective norms or simply collectivity". The basic moral relationship is, according to Nykänen, "constituted by conscience which is a fundamental engagement between human beings." Instead of engagement,

Nykänen says that "one should perhaps speak about sympathy or, better yet, love."

Patrik Kjærsdam Telléus' article addresses "the relationship between ethics as a philosophical or theoretical discipline, on the one hand, and ethics as an applied or normative form of action and reasoning, on the other, in the context of teaching practices". Telléus discusses the role of ethical theories in courses on applied ethics to, for example, medical school students. According to Telléus, "a controversy between a theoretical approach and an applied approach can be summed up in the question of whether to teach ethical theories in applied ethics courses." He claims "that the conditional settings, with the actual lecturer as a key figure, constitute the balance between ... 'moral notions' and 'moral phenomena' necessary to generate the intended moral reasoning."

New social media is a digital way of achieving relationships among people where proximity and presence are perceived, even with fictional characters. As a starting point for clarifying the ethical challenges involved, Thessa Jensen refers to a Danish theologian, K.E. Løgstrup. His ethical theory about the "sovereign expressions of life" – mercy, honesty, trust, nonviolence – is based on the fundamental social life of human beings. Thereby, Jensen can illuminate the variety of relationships mediated by new social media and their characteristic ethical challenges.

According to Veselin Mitrovic, "Transhumanism justifies the use of the new enhancement technologies, not just for the sake of treatment and disease control, but – more strongly – for the sake of enhancing, improving human capacities and traits, and transference from humanist to post-humanist society". Conversely, "bioconservatives express their opposition regarding these ways of changing human beings." There is also a 'middle approach', amounting to the view "that the constant growth of technology renders the bioconservative position untenable, because once the research is initiated in countries of market economy, and once their effects, like the improvement of life quality and greater life expectancy, are manifested, it cannot easily be obstructed any more"

References

Kant, I. 1785. Grundlegung der Metaphysik der Sitten, in: *Moralische Schriften von Immanuel Kant*, Leipzig 1920: Inselverlag, p. 11-101.

Wittgenstein, L. 1929. A Lecture on Ethics, in: Klagge J. and Nordmann A., eds. 1993, *Ludwig Wittgenstein, Philosophical Occasions, 1912-1951*; Indianapolis: Hacket Publishing Company, p. 36-44.

Tito Magri

First persons

Persons and personal identity, according to our different conceptions of them, play an all-important role in practical philosophy: in connection to normative issues, think of the debate between consequentialism and deontology; in connection to metaethics, think of the conditions and structure of agency and reason. But this whole area is messy. Ordinary reflection and philosophical theory manifest contrasting views of the self as, for example, the personal principle of understanding and will, or as the embodied subject of sensations and sentiments, or as a self-construing and deliberating agent. The identity of moral persons is seen as necessarily determined by its criteria, or as relative and plural, or as no identity at all. The metaphysics and the epistemology of persons is shot through with difficulties: what sort of entities are persons; do they belong to the ultimate furniture of the world; do they come into view from an objective standpoint? One particular source of complications is whether there is an essential first-person dimension to persons and personal identity that any appropriate conception of them must characterize, explain, and vindicate. This issue is not only controversial in itself: it underlies drastic alternatives in moral philosophy. At one extreme, we have Derek Parfit's idea that persons – as entities that have brains and bodies, thoughts and desires – can be reductively understood in terms of facts described in an impersonal way – an idea that implies normative implications of consequentialism and metaethical implications of realism.[1] At the other ex-

---

1   See Parfit 1984, pp. 210-211, 216-217, 250-252.

treme, we have the first-person understanding of practical identity from the perspective of and of the standpoint of deliberation and choice which is characteristic of Kantian-constructivist positions.² And someone like B. Williams takes an intermediate ground, with his attention to the central role of character, projects, and internal reasons for the conception personal identity, agency, and ethics.³ I think that those who insist on the essential first-person dimension of persons and their identity are right. But rather than exploring and assessing the implications of this claim for moral philosophy – for a conception of agency, of practical deliberation, of reasons and norms – I want to add to the messiness by saying something about the very concept of the first person, about its logical and metaphysical structure. In particular, I want to raise doubts as to whether there is a coherent, not merely disjunctive, way of forming this concept and, *pro tanto*, of framing a conception of person and personal identity. I have not yet made a decision about the extent to, and direction toward which, such doubts could generalize and have ramifications for practical philosophy. However, I think that the considerations I sketch out deserve some attention.

Persons and the first person: Persons and perspectives

My background is the study of the close interconnection among: the conceptual perspective through which persons come into view; the modes of presentation under which they can recognize themselves as persons; and the constitutive conditions for their counting at all as persons. This background is one many can share.⁴ To summarize: The conceptual perspective makes it possible to think of persons in intentional and nor-

---

2 See Korsgaard 1996, pp. 363-397 (p. 378: "from the practical point of view our relationship to our actions and choices is essentially *authorial: from it, we view them as our own*").

3 See the papers collected in Williams 198).

4 This apparatus is applied in different ways. It can hold water as a constitutive thesis: Being a person can be equated with having a viewpoint. The concept of a person is in part constituted by that of viewpoint, in particular, that of the first-personal viewpoint (Rudder Baker, 2000). But it can be regarded also as a 'logical' view, as a view about the logical space to which the concept of a person belongs. Persons can be conceived of only as 'emerging' under the 'personal' perspective on the world (like in Hornsby 1997); or where subjective and objective views license deeply different conceptions of persons (like in Nagel 1986 and in Bilgrami 2006).

mative terms, as subjects of thought, of cognitive and practical commitments. This perspective also defines a viewpoint to which only persons can have access: it is personal in that it can be taken only by persons. Finally, this view is also essentially reflexive, in the important sense that it is that persons must take toward themselves, in the first person, in order to count fully as persons. The personal viewpoint leads quite naturally to a constitutive thesis: counting as a person involves being in a position to regard and recognize oneself as person; it involves thinking and knowing and acting – existing, so to speak – in the first person. The personal status is also essentially first personal.

The minimal first-person viewpoint

This is the background. The first-person viewpoint and how it contributes to personhood have been variously articulated in terms of unique and ineffable modes of presentation; *de se* attitudes; essential indexicals; I-thoughts; what-is-it-likes; self-constitution; immediate self-presence; deliberative commitments; and avowals. Since I am going to raise some questions about the first-person viewpoint, I will start with a preliminary, minimal characterization. The first-person viewpoint can be articulated in epistemic or agential ways: in the form of self-knowledge, of the self-reference involved in framing intentions, or even of self-constitution. The first seems to be more fundamental. Reflexivity in itself raises special problems.[5] But one can leave those problems aside and concentrate on the objects and modes of presentation that are characteristic of the first-person viewpoint, that is, those that amount to an understanding of oneself as a person. Such understanding can be as implicit as one likes, but still it answers to and expresses mandatory content for the first-person viewpoint: the complex of content, attitudes, commitments, mental and bodily states we hold or have; the sense of being the subjects of certain experiences, cognitions, and actions; the sense of time and of egocentric spatial location. These contents – objects and modes of presentation – are given in an essentially reflexive way, or in an indirect-reflexive voice.[6] The first person viewpoint is thus one I and only I can take toward myself and which only I can take immediately and knowingly. On all these accounts,

---

5   See, for instance, Perry (2001) and de Gaynesford 2006.
6   As Anscombe 1975, p. 22, puts it.

it cannot be reduced to third-person viewpoints and to nonessentially or only directly reflexive self-referential stances. And access to this viewpoint constitutively contributes to the status of being a person.

The rub

This is the general, minimal character of the first-person viewpoint, but there's the rub. Here is where some serious conceptual tensions arise: the first-person viewpoint is no safe haven for the understanding of persons and their identity. Of course, to commit to a first-person construal of persons is to commit to the idea that the essential features of persons are not present in any impersonal perspective. But once impersonal, objective considerations have been ruled out, there are radical alternatives about what is to conceive first-personally of oneself and of persons in general. The use of the "I" as subject, the indirect reflexive, is not univocal: it seems to include different ways to think; to feel, know, and act; to exist first personally.[7]

I suggest that there are different modes of the first-person viewpoint. Their difference has been scarcely recognized but invests the logical and ontological grounds of the first person. While my aim is to give *a priori* grounds for recognizing different conceptual layers or dimensions in the first person, there are some clear hints in the philosophical and psychological discussion of persons, personal identity, and self-knowledge, which point in this direction. I will mention some of them now, briefly.

Sorabji's self

A firm hold on the complexities of the first person is provided by a careful historical reconstruction of the idea of self we owe to Richard Sorabji. Sorabji's research is based on two main notions of a person:

1. a person owns psychological states and actions; owns a body and bodily characteristics; is an individual embodied owner; and
2. there is a need to see the world in terms of Me and Me Again.[8]

---

7 Beatrice Longuenesse has important work in progress on "Two Uses of "I" as Subject" from which I have learned much.
8 Sorabji 2006, p. 21, 22, 31, 33.

Either notion articulates in a distinct way the reflexive relation in which persons must stand to themselves and can stand only to themselves; the first-person and person-constituting relation. As a gloss on the first notion, Sorabji writes: "Talk of me is, roughly speaking, talk of this person" (where the import of the demonstrative is reflexively grounded); "a person is something that has psychological states and does things; for short owns psychological states and actions" (ownership, authorship, primitive endorsementary first-person notions).[9] We can read as a gloss on the second notion Sorabji's paraphrase and commentary of Augustine: "The soul knows itself by being present (*praesens*) to itself, not absent […] So the soul does not need to seek itself. If it did have to seek itself, it would fail, for then it would find only images and traces."[10] On a first approximation, the alternative modes of the personal viewpoint are thus (1) the immediate presence of one to oneself as Me and Me Again; and (2) the intimate and unique relation of ownership, authorship, and authority to one's own psyche and body, opinions and actions. The difference between these two notions of the self marks off two different notions of the first-person viewpoint: the difference between seeing oneself as individual embodied owner and Me and Me Again is a difference in the reflexive dimension of being, of counting, as a person. The common features that make either a notion of person and a form of the first-personal viewpoint have already been outlined: reflexivity; reference to one's own contents, commitments, bodily states; the sense of being a subject and having a viewpoint. But these common features are articulated in radically different ways and with radically different implications; at most, they define a disjunctive conception of the first person. Now we must say something more about their different logic and ontology.[11]

---

9   Sorabji 2006, p. 265.

10 Sorabji 2006, p. 212. Sorabji refers to De Trinitate, 10 (3, 7, 9, 10). This is nicely summarized in Rudder Baker 2007, p. 345: "In my opinion, there is no informative noncircular answer to the question: 'In virtue of what do person P1 at t1 and person P2 at t2 have the same first-person perspective over time?' It is just a primitive, unanalysable fact that some future person is I; but there is a fact of the matter nonetheless." See also Chisholm 1981, pp. 89-90.

11 The interplay of these models is pervasive in contemporary philosophical discussion – also within widely disparate frameworks. Thus, Rey 1976, p. 46 remarks that what matters in and what conditions constitute survival must be derived from synchronic concern, the "experiential relation," the relation between one person and "usually only her own present experience" even though his final position comes closer to the first notion distinguished by Sorabji. And Perry 1976, pp. 78-84 outlines some of

Rational Living Body: *Situated first persons*

One way of framing the first notion is the following: individuals think first personally in terms of their own living bodily existence and of their own cognitive and practical mental engagements ("their own" is indirect-reflexive). This mode of first-person thinking – which is a condition of their counting as persons – consists of owning and engaging in bodily and mental states.[12] This conforms to the minimal content of first-personal thinking as above sketched. Ownership of a complex of diverse and internally related attitudes substantiates and regulate first-personal thinking: these include cognitive, evaluative, practical contents and bodily capacities and activities; and authorship of particular commitments and actions -- at this time and place, in my own perceptual and motivational situation. Of course, the character and content of the first-person viewpoint answers the question of what it takes for these objects and relations of ownership and authorship to be determined. The first-person viewpoint thus specified is, in turn, an essential aspect of what is to count as a person. The mark of personhood and the general content of the first-personal viewpoint are thus reflexively presented in embodied, rational living. Something close to this view could be framed on the basis of far different metaphysics: the substantial unity of *res cogitans* and *extensa*; the finite subject of rational will; the psychological and physical structure of natural minds. But I would place my bet on the broadly Aristotelian position implicit in my own formulation. This notion of personhood and the first person is fitting to different explanatory and conversational

---

the features that might figure in a conception of personal identity connected with the explanation of special concern for self-directed identification and with the importance and value of private and ego-involving situations and projects; at the same time, however, he denies that anything especially first-personal is required for the explanation of such features.

12 A very clear and authoritative formulation of this view can be found in Wittgenstein 1965, pp. 66-67: "Now the idea that the real I lives in my body is connected with the peculiar grammar of the word 'I,' and the misunderstandings this grammar is liable to give rise to. There are two different cases in the use of the word 'I' (or 'my') that I might call 'the use as object' and 'the use as subject.' Examples of the first kind of use are these: 'My arm is broken,' 'I have grown six inches,' 'I have a bump on my forehead,' 'The wind blows my hair about.' Examples of the second kind are: 'I see so-and-so,' 'I hear so-and-so,' 'I try to lift my arm,' 'I think it will rain,' 'I have a toothache.' One can point to the difference between these two categories by saying that the cases of the first category involve the recognition of a particular person, and there is in these cases the possibility of an error. Or, as I should put it instead: the possibility of an error has been provided for."

contexts. A particularly important application of it is that of Strawsonian reactive attitudes: rational living bodies are the appropriate objects of the practice, say, of praising and blaming. Many accounts of moral motivation and of deliberation seem to rely on this situated conception of persons. This conception does not seem to raise intractable problems. It can be difficult to apply; it can raise epistemologically challenging tasks; but conceptually and ontologically it is reasonably clear. It is not by chance that it had a considerable fortune in the history of philosophy.[13]

De se

The main problem with this conception is how to articulate its first-personal import, its indirect-reflexive mode. The matters it takes into consideration -- embodiment, life, rationality – are not especially first-personal; the same holds true of other versions of this general idea. Of course, we are assuming the essential reflexive attitude to such matters. But still it must be shown that such an attitude is not extrinsic to the contents it takes; it constitutes a way of conceiving of one's own body, life, and rationality that is not only viable but in some sense mandatory. There must be compelling grounds for regarding oneself first personally as a Rational Living Body if these elements are to deliver a conception which is truly of persons and the first person; the idea of one's Rational Living Body must be plausible as a realization of the I as subject. However, there are conceptual apparatuses like *de se* attitudes (Lewis) or direct self-attributions (Chisholm) or essential indexicals (Perry) or I-thoughts (Evans) which seem to establish that the conception of oneself as this Rational Living Body includes the required first-personal dimension. Any adequate construal of cognition and action that takes into account

---

[13] For a careful non-Aristotelian discussion of something very close to the notion of Rational Living Body as a person, see Shoemaker's 1976, pp. 110-119, in which he discusses "volitional" and "sensorial embodiment." See also Wiggins 1976, pp. 152-153, 168. But this is the conception of a person as "an entity that has a brain and a body, and has particular thoughts, desires, and so on" which Parfit 1984, pp. 211, 217, regards as the best one among those which postulate that persons are not reducible entities and which discards for this reason. This is also broadly the conception of a person that underlies Lewis' criticism of Parfit's views in Lewis (1976). Some of the views advanced in Roessler and Eilan 2003 fall broadly into this category, especially with regard to the connection between first person and awareness and production and authorship of actions. See Peacocke 2003, pp. 97, 103; Dokic 2003, pp. 328-329, 333, 337; O'Brien 2003, pp. 378-379.

location in time and space and particularistic conditions on perception and motivation, and that is thus *pro tanto* germane to the view of persons as rational living bodies, does and must include conditions that mandate first-personal thinking. Taking our lead from David Lewis, we maintain that *de se* beliefs -- which have self-locating properties as their objects and consist in self-attributing such properties, correctly or incorrectly – are indispensable and fundamental to the individuation of all other sorts of cognitive attitudes, as well as to the cognition that individuals have of their own location and perceptual situation. In this way, *de se* beliefs provide essential information by which individuals can know who they are: "which was which." Other attitudes, primarily desires, follow suit.[14]

A basic role of *de se* attitudes is thus to secure that one "is in a position to self-ascribe the property of being in a certain perceptual situation" where "exactly one person is" (in that world): himself.[15] The conceptual apparatus of *de se* attitudes in this way makes an essential, non-reducible contribution to cognition and agency, by making it possible to know and to want more than what falls under the scope of propositional objects or of *de dicto* attitudes.[16] This is identical to first-personal cognition in general; correspondingly, the *de se* apparatus is essentially reflexive and confers a dimension of reflexivity to cognition and agency in general. But the sort of objects which *de se* attitudes take – self-ascribed properties having to do with location in space and time, perceptual situation, particularistic desired properties – are also the indispensable elements of the notion of person as Rational Living Body. Therefore, this apparatus, applied to the matters of self-knowledge – one's living body, mental states, actions – makes such cognition essentially first-personal, in the required first-personal and person-constituting way. To think of and to individuate oneself as this Rational Living Body is to entertain an array of *de se* attitudes. But therefore this sort of thinking is necessarily first-personal: on Lewisian grounds (not particularly sympathetic to first-personal considerations), the Rational Living Body is a perfectly good version of I as subject.

---

14 Lewis 1979, p. 136-139, 145. See Chisholm 1981, for a systematic development of a closely related idea, the epistemically foundational position of direct self-attribution of properties.

15 Lewis 1979, p. 138.

16 Lewis 1979, p. 144, 146.

Me and Me Again: Presence to self

Regarding the second notion that I am distinguishing, being a person is just being me: the simple awareness of being me, with the elementary recognitional element me again. I am a person simply by having or occupying a viewpoint – my own viewpoint, of course: whose else could it be? – or by engaging with the world with my eyes, from my standpoint.[17] A slightly more developed, phenomenological understanding of what is to be a person in this sense and of the character of the relevant first person perspective could be drawn from the what-is-it-like dimension of experience or from the special involvement we have with certain important concerns. But one can also think of the essential aspect of self-understanding and self-trust that accompanies any simple or sophisticated rational engagement. At a more refined level, the deliberative and agential standpoint can be articulated, not only in terms of our reflexive relation to our mental and bodily activities, but also in terms of the immediate sense of our practical freedom and engagement. The most obvious philosophical model for this conception of a person is (apart from Augustine) Descartes' *ego cogito*, if stripped of any (dubious) implication of my counting as *res cogitans*. Perhaps also Kant's *Ich denke* can be related to this view of person and identity, but I hesitate to do so. The formality of this concept and its connection to the issue of the unity of representation is not primarily one of personal identity. And, of course, I also take into account the minimal understanding of the Kantian idea of autonomous willing. But contemporary discussions of persons and agency sometimes welcome this view of the first person and are even keen to distinguish it from alternative views.[18] This notion of a person is primitive and elementary as to its character and position: it is immediate presence to oneself,

---

17   See Marcel 2003, pp. 84-87, who characterizes the primitive form of self-ownership in terms of a property of the phenomenology of action, that is, the awareness of oneself as the perspectival source of action, the egocentric spatial viewpoint one is aware of occupying. This is close to the simple, primitive first person viewpoint I am describing. If Marcel's idea is seen in this light, the misgivings voiced in Peacocke 2003, p. 97 – which are essentially addressed to a kind of Rational Living Body conception – fail to apply. In general, the complex and enormously interesting dialectic of Marcel's paper is well understood in terms of the distinction I am drawing between forms of the first-person viewpoint.

18   Something like this conception of the first person is suggested in Chisholm 1976, pp. 33. (See also the references to Frege and Husserl in footnotes 19-21, 51-52, 106-108, 110-112, in the context of discussions of the presence of self in experience and of persons as entia per se. See also Swinburne 1984.

the simple thought or sense of being me, with the minimum of recognition of being me again. It is the form of personhood and first person involved in the simplest mental and agential exercises, but also in the most complex, conceptual ones. It is the condition of our relying on ourselves as self-movers and as cognitive agents: no matter how complicated the structure and consequences of movements and actions, we see ourselves as engaging in them. It is the basis on which we take at face value perceptual appearances and introspective experiences, the basis of the primary distinction we make between the inner and the outer, the character of 'I'.

Immediately first personal

Me and Me Again construes the first-personal viewpoint in a different way from the Rational Living Body, from my being in a position to have certain *de se* attitudes. The basic and prominent difference is – in a first approximation – that the thought "Me and Me Again" is, by construction, primitively first-personal. The first-person mode of presentation that is distinctive of it is primary, does not depend on further conditions, and cannot be further analyzed or explained. By contrast, the first-personal import of the thought of oneself as Rational Living Body depends on the general *de se* character of such thought and on the matters or objects it takes. The consideration that cognition of one's living body and mental life is necessarily first-personal is perfectly consistent with the first-personal import of Rational Living Body being composite. These thoughts are first-personal because they are *de se* and involve one's mental and bodily properties. In Rational Living Body, the order of determination goes from the conditions for being this particular Rational Living Body, to the (mandatory) *de se* access of these conditions, to self-knowledge as owner and author of mental states and actions. In Me and Me Again, the order of determination is from simply being present as Me and Me Again to whatever it takes – in terms of contents, attitudes, states, life, embodiment – to be a person who is susceptible to such self-presence. Even if we identify what it takes to actually be a person in a Rational Living Body – an eminently plausible metaphysical move – the difference in order of determination and in the character of modes of presentation remains. The simplicity of the thought "Me and Me Again," the difficulty of further characterizing it, are such this mode of first person appears to harbor no mystery at all. Once we gain access to this way of being present to oneself, to the primitive difference between me and everything else – something we do almost at birth – any related issues of personal identity appear peculiarly unmysterious. It can only be a question of whether I am Me and Me Again. Either it is Me and Me Again so that there is nothing else to worry about, or it is not, so that there is no one here to do the worrying.

Why Me Again?

Might this conception of the first-personal viewpoint be stated as "Me, but not" and "Me Again"? I doubt that this is possible. It makes no sense to think of personhood and first person in absence of any minimally articulated contents and structures of the sort involved in recognition, even those that are involved in simply wondering who I am and who I was.[19] Some sort of conception of oneself must accompany the primitive act of self-awareness in terms of Me; this conception would scarcely be intelligible if it did not open the possibility of framing a notion of my own perduring, in other words, my possibly being Me again in some specific way. In general, the contents of the Me and Me Again conception, the ways in which by entertaining this thought I end up thinking of myself as me again, could be radically diverse. This seems to follow from the priority of this first-person mode of presentation on the objects it takes. But while it is not an easy task to determine what contents can realize my recognition of myself as me again, it seems indispensable that there are such contents, allowing for some sort of generalization of my primitive presence to myself. Perhaps this content is drawn from the same elements of Rational Living Body, or of some other conception of persons as individual substances and of the first person as the indirect-reflexive attitude of individual substances. In fact, the two notions of the first person, while radically different, are perfectly consistent. But, perhaps, the special, unique features of this mode of the first person require a different, nonepistemological, but rather agential, frame of reference. This would to some extent mandate a revision of the character of Rational Living Body if

---

19 The need of some act of identification for the correct use of "I" has been persuasively defended against the traditional denial that any such act is required, by de Gaynesford 2006. A closely related thesis could be advanced for first-personal thought in general, a fortiori in its Me and Me Again form.

the two notions must be kept consistent.[20] However, I can only mention in passing these important questions.[21]

Two logics of the first person: A deep difference

I have outlined two different, if consistent, forms of the first person. But are these forms deeply different? Does their difference amount to a duality in the conception of the first person? I answer in the affirmative. The background here is the minimal conception outlined earlier. Being a person is a condition that is constituted by capacities and exercises such as consciousness and memory, feeling and affections; understanding and commitment in cognition and in action; grasp and endorsement of rational relations. These actions are realized in embodied life, all under the essential condition of indirect reflexivity. Persons are necessarily in the first person. Against this background – as the consideration of the different first-person modes has begun to show – first-person thought turns out to be more complicated but also perhaps more flexible and productive than one might think. My claim is that there is no metaphysical factor common to the two modes of the first person, and that their logical structures, the character and individuation of their contents, are deeply different. Rational Living Body and Me and Me Again allow genuinely different possibilities of thinking and being in the first person. If this is true, it could be doubted that there is an ontologically sound and explanatorily indispensable concept of the first person that synthesizes the features of the two notions, rather than leaving the issue open as to open whether to apply

---

20 An agency-grounded, normative account of the conceptual conditions and apparatus of self-knowledge is carefully articulated in Bilgrami 2006.

21 de Gaynesford 2006 also argues for a revision of the principle of Immunity to Error through Misidentification relative to "I", shifting it from semantics to pragmatics, from meaning-constitution to factual conditions on the use of the first-person pronoun. Again, a similar view should be advanced about first-personal thought, perhaps taking a start from Shoemaker's distinction between de facto and logical immunity to error. See the careful and insightful discussion in Coliva 2006, pp. 20-22. The catch would be to extend de facto immunity to all sorts of first-personal thought and then modally articulate the factual, substantively conceptual conditions differently for the different varieties of the first-person. But of course I can only hint at this development.

one or the other. Perhaps there is only a disjunctive concept of the first person that encompasses both forms.[22]

The logic of Rational Living Body: Starting from Rational Living Body

One can at least conceptually distinguish the mandatory objects of the first-person viewpoint from the *de se* attitudes that constitute its essential reflexive dimension. Given that – as I am claiming in general – essential reflexivity does not alter the nature of contents, the important properties of these contents are preserved in the first-person viewpoint. Here, the crucial idea is that the mental and bodily matters that figure essentially in Rational Living Body have a necessary grounding in the actual world. *De se* attitudes, which locate thinkers or agents within a possible world, must be interpreted relative to centered worlds. In order to give the contents of the first person in the Rational Living Body conception, the centered world must be the actual world (the world of the actual persons whose first-person viewpoint is to be determined), because such contents depend upon embodiment, life, and rationality. The following issues can only be determined with reference to how it actually is what a living body is and whether it is the same or not with another; what a conscious, cognitive and motivational mind is and whether it the same or not with another; what Rational Living Body I am and whether I am the same or not with some Rational Living Body. Living bodies have essential properties by way of belonging to natural species and of being composed of natural substances. Such properties are individuated *a posteriori* and cannot be different from what they actually are. Contents involved in the attitudes and activities of rational minds are externally individuated, in connection with both bodily

---

22 Sorabji 2006, p. 49, denies that there is any incompatibility between the first-personal self and our objective existence as human beings and affirms that "interest in 'me'-ness [...] would not arise if there were such things as persons and higher animals that could be described in more objective terms." We can also add that there would not be persons at all. But this point about the unity in actuality of the dimensions of the first person simply fails to address the conceptual and ontological question of how they differ in form and implications. To clarify: Of course I am not denying that being Me and Me Again entails having one's own body, life, and mind. I only say that it is not the same with being an individual substance immediately reflexively individuated.

and environmental conditions. It is notoriously controversial whether content-externalism is consistent with self-knowledge. However, they seem to be in the approach I am proposing, where reflexivity *per se* does not alter contents and (as we will see) the epistemic privilege of self-knowledge is not a priority.

Thus, being a person – which involves being in the first person -- in this conception is to be in a position to have *de se* attitudes toward the constitutive elements of one's rational, bodily life. But these elements are necessarily what they actually are; they can only be determined in relation to actuality. Therefore, what is possible and knowable in connection with this form of the first person is determined by how it is with the actual world, just as it is with regard to what is knowable and possible with water, gold, and natural elements. The Rational Living Body that I could be cannot be different – as to its constitution – from the one I am. Essential reflexivity does not alter this modal condition of the contents' first person; in fact, it transposes it to become a condition of my being a person. The notion of possibility here is counterfactual: possibility relative to the actual world as actual. With reference to possible worlds as counterfactual – as is mandated by the nature of *de se* attitudes and of rational living bodies -- it is not possible, given what Rational Living Body a person actually is, that this very person is present if this very Rational Living Body is altered in its nature. Rational Living Bodies are persons in the way of individual substances; their nature, their sameness and difference have the necessity of substantial constitution and identity. [23]

Secondary first-person viewpoint

The first-person viewpoint licensed by Rational Living Body is certainly *a posteriori*. First, knowledge of one's body and mind, in this construal, is *a posteriori* because it depends on specific information about the actual

---

[23] There are two different concepts of possibility here at play, one relative to counterfactual worlds (possibilities and necessities are assessed from how it is in the actual world, on an a posteriori basis), the other relative to possible worlds (possibilities and necessities are determined on an a priori basis and are assessed in terms of what world is the actual world). This general conception of metaphysical possibility is thoughtfully and carefully constructed in Chalmers 2006. For the view that that of a person is a natural kind concept and that this determines its semantic status and behavior, see the thoughtful discussion in Wiggins (1976).

world; it responds to states of affairs in the actual world.[24] Second, essential reflexivity does not alter the character of cognitive contents and of their acquisition; therefore, the perspective in the first person, which simply consists in indirect-reflexive cognition of self, also is accessible *a posteriori*. The substantive, categorical possibilities that define my personal identity as Rational Living Body are not accessible only by imagination and conception; they can only be known (if at all) on the basis of information concerning how it actually is with my Rational Living Body. We can generalize this claim by saying that the contents that are grasped indirect-reflexively in Rational Living Body function semantically and cognitively according to their secondary intentions. That which individuates what and how I think first personally and thus how I count as person are the extensions of my first-person thoughts, which lock them onto the actual world. These thoughts are conformable to the nature of persons and of the first-person viewpoint, thus conceived.[25] Notice that this is no obstacle to self-knowledge and first-personal thoughts being especially authoritative, nonobservational and noninferential, at least in a reasonable understanding of these conditions. The epistemic privilege of the first person, in the present conception, is not to be equated with *a priori* status: it is rather a matter of almost complete reliability. Furthermore, *a posteriori* status depends on the sources of justificatory grounds, not on the details of the processes of cognitive acquisition. The latter can be widely different while the *a posteriori* status is kept firm. Acquaintance with contingent facts concerning one's bodily and mental states can be *a posteriori*, if it involves and is justified by information on the actual world; but still it can be a cognitive operation different from observation and inference, in particular by not involving any sort of epistemic detachment or mediation, both of which are out of place in first-personal thinking.

The logic of Me and Me Again

The logic is radically different. Of course, the minimal features of the general, I think disjunctive, first-person viewpoint still hold. Thinking first personally in the Me and Me Again mode must not be severed from the world being presented and addressed in cognition or action. It can

---

24 Concerning this conception of the a posteriori, see Evans 1979, pp. 205-206.
25 For a good introduction to Two-Dimensional Semantics, see Schroeter 2010.

be viable as a form of the first person viewpoint precisely because it allows one to refer to oneself as an individual located in and engaged with a world. Otherwise it could be doubted that the first-person viewpoint would license entertaining any thoughts and counting as a person. Rational Living Body and Me and Me Again do not profoundly differ in this respect. Still, they do differ deeply; the elements involved in my Me and Me Again thinking must share some feature which constitutes this primitive, simple mode of self-presence.

What more can we say of this special mode of presentation? To begin characterizing it, I propose to understand Me and Me Again thoughts as reference fixers or determinants of the world-relative extension of contents or (drawing on unpublished work by Saul Kripke) as acquaintance guiders, rather than as world-determined referents or in their extensions or as items of acquaintance.[26] The kind of semantic and cognitive role that is relevant for characterizing this form of the first person is the internal – internal to thinking, to attitude, to awareness -- determination of possible reference and acquaintance. This stands in contrast to the kind of role that is associated with referents or extensions and to objects of acquaintance, consisting of the external determination of what one is actually thinking, and of the mental states in which one is. The rationale for the proposal is the following. In the Me and Me Again form of the first-person viewpoint, priority is given to availability of the simple, prime reflexive thought of one's presence. On the basis of the minimal concept, we can say that first-person thinking in this mode is addressed to one's bodily and mental states; but still, as I pointed out, it has to be reflexively manifest in a primitive and prime way. The specific features of modes of presentation in which such prime and primitive self-presence would consist must be left for future enquiry. Until very recently, scarcely any attention had been dedicated to this topic by analytic philosophers, in contrast with continental, phenomenology-oriented ones. But the general point can be made that all contents that can contribute to Me and Me Again must work se-

---

26 Kripke (Unpublished), pp. 38-40. There is affinity between my proposal that at least one form of the first person is defined at the level of primary intensions and Anscombe's claim that "I" is not at all referring expression. See Anscombe 1975, p. 32: "Getting hold of the wrong object is excluded, and that makes us think that getting hold of the right object is guaranteed. But the reason is that there is no getting hold of an object at all. With names, or denoting expressions (in Russell's sense) there are two things: the kind of use, and what to apply them to from time to time. With 'I' there is only the use."

mantically and cognitively according to their primary intentions. Primary intensions are pure modes of presentation or ways of determining extensions (secondary intensions) which are considered *per se*, that is, in and for what they manifest or specify or in and for the appearance they give of their referents. Primary intensions determine and shape the inner presence of objects to conscious cognition, their phenomenal or conceptual manifestation to thinkers. I think that the primitively reflexive, first-personal import of Me and Me Again is best or perhaps uniquely individuated and understood at the semantic and cognitive level of primary intensions. This form of the first person is essentially nothing other than the primitive and simple presence or manifestation of oneself to oneself; primary intations make possible this sort of immediate, cognitive, possibly conceptually, conscious presence or manifestation. This form of the first person is not externally constituted, like Rational Living Body: it is not the indirect-reflexive grasp and cognition of the actual mental and bodily properties that are the secondary intensions of these sorts of first-personal thoughts. Me and Me Again is, so to speak, the first- person viewpoint from inside, the mere sense of my presence – whatever and whoever I am. This sense, primary and primitive, is realized directly at the level of the primary intensions of first-person thoughts that shape our conscious, indirect-reflexive acquaintance to ourselves. Me and Me Again is primitive and prime precisely because its contents are not determined starting from constitutive or causal relations between the self, her mental and bodily states, and the world. It is first-personal thinking whose essential reflexivity does not consist in having certain *de se* attitudes, but simply and primitively in being present to oneself as oneself. The specification of this self-presence is completely determined in connection with primary intensions, just as it is with phenomenal or conceptual manifestations in general (water as the transparent liquid forming rivers and seas rather than as H_2O; direction as spatial orientation and progression rather than parallel lines). Of course, this gives only a necessary condition for the Me and Me Again viewpoint: what specific contents contribute to Me and Me Again thoughts, apart from their working at the level of primary intensions, is a further, difficult question that I will not address here.[27]

---

27 Of course, primary intensions are also necessarily involved in Rational Living Body first-personal thoughts: the primary/secondary intension distinction holds across the board. But it is secondary intensions that define in this case the first person viewpoint. The primary intensions that are characteristic of Me and Me Again

Two metaphysics of the first person: Necessary *a posteriori* first persons

We have now arrived at the frontier of the metaphysics of the first person. Rational Living Body is *a posteriori* but still expresses a necessity. The argument for this proceeds from the constitutive connection between the first-person viewpoint (however we conceive of it) and the status of being a person, because this includes the condition of thinking first personally. According to one perspective, the viewpoint consists of *de se* attitudes to one's bodily and mental states or whatever individuates rational living bodies. These *de se* contents, as I have already suggested, are grounded in the actual world and express the necessity of natural kinds and substances, as certainly befits rational living bodies. Since reflexivity in general does not alter contents, the first person viewpoint is itself the expression of such necessity. It follows that I am a person and this person is itself a matter of necessity. My Rational Living Body would not be the same if my constitution were altered in some essential respect (i.e., in a way respect that decides the kind to which it belongs, or the substance of which it consists, or the individual it is). In order to count as a person, I must be in a position to address myself, in the indirect-reflexive way, as a Rational Living Body. But the contents and attitudes that define my first-person viewpoint are, in turn, naturally necessary, precisely on the same grounds that determine the necessity of my being the individual substance I am. But certainly what contents are in this way determined for my own *de se* attitudes and how these attitudes shape my mental and bodily activities, how they shape what compliments my life and my rational commitments, are matters that can be known *a priori*. No more than my being this Rational Living Body is *a priori*. This form of the first person and personhood is a case of the necessary *a posteriori*.

Contingent *a priori* first persons

The Me and Me Again first-person viewpoint and the possibilities it defines are not anchored onto the actual world; they do not have to lock on existents in order to be individuated. There is no external determination of them; therefore, there is no expression of natural necessity that is es-

---

thoughts do not necessarily determine the same secondary intensions as those of Rational Living Body thoughts; this can well be, depending on what world is the actual world; but it is not necessary.

sentially associated with Me and Me Again thoughts and possibilities; this first person viewpoint is determined at the level of primary intensions. Me and Me Again is simple, prime self-presence and as such is fully individuated in terms of pure modes of consciousness, thinking, or cognition. This has important metaphysical implications. It follows from the minimal conception of persons that Me and Me Again, as mode of the first person, is constitutive of personhood, of the status of being a person. But this is not by way of expressing, and depending on, the actual identity and nature of an individual rational substance but by defining an *a priori* condition: whomever the primary intensions that define my first-person viewpoint pick up in any possible world is the person I am. That person is Me and Me Again. This is a condition of the constitutive identification of persons, but it is important to be clear about the character of this picking up. What is constitutively and necessarily identifying of persons, here, are not the referents or secondary intensions that actual primary intensions individuate in a possible world. This, as we will see presently, is an *a posteriori* and contingent matter.

The constitutive identification of persons discussed here proceeds from the pure modes of self-presentation, in relation to the primary intensions that form their first- person viewpoints. Such identification, therefore, can only depend on the sameness of such primary intensions – first-person primary intensions. Picking up who is Me and Me Again in a possible world fits the following criterion: thinking the same first-person primary intensions, or I am whoever thinks my same Me and Me Again thoughts or has my same Me and Me Again viewpoint.[28] This is the logical and metaphysical core of this form of first person. This condition of personhood and the first person is *a priori*, precisely because it is defined by primary intensions: in any possible world, the truth about who I am is determined by the primary intensions of my actual first-person thoughts. I am Me and Me Again. But the nature of *a priori* truth can be understood as the truth in all worlds of the primary intensions of thoughts. Certainly, such a truth is one that can be known *a priori*.

---

28 For a closely related point, see Anscombe 1975, p. 31. "If 'I' is a referring expression, then Descartes was right about what the referent was, a 'Cartesian Ego, the thinking that thinks this thought,' which is what is guaranteed by 'cogito.'" Of course, Anscombe rejects the idea that 'I' is a referring expression. But I hold the somehow related view that thinking these first-person thoughts individuates Me and Me Again first- person viewpoints qua specification of primary and not secondary intensions.

Therefore, in this form of the first person, imagination and conception are safe guides as we grasp and assess the possibilities concerning personhood and personal identity.

On the other hand, the individuation of persons, in this mode of the first person, assumes that who it is that, in any possible world is individuated by thinking my same Me and Me Again thoughts, involves a contingent dimension. The content of Me and Me Again is not determined by how it is with the actual world, in the same way as the content of Rational Living Body. Therefore, such content does not individuate what individual rational substance in the actual world I am: it only defines my own prime and primitive first-person viewpoint. But therefore, in this mode of the first person, there is no ground in the actual world, no state of affairs, no substantial feature, no belonging to natural kinds, that necessitates who I am in any possible world. The only necessitating principle is the sameness of primary intension. And these prime and primitive viewpoints have a completely different semantic and cognitive role than the secondary ones. (This is the truth in Frege's idea of a first-person mode of presentation that is accessible only to oneself and incommunicable.) But then, from the point of view of the secondary intensions, of the referent on which the primary intensions of Me and Me Again thoughts determine in any possible world what individual substance I am, on which my bodily and mental constitution are contingent. (Of course, the minimal conception of persons must be satisfied.) There is no counterfactual necessity to the secondary intensions of Me and Me Again primary intensions. As said above, I am whoever thinks my Me and Me Again thoughts. Whatever else is required for existing as a person in this way, whatever mental or physical constitution enables me to be Me and Me Again, it is just that: a contingent condition. It is not what makes me a person. Me and Me Again lets this dimension of personhood, mental and bodily constitution, vary across counterfactual possible worlds: it is a case of the contingent *a priori*.[29]

In the actual world, the two forms of the first person are coextensional: Me and Me Again thoughts have the same reference as those of Rational Living Body if the latter is the true metaphysical constitution of persons and if the former is a viable mode of essential reflexivity. The two modes

---

29 Something close to this was pointed out by H. Frankfurt and is endorsed in Kripke 2011, pp. 304-305.

of the first person are the same in actuality.[30] They are consistent and jointly mark the constitution of persons as we know them. But this encompassing understanding of the first person is only disjunctive. What is common to the two modes of the first person is only what is expressed in the minimal conception I have given, but then a deep modal difference comes into view. Each conception licenses different possibilities and determines differently the dimension of the first person that is preserved across possible worlds. It is either the identity of the Rational Living Body I actually am, as this is individuated by the secondary intensions of person-constituting first-person thoughts (of the relevant, externally determined, sort); or it is the identity of primitively reflexive, reference-fixing modes of presentation or primary intensions, the identity of the way one is primitively present to herself. On Me and Me Again, sameness of the first person consists in sameness of the first-person primary intensions that shape how one is present to oneself in a simple and primitive way. And the same holds true of the identity of persons. In Rational Living Body, the first-person viewpoint and the identity of persons are individuated from the existence, the constitution, and the sameness of an individual substance. Identity-determining thoughts are *de se* thoughts of an individual thinking substance, which give indirect-reflexive cognition of her location in space and time and of her engagement in perception and agency.[31]

---

30 The complex and almost tormented conclusion of Anscombe 1975, pp. 33-36, is to some extent evidence of the theoretical need of keeping together but at the same time deeply distinguishing the dimensions of the first person that can be likened to those I am discussing here.

31 The idea of the sameness in actuality and the formal and modal difference between the two modes of the first person suggests a way of treating certain paradoxical intuitions about persons and personal identity. They have been held to indicate that there is an essential indeterminateness as to whether the same person is present in certain circumstances; by implication, the concept of a person is a reducible concept and persons are not essentially first-personal. In brief, this is the master argument of Parfit 1984. In these cases – the branching or the merging together of life-lines – there is an authentic clash of intuitions only if we attempt to occupy at once, with reference to purely modal conditions, the two different first-person viewpoints. In Me and Me Again, it is a priori that, in any of the branching life-lines, I am who thinks my same first person thoughts (same in primary intensions) and, in the merging case, whether I am present at all depends on whether my first-person thoughts are thought at all. In Rational Living Body, in any of the branching life-lines, I am who owns my actual mental and bodily states and is author of my actual actions and, in the merging case, whether I am there depends on whether some actual bodily and mental states and actions are mine. This would be an a posteriori matter; at it may well be held that in the

Contingent and necessary first person

These points can be construed in a more explicit metaphysical way. To appreciate the dimension of contingency that Me and Me Again introduces in personhood and personal identity, we must say something more about how the primary intensions that constitute this mode of the first person pick up persons in different worlds. This could be done in two steps. First, persons are identified in terms of sameness of primitively indirect-reflexive thoughts, which define the first-person viewpoint at the level of primary intensions. I suggested a condition such as thinking the same indirectly-reflexive primary intensions. Secondly, the elements are given for individuating a person who, in any possible world, is having such thoughts or thinking in these ways; a person who (say, what unity of mental and bodily states; or maybe what Cartesian unity of thinking and extended substance; or whatever else) is determined by the reference-fixers that form these reflexive thoughts. The metaphysics of persons will of course be all important to this step. At both steps, we handle questions of personhood and of the first-person as these are defined by the general, disjunctive concept of a person. But in Me and Me Again there is a necessity to the identity of persons and of first-person viewpoints only in relation to the first step. There is not necessity of, but contingency for, the further identification of persons with this or that thinking substance, precisely because this sort of identification is derivative from the person-identifying sameness of primary intensions, together with what the circumstances are in that possible world and given, of course, the right metaphysics of persons. (So we reach a double-edged reading of the formula: I am whoever is thinking my same reflexive thoughts.)

Think of this in contrast with the other conception. There is a sense in which I might not have been the Rational Living Body I am and

---

described circumstances it is undetermined. But here we simply have a case in which the two forms of the first person, while coinciding in actuality, license different modal conclusions; it is this divergence that generates the feeling of paradox. But if this duality in the first-person viewpoint is the normal structure of our first-personal thoughts and is given some philosophical grounding, the perplexities that can arise on this account cannot impel us to discard the first-personal viewpoint itself. By keeping distinct their logic and the underlying metaphysics, I am also confident that we can block the risk of a slide from the duality of forms of the first-person into metaphysical dualism – a risk to which Descartes and Swinburne are witness.

which I have *de se* attitudes to – even though I could not fail the Rational Living Body I actually am; it must just as well have been the case that water is not H_2O, even though it is not possible that water is not what it actually is, H2O. Truths about persons as individual substances are deeply contingent: they depend on states of affairs in the actual world that make them true, including the holding of the relevant *de se* attitudes. But there is necessity to my being the Rational Living Body I am: in all possible counterfactual worlds in which I exist, I am the Rational Living Body I actually am with my actual *de se* attitudes. Rational Living Body is the deeply contingent, superficially necessary form of the first person. A symmetrical thesis holds true of Me and Me Again. There is necessity to my being Me and Me Again; there is indeed deep necessity. In any possible world in which I exist, I am the thinker of my same (in primary intensions) actual Me and Me Again thoughts, regardless of the actual world. But this condition is also superficially contingent because in some (indeed, at indefinitely many) possible worlds the primary intensions of my Me and Me Again thoughts determine different thinking substances. To be a certain person in the Me and Me Again sense is to have certain primitive indirect-reflexive thoughts, individuated in their primary intensions. This is an *a priori* condition, just as it is *a priori* that the Paris meter stick is one meter long. But who or what the primary intensions of Me and Me Again thoughts pick up at different worlds is a variable, thus a contingent matter – just as it is a contingent fact that this is the actual length of the Paris meter stick. The secondary intensions of these thoughts, which determine the actual entities, the individual substances – possibly but not necessarily rational living bodies -- who are thinking these reflexive thoughts can well be different in different possible worlds. (The concept of person that is appropriate to express these points is the disjunctive, minimal one: we do not want to predicate contingency of the first person at the level of primary intensions; still, agency and cognition, mental and bodily activities, and the ground of their self-ascriptions, are dimensions of being a person.) This aspect of contingency is connected to personhood and the first person. So we can say that Me and Me Again is the superficially contingent, deeply necessary form of the first person. There is a clear and deep metaphysical difference between two modes of being first personally as a person.

Conclusion

We have first-person thoughts of either form. One can think of oneself as a person, as one and the same person, and in the first person in either form. I would say that we do this all the time. The resilience of the Cartesian intuitions concerning what is to exist and to view oneself in the first person and that of Aristotelian or other 'situated' views are philosophical expressions of this fact. I think that there is no inconsistency between these forms of first-personal being: both are indispensable and the idea of a choice is preposterous. But there are drastic limits to how they are conceptually interrelated: it is here that philosophical responsibilities must be faced. Ultimately, we have available only a disjunctive conception of persons and their identities, also and primarily when we engage first personally. We do not seem to have available a unitary and deeply grounded conceptual, inferential, and explanatory framework, which puts us in a position to form views and draw conclusions about persons, personal identity, and the first person in one of these modes on the basis of premises drawn from the other. Any attempt to merge conceptually the two modes of the first person would be ill fated; it would be a spurious concept without a consistent logic and determinate metaphysical content. The neglect of this duality is perhaps an important source of some difficulties we meet in practical philosophy and epistemology when framing conceptions of agency and of cognition, of affective and evaluative experience, from a first-person, rather than third-person or impersonal, perspective.

References

Anscombe, E. A. 1975. The First Person, in: E.A. Anscombe 1981, *Metaphysics and the Philosophy of Mind*, Oxford: Blackwell, p. 21-36.

Bilgrami, A. 2006. *Self-Knowledge and Resentment*, Cambridge (Mass.) and London: Harvard University Press.

Chalmers, D. 2006. The Foundations of Two-Dimensional Semantics, in: García-Carpintero, M. and Macià, J., eds. 2006, *Two-Dimensional Semantics*, Oxford: Clarendon Press, p. 55-140.

Chisholm, R. 1976. *Person and Object*, Chicago & La Salle: Open Court.

Chisholm, R. 1981. *The First Person*, Minneapolis: University of Minnesota Press.

Coliva, A. 2006. Error through Misidentification: Some Varieties, in: *The Journal of Philosophy*, 103, p. 403-425.

de Gaynesford, M. 2006. *The Meaning of the First-Person Term*, Oxford: Clarendon Press.

Dokic, J. 2003. The Sense of Ownership: An Analogy between Sensation and Action, in: Roessler & Eilan 2003, p. 321-344.

Evans, G. 1979. Reference and Contingency, in: Evans, G. 1985, *Collected Papers*, Oxford: Clarendon Press, p. 178-213.

Hornsby, J. 1997. *Simple-Mindedness*, Cambridge (Mass.): Harvard University Press.

Korsgaard, C. 1996. Personal Identity and Unity of Agency, in: *Creating the Kingdom of Ends*, Cambridge: Cambridge University Press, pp. 363-397.

Kripke, S. 1986. *Rigid Designation and the Contingent A Priori. The Meter Stick Revisited*, Unpublished.

Kripke, S. 2011. The First Person, in: Kripke, S. 2011, *Philosophical Troubles*, New York: Oxford University Press, p. 292-321.

Lewis, D. 1976. Survival and Identity, in: Rorty 1976, p. 17-40.

Lewis, D. 1979. Attitudes *De Dicto* and *De Se*, in: Lewis, D. 1983, *Philosophical Papers*, I, Oxford and New York: Oxford University Press, p. 133-155.

Loux, M. J., ed. 2008. *Metaphysics. Contemporary Readings*, London: Routledge.

Marcel, A. 2003. The Sense of Agency: Awareness and Ownership of Action, in: Roessler & Eilan, 2003, p. 48-93.

Nagel, T. 1986. *The View from Nowhere*, Oxford and New York: Oxford University Press.

O'Brien, L. 2003. On Knowing One's Own Action, in: Roessler & Eilan 2003, p. 358-382.
Parfit, D. 1984. *Reasons and Persons*, Oxford: Clarendon Press.
Peacocke, C. 2003. Action: Awareness, Ownership, Knowledge, in: Roessler & Eilan (2003), p. 94-110.
Perry, J. 1976. The Importance of Being Identical, in: Rorty 1976, p. 67-90.
Perry, J. 2001. *Reference and Reflexivity*, Stanford: CSLI Publications.
Rey, G. 1976. Survival, in: Rorty 1976, p. 41-66.
Roessler, J. & Eilan, N., eds. 2003. *Agency and Self-Awareness*, Oxford: Clarendon Press.
Rorty, A. O., ed. 1976. *The Identities of Persons*, Berkeley and Los Angeles: The University of California Press.
Rudder Baker, L. 2000. *Persons and Bodies*, Cambridge: Cambridge University Press.
Rudder Baker, L. 2007. Persons and the Metaphysics of Resurrection, *Religious Studies*, 43, 2007, p. 333-348.
Schroeter, L., Two-Dimensional Semantics, in: *The Stanford Encyclopedia of Philosophy* http://plato.stanford.edu/entries/two-dimensional-semantics/
Shoemaker, S. 1976. Embodiment and Behavior, in Rorty: 1976, p. 109-138.
Sorabji, R. 2006. *Self. Ancient and Modern Insights about Individuality, Life, and Death*, Chicago: The University of Chicago Press.
Swinburne, R. 1984. Personal Identity: The Dualist Theory, in: Loux 2008, p. 510-538.
Wiggins, D. 1976. Locke, Butler and the Stream of Consciousness: and Men as a Natural Kind, in: Rorty 1976, p. 139-174.
Williams, B. 1981. *Moral Luck*, Cambridge: Cambridge University Press.
Wittgenstein, L. 1965. *The Blue and Brown Books*, New York: Harper Torchbooks.

Finn Arler

A five-step model for ethically informed decision-making

Introduction

What is ethical theory good for? One may sometimes wonder, given the fact that some people make good decisions without much knowledge of ethical theory, whereas other people make terrible decisions even though they are quite familiar with these theories. Similarly, in a number of cases, people agree about which decisions are decent and appropriate even though they disagree strongly about ethical theories. On the other hand, in just as many cases, people disagree about specific decisions despite the fact that they agree in general about ethical theories.

There seems to be a certain gap between theories and decisions. If this gap is very large, discussions about theories become superfluous or of academic interest at best. If the gap is small, on the other hand, at least some discussions of theories can be expected to influence practical decisions. This also means that actual decisions, particularly in difficult or unusual cases, can be expected to lead to theoretical discussions and sometimes to revisions of ethical theories. How large is the gap between theory and practical decisions? The answer has significant impact on how to teach ethics to students, who will be dealing with ethical questions in their professions but who have no particular interest in academic discussions of ethical theories. If the gap is very large, it seems reasonable to drop thorough presentations of theories. If the gap is quite small, on the other hand, and theories play a significant role in decision-making, it becomes much more important to introduce students to ethical theories. The question, though, is how.

A five-step model for ethically informed decision-making

In this this paper I will introduce a five-step model for decision-making that is informed by ethical theory (or by a variety of theories). In this way I hope not only to show that ethical theory does have a role to play, but also to present a cogent way to introduce students (as well as other groups) to ethical theories and their role in decision-making. The five-step model has been developed (and simplified) over some time. It has been used in relation to the education of planners and other groups of university students, who have only sparse knowledge of ethical theory.

The model is designed to do two things at the same time. First, it presents a number of fairly basic ethical themes that the students now face or will be facing in their daily work. Second, it intends to clarify the kinds of ethical considerations that lie at the foundation of some of the methods, procedures, and institutions they will be acquainted with whenever they try to handle ethical issues. Because of the limited time that is usually reserved for teaching ethics, but also in order to make it part of the students' intellectual backbone, the model must be fairly simple and accessible, and easy to remember and apply.

The model does not reflect directly any actual decision procedures, but it should be close enough to serve its purpose. Nor does it intend to serve as a role model for a wide range of public decisions. Although I assume it can be helpful in a significant number of situations, the model may either be too simple or too complex in others. The initial purpose was didactic. It aimed to make people, who are or will be involved in decision-making processes, aware of a variety of ethical aspects that arise in different parts of the processes. Once developed, however, I myself have found the model quite helpful as a reference and checklist to which I can return when dealing with complex ethical issues of various sorts. I hope others will find it helpful this way, too.

At the end of this paper, I shall return to the question of the role of theories, but just a few words may be helpful to start. First of all, I do not try to defend one specific ethical theory as, for example, Kantian deontology, virtue ethics, utilitarianism, or perfectionism, even though I find some theories more helpful than others. I tend to think of myself as an ethical pluralist, who finds reasonable ideas about nonreducible values (e.g., happiness, freedom, beauty, autonomy, friendship, love, depth, meaningfulness, and quality improvement); obligations (to oneself, one's family, friends, neighbours, nation, international community, future generations, members of other species, etc.); virtues (self-control, justice, solicitousness, patience, scrupulousness, courage, etc.); applicable points and principles (e.g., the golden rule, fairness, equity, universalization, and impartiality); and reasonable methods and procedures (e.g., consequence assessment, stakeholder participation, and deliberation) developed in several mutually supplementary, complementary and sometimes (actually or apparently) competing theories.

Pluralism must not be confused with relativism, at least not as this word is traditionally understood. The pluralism I uphold is certainly not relativist in the sense that anything goes anywhere at any time. Nor does it say that all theories or approaches are equally good, or that they should all be included without further argument. On the other hand, pluralism can actually be called relativist in another, almost opposite sense: the worth of each theory's principles and recommendations may be relative to specific situations, where decisions need to be made – sometimes points and values highlighted in one theory are more relevant than those emphasized by another – or in the sense that relative to a specific situation there may be a limited spectrum of relevant values, good reasons, and applicable procedures to be retrieved from each of the theories.

I will not exclude the possibility of boiling down all the most reasonable values and points in partially competing theories to a single theory concentrate. I actually find that a number of standard textbook divergences among theories often are sharpened much more than needed; setting up "straw men" is a widespread academic practice. Some may even consider the model presented here a first step in the production of a complex theory that integrates a variety of considerations highlighted by other theories. If so, it is only a small initial step, and my aim has not been to undertake a systematic integration of apparently conflicting values and obligations, principles and assumptions that hold prominent positions in significant ethical theories, but only to present an easily accessible model that highlights the most important elements that typically are relevant when complex ethical issues need to be dealt with.

Why ethics?

Ethics are practical. Their purpose is to give reasonable answers to questions about what to do, not in a merely pragmatic sense, where goals are already settled in detail, and all that remains are technicalities, but in a broader sense where both goals and means are up for discussion. The overall purpose is to identify actions, projects, rules, plans, institutions, etc. that can be justified with reasons that one believes ought to be universally acceptable in a given set of circumstances. The core of ethics, and the starting point of ethical theory, is justifying one's actions, projects, etc., to oneself as well as to others. In order to do this properly, one has to use the same arguments in both cases, i.e., one cannot use special standards for oneself or for people close to oneself.

This does not mean that one's arguments fail if it turns out to be impossible to convince everybody else or even the majority about their validity. The point is only that one must believe that everybody who seriously tries to understand and evaluate one's arguments ought to acknowledge them as convincing or at least acceptable. Otherwise, one has to change either the arguments or the actions. Sometimes it is necessary to stand up against a majority, who are not convinced by the arguments. This is a fine occasion to reconsider one's own reasons and conclusions, of course, but if one still finds the arguments convincing, one must have the courage to keep on defending the conclusions that follow from them.

The point of view in ethics is that of impartiality in the sense that one should not use special arguments for oneself, or for one's relatives, or for other people one is particularly fond of, but recognize the same standards for everyone. This is the case unless, of course, one has separate reasons for making distinctions that one seriously believes that everybody else ought to endorse, too, or at least accept. The same point can also be expressed in terms of universalization: one must be prepared to accept that whenever one decides to do something, on the basis of the best arguments available, everybody else, who is similar in all relevant respects, should be allowed (or sometimes committed) to act similarly for similar reasons in similar situations. Four qualifications need to be made here.

First, impartiality towards persons should not be confused with neutrality towards conceptions of the good. One may be firmly convinced, for instance, that scientific research and artistic expression are such basic parts of the good life in a (modern) society that they should be furthered by public means, and yet be impartial in judgments about which persons are most capable of carrying out these activities in a qualified way. Similarly, one may support the protection of certain wilderness areas or buildings of high cultural significance, even if one has little personal interest in them and hardly knows anybody who would spend time visiting them.

It is sometimes claimed that the state can only remain impartial, if it stays completely neutral to all conceptions of the good (Rawls 1971; Raz 1986; Kymlicka 2002), and that the weighing of people's conceptions of the good, or rather, of the preferences that spring from these conceptions, should be left to individual choice, processed in apolitical regulatory mechanisms, primarily the market. This assertion is far from neutral itself, however, but rests on non-neutral assumptions. A claim that all prioritisations ought to be left to consumers' choices, and processed on the market, is based on a fairly controversial conception of how a good society must be organised. Not only does it ignore that democratic procedures, through which political prioritisations are laid down, can be constructed in impartial ways as well, and yet end up supporting policies that are closer to certain conceptions of the good than to others. It also disregards the very possibility of arguing about values in impartial ways, probably because values are confused with person-related preferences.

Second, as indicated already, impartiality does not imply that all persons (or all organisms for that matter) should be treated in exactly the same manner, no matter how different they may happen to be in various respects. That would be absurd. All that is implied by impartiality is that whatever differences one recognizes in one's treatment of other people, one should be able to justify these differences as relevant and appropriate using arguments that one believes that everybody ought to accept. The arguments for different treatment should never be biased in a way that systematically favours certain groups above others.

Third, one has to distinguish between two kinds of impartiality (cf. Wenz 1988, Barry 1995). First order impartiality means that an actor should treat all persons equally, no matter what their relation to the actor may happen to be. This kind of impartiality is implausible in most cases. If, for instance, you want to give birthday presents to your children, first order impartiality demands you to give birthday presents to every human being in the world. Or, to cite another example, if a country decides to support its weakest members, it should be prepared to support the weakest members of all societies.

Second order impartiality, on the other hand, demands only that differences in your treatment of other people must be justified with arguments that you believe everybody ought to accept. If you give birthday presents only to your own children, you should accept it as a general rule that everybody is allowed to give birthday presents to his or her own children without being committed to give presents to everybody else. Similarly, if a country supports the weakest members of its own national community to a much larger extent than citizens of other countries, it should accept parallel arrangements in other countries as well.

Fourth, we should separate the two kinds of ethics, which the German philosopher Karl-Otto Apel has called Ethics A and Ethics B (Apel 1973). Ethics A deals with principles that are appropriate under ideal circumstances, where everybody is willing to act in accordance with such reasonable principles, assuming that others will do likewise. Ethics B, on the other hand, deals with situations where this is not the case, i.e., where some actors have an eye only for their own narrow self-interest and are willing to sacrifice principles that work against their immediate interest. This forces other actors to think in more strategic ways, for instance, to search for arrangements that are favourable to the obstinate parties. When such arrangements are not satisfactory from an impartial point of view, actors need to consider how far they dare act as if the ideal circumstances, which they find it worth to further, were already established. This involves a risk that needs to be taken into account, and nobody can be expected to move very far beyond anyone else.

Besides impartiality and universalization, a number of other general criteria are used in ethical argumentation, but these are typically the same as for other kinds of argumentation. Ethical argumentation parallels science in its demand for consistency and coherence, for precision and sensitivity to difference, as well as for relevance and appropriateness.

It is often asked what motivation one may have to take impartial or universalisable considerations into account instead of simply acting selfishly. One could call attention to the fact that even from a selfish point of view it is quite often favourable to think in terms of impartiality in order to avoid other people's negative reaction and that it would therefore be advantageous to develop this way of thinking as a habit (Hare 1981). In a number of cases, however, e.g., the treatment of future generations and other species, this would not be the case, because they would not be able to hurt current people (Hume 1751/1966; Barry 1989; Arler 1996). The motivation must be of a different kind.

The best answer is undoubtedly that self-respect is a fundamental need in human lives, and that self-respect (similar to respect from others) demands that one can defend one's actions with arguments that everybody else ought to accept as reasonable and sufficient.

Environmental ethics

Environmental ethics is the part of ethics that is concerned with the good and the right in relation to human impact on our actual and/or future environment. This is quite a broad subject area, which overlaps with several other kinds of ethics (e.g., bioethics, social ethics, or international ethics). Environmental ethics are never sharply separated from ethics in general by some sort of insuperable barrier.

One point, however, does become more obvious in environmental ethics than in most traditional discussions of ethics. When environmental issues are at stake, it is often not sufficient to ask whether one's actions can be justified before an audience that includes only one's contemporary fellow citizens. One must further include not only people from other nations and cultures, but also people from distant generations, and even, in principle, members of other species. When live discussions take place about environmental issues, future generations and members of other species often need to be represented somehow by current advocates, either directly by people taking on this role or indirectly as scrutinizing representatives of certain standpoints in our inner dialogues. The very questions of how and to what extent future generations and other species ought to be taken into consideration has been a recurring issue in environmental ethics.

The main purpose of environmental ethics is to make ethical evaluations of decisions that may lead to serious short-term or long-term changes in the environment of humans. This is the case in relation to various kinds of decisions:

- projects (e.g., would a new bridge be a good idea?);
- technologies (e.g., should we allow GMO crops?);
- plans (e.g., do the new nature plans focus on the right issues?);
- rules (e.g., in which cases is the Polluter Pays Principle the right rule to use?);
- laws (e.g., is EU's Water Framework Directive too demanding?);
- social models (e.g., can modern market societies ever become sustainable?); and
- methods (e.g., should we use CBA or LCA when weighing environmental consequences?).

A five-step model for ethically informed decision-making

These are all complex issues, and one cannot expect to be able to find one right solution to each problem simply by knowing ethical theory. Many decision makers are not even aware that their decisions can properly be termed ethical. Quite often, they see ethics as a peripheral aspect that comes last in line after the much more important economic, political, social, or military aspects. What is seldom realised is that these apparently different aspects are actually various ways of applying ethics, or, to put it more mildly, that ethics is there all along, even when one discusses these other aspects.

Ethical theories and the five-step model

Let us now turn to ethical theories and their roles in decision-making. I hope to show that – from a pluralist and complementary point of view – the contributions of some major ethical theories are best understood and employed using a five-step model that reflects, or rather stylises, the processes used in actual decision-making. This model can also serve as

Fig. 1. The five-step model of ethically informed decision-making

the backbone for checklists of relevant ethical aspects in specific cases. It is not only intended to be useful as a heuristic advice to raise general awareness about ethical theories and concerns. It may also serve as guidance for policy-advisors and decision-makers in their effort to make ethically informed decisions without being forced to make an *a priori* choice of theory.

The model starts with a situation where there is a need for decision-making in a complex case. More than one solution is possible, because several goods are at stake and a number of considerations seem relevant but point in different directions. Ethics works continually behind the scene, but explicit ethical debates become particularly important in difficult decision-making cases marked by internal or external conflict.

Step 1. Assessment of consequences

The first step in the model is an important element in all ethical theories, but is particularly prominent in consequentialist or teleological theories. The purpose here is to identify and weigh the various consequences that are likely to occur in order to find the solution, which either maximizes or optimizes the total of good consequences (and/or minimizes the bad consequences) of an action, a rule, a law, a method, etc. This analysis is seldom easy, because consequences typically come out in very different shapes. Building a road, for instance, may save travellers time by making it easier and more comfortable to get from point A to point B, and this may attract business and industry. However, it is also likely to disturb neighbours and affect wildlife, change local traffic patterns, cause or prevent accidents, change emission levels, etc.

If it were possible to compare all the different kinds of consequences using only one common denominator, which is neutral to varied subjective conceptions of the good, it would make assessments of consequences much easier. Consequentialists have therefore come up with a number of suggestions about denominators they expect will match human intuitions. The first of these is pleasure, happiness, well-being or welfare suggesting that what counts in the end is the subjective state of human beings (or of sensitive animals in general). In order for a decision to be good, it must be good or pleasant for someone, who then becomes happier.

Even if one accepts this controversial premise, and further, as recommended by Jeremy Bentham, abstracts from differences in personal circumstances and individual sensibilities (Bentham 1789/1996), it is still not easy to weigh the broad variety of consequences that occur in complex cases with impacts appearing over long periods of time. States of happiness are notoriously difficult to measure, as Bentham's followers noticed (Jevons 1888), and even though one can sometimes do with ordinal (more or less) values rather than numerical cardinal values in simpler cases, complex cases seem to demand more precise measures because several separate considerations are at stake at the same time.

It has therefore been suggested to use preference satisfaction either as a) a proxy for happiness, which then remains the final measure, or b) as an independent criterion (Singer 1993). If preference satisfaction is used as a proxy, the idea is that, if people get their preferences satisfied, happiness is likely to result. The stronger the preference, the more happiness can be expected to follow, when it is satisfied. If preference satisfaction is used as an independent criterion, it must be emphasized that it does not always lead to happiness. A junkie may have strong preferences for drugs, for instance, even though he or she knows perfectly well that drug use is likely to end in misery (Pareto 1927/1971). Theorists who defend preference satisfaction as an independent criterion would typically use one of two arguments, either a) most people's preferences are after all fairly considered, and on average more preference satisfaction will lead to more happiness (Marshall 1920/1946); or b) there are goals other than happiness related to the pursuit of preference satisfaction, primarily the freedom to choose (Sen 1987). When more preferences are satisfied, more people will be capable of having some of their dreams come true, even if a fraction of these fulfilled dreams causes more misery than happiness.

But is it easier to measure preference satisfaction than happiness? The answer can hardly be positive, unless one accepts one further assumption, which already Bentham defended, namely, that the total amount of possible preference satisfaction relies on the total purchasing power of people as consumers. If a society is wealthy, more people can have their preferences satisfied and are therefore more likely to feel free and/or be happy (Bentham 1887). Consequently, economic wealth becomes a measurable proxy for preference satisfaction, which again may be a proxy for happiness and freedom. If this is true, and if happiness and freedom are the ultimate goals, economic growth must be a main, maybe even the main (deduced) goal in society.

Some reservations have to be noted, though, before this conclusion can be accepted. First, regardless of whether happiness, freedom or preference satisfaction itself is the goal, it will not be possible to maximize the totality of good consequences for individuals if means, capacities, or opportunities are distributed very unevenly. The marginal value of means and opportunities, measured in terms of economic value, will inevitably diminish the further one gets beyond a certain minimum level. This means that in order to maximize happiness, freedom, or satisfaction of preferences, the goal of maximizing economic wealth at least has to be combined with a reasonable distribution of this wealth.

Second, commodities bought on the market cannot satisfy all individual preferences nor can all kinds of goods be obtained with money (e.g., Walzer 1983; Sandel 2012). This is not only the case with superior goods like love, friendship, life and death, or with public goods like scientific truth, political influence, and public offices, but also with important goods like free time, which often disappears in the struggle for wealth, or biodiversity and other kinds of environmental goods that are often threatened by an expansions of economic activities. These goods all have some kind of economic value, of course, but they are treated as externalities, not only because there are no actual markets where they are for sale or because they are difficult to monetize on virtual markets, but because something basic in human life is betrayed if they are bought and sold on the market.

Third, it is hard to talk about happiness, wellbeing, preference-satisfaction, or economic wealth as major goals if people are happy and feel good for all the wrong reasons, or if the preferences they pursue are unconsidered and lead in bad directions. Likewise, one enjoys a very constrained kind of freedom if it is used to achieve goods that one would never pursue if one had had just a little time for calm and sober reflection. It is important to leave plenty of room for mistakes, and we certainly all need to be tolerant about the way people choose to live, but this cannot imply that one must always keep the door closed to rational discussion about worthwhile life goals. Even some utilitarians agree about this, and therefore only want to measure satisfaction of informed desires in their accounts of consequences, although this obviously undermines any insistence on neutrality (Griffin 1986).

Happiness, preference satisfaction, and economic value are not the only candidates for neutral measures. Yet another apparently neutral measure has been used, particularly in the health care sector (e.g., Weinstein et al.

2009; Nord et al. 2009): QALYs, quality adjusted life years (or HALYs: health adjusted life years, or DALYs: disability adjusted life years). A fully healthy person's life year counts as one, whereas sick, injured or disabled people's life years count for less, dependent on the seriousness of their decease or injury.

The point is that we should always try to maximize the total number of QALYs when making decisions about allocation of economic and other resources to various sectors or projects. The closer a person's life gets to a baseline state of full quality, the more it counts, and society should therefore try to avoid injuries or eventually upgrade injured lives, particularly of younger persons, where upgrading has more durable effects than with older people. According to these standards, improving younger lives will have first priority in the health care system, even though it was the elderly people who built the system in the first place. By default, fairness and equity are absent from these calculations; distributive criteria like equality or desert have no place in this system.

The weighing of consequences does not necessarily depend on the use of neutral quantitative measures, though, nor is maximisation the only possible standard to use when consequences are assessed. Instead, one may proceed by making qualitative assessments on two levels. Firstly, one can try to consider which kinds of basic goods or values are needed in order to lead a good life from cradle to grave, almost no matter what else one's conception of the good includes. Apart from food, shelter, security, and other kinds of physical goods, obvious candidates are mutual recognition, social inclusion, personal relationships, beautiful surroundings, meaningfulness, education, etc. If the consequences of a project are likely to do damage to one or more of these basic values, it should be avoided. If, on the other hand, the consequences of the project are neutral to or enhance the basic goods, it should be allowed or even furthered.

Second, in addition to stating the basic requirements of a good life for everybody, one could set up a number of non-neutral goals, the achievement of which may qualify the good life in society even further. One could argue, for instance, that curiosity, reflectivity, and virtuosity are virtues that should be encouraged, and that establishing institutions for sciences and arts will bring life in society to a higher and more desirable level. This does not necessarily make people happier in any easily measurable sense. Practising science and art is dependent on discipline, and it may for this reason alone disturb other parts of life. It can also be terribly annoying if a problem is hard to crack. Still, one can argue, as John Stuart Mill famously did, that it is preferable to be a dissatisfied Socrates than a happy pig, because human development is the most meaningful goal one can devise (Mill 1957).

Step 2. Justice, care, and rights

Consequentialism occurs in many forms, but it is more often concerned with the total impact of an action, a project, or a rule than with the distribution of consequences on individuals. In economics, for instance, the widely used Kaldor-Hicks criterion says that an action should be continued if the gains from the action can, in principle, compensate all losses, but that compensations need not actually be provided. Other kinds of ethics are more oriented toward the destiny of individuals, however, and are much more tentative in cases of where the wellbeing of individuals is sacrificed for the common good.

Some of the main concepts in ethical theories, which focus on the fate of individuals, are human rights, equity, fairness, and justice (e.g., Rawls 1971; Dworkin 1977; Barry 1989; Griffin 2008). It is not enough that the social pool of goods is growing due to a project or a rule if it leaves some individuals significantly worse off. It is not always enough that a larger pool gives losing individuals better chances to improve their situation in the future. Nor is a project acceptable if it leads to an unfair distribution of goods and damages. As Rawls has put it, consequentialists often forget to take seriously the distinction between people.

If, for instance, a calculus indicates that the total economic outcome would be greater (primarily to the advantage of few shareholders and managers) if heavily polluting industries are not forced to improve their environmental standards, but instead are placed in countries where local people are willing to work for low wages despite the significant risks, the unfair allocation of costs and benefits would alarm ethicists, whose main focus is on human rights, justice, and equity.

Often ethical theories that focus on justice, care, and the rights of individuals can be seen as complementary to consequentialist accounts. One does not have to rely on any comprehensive theory of individuals' rights in order to find it appropriate to take the distribution of good and bad consequences into account. Measured in terms of total impact, it may be a good idea, for instance, to catch young healthy people and use them in medical experiments that are assumed to help save hundreds of lives. Consequentialists have argued that this is only a good idea if it is done in secrecy; otherwise fear would spread throughout society. Most people, however, whether they rely on specific rights-oriented theories or not, would be appalled more immediately by the practice and try to stop it at once. The harm done to innocent and involuntarily involved people would be much too serious to be acceptable.

However, one should be careful not to exaggerate the difference between consequentialism and ethical theories focusing on individuals. There is a great deal of concern for individuals in consequentialism, too. Look again at economics, where a basic individualist assumption is that there is no common good apart from the aggregation of individual goods (or preference satisfactions). In general, utilitarianism is based on the fundamental premise that everybody has an equal right to have his or her feelings and/or preferences included in the total account. Everybody should count for one and nobody for more than one (Singer 1993). Most utilitarians are also aware of the law of the diminishing value of incremental income or wealth, stating that poor people get more happiness out of an extra amount of money than rich people. A more equal distribution of money and goods therefore contributes positively to total happiness. Finally, qualitatively oriented consequentialists, who care more about the quality of life in society than about quantities of money or goods, would certainly be upset if major injustices are among the inevitable consequences of otherwise reasonable decisions.

It is also important to notice that situations are seldom as clear cut as in the medical experiment example just mentioned. It is not always obvious which potential victims are entitled to extra protection. Nor is it always easy to determine how serious damage to individuals must be in order to be merit special protection. For instance, most people would agree that in order to reduce inconveniences for the immediate neighbours, road building in urban areas necessitates erecting noise barriers. On the other hand, it is a matter of controversy whether special considerations should be shown to distant neighbours of wind turbines just because the sight of moving wings disturbs them.

Bridges for crossing animals are even more controversial, because not everybody accepts animals, at least not wild animals, as proper objects for care (cf. e.g., Attfield 1983/1991; Regan 1983; Taylor 1986; O'Neill 1996; Arler 2009). Or take the likely future disappearance of land due to the drop in sea level caused by climate change. The needs of the people who own the land are seldom even mentioned when road projects are discussed. This is partly due to the fact that the connection between the new road and the flooding of distant islands is anything but straightforward. Another reason is that they live so far away in both space and time that one might question whether they should be considered participants of our morally binding community, or at least how far our obligations can be toward them (cf. e.g., Beitz 1979; Miller 1995 and 2007; Rawls 1999; Caney 2005). If the criterion is that one should select projects that help those who are least fortunate, no matter where they live in space and (current and future) time, money used for road building could be better used elsewhere.

Step 3. Virtues, judgment, and reflective equilibrium

We have seen so far that there are at least two traditions of ethics, one focusing mainly on the total outcome, the other one focusing on justice and the rights of individuals. We have only to scratch the surface before it becomes obvious that there are a number of similarities across the two traditions, and that each tradition includes subtraditions with highly different approaches based on divergent assumptions. Intense philosophical analysis may lead to a reduction of the number of competing serious approaches, but even if this happens, it is quite unlikely that everybody will end up agreeing on one universal ethical approach or method that makes it possible to solve all ethical dilemmas or conflicts whenever they occur.

We are thus faced with a certain amount of theoretical pluralism or at least a plurality of approaches and considerations. Different theories and approaches appear in the decision-making process, each with their specific set of reasonable points and suggestions for principles and methods; however, none of them are capable of convincing everybody once and for all in a way that makes other positions superfluous. How do we proceed? Basically, what is needed is an example that is capable of doing two things. First, it must be able to identify reasonable points from the various theoretical approaches that are relevant to the specific case at hand; second, it must be capable of weighing these points in a suitable way. This instance cannot be some unique device that relies on one particular method, because we have already seen that methods are based on controversial assumptions that need correction from other approaches.

The only instance that we may actually rely on is the good judge, politician, or planner, i.e., a human being who possesses the necessary skills and virtues that make it possible for him or her to weigh and judge a plurality of arguments arriving from different theories in complex situations. This is the basic point in virtue ethics: ethics are not a game for automatons; at the end of the day it all comes down to judgments made by sensitive, reasoning human beings. In order to qualify these judgments, it is necessary not only to know the relevant facts, opinions, and potential obligations related to a case. One must also develop virtues that make it possible to deal with complex issues in a proper way.

Which kinds of virtues are we talking about? Some are of a general nature, such as self-control, critical self-knowledge, caring, and honesty. Courage is important in cases of conflict. Temperance, prudence, moderation, and a refined sense of justice are particularly important when ethical questions are at stake. Some virtues are important in order to keep morality free from rigid moralism: tolerance, generosity, magnanimity, taste, humour, openness, and an appropriate dose of cheerfulness. Wisdom is a virtue that sums up a number of important character traits. A person who possesses an adequate amount of these virtues is likely to have a sufficient amount of judgment to balance different kinds of considerations.

What does a person with sufficient virtues and judgment do when he or she weighs arguments, claims, and considerations? The most important element is the search for coherence among all well-considered arguments and claims that are relevant in specific cases. This includes bits and pieces from both ethical and scientific theories that one believes to be valid; principles that usually appear acceptable in use; empirical facts about the specific case; experiences and considered judgments from similar cases; and intuitions related to possible consequences. If the considered claims and judgments are so much in conflict that a coherent combination is out of the question, it will be necessary to adjust one or more of the beliefs or intuitions until a fairly stable balance has been established. This is what Rawls has called establishing or restoring a 'reflective equilibrium' (Rawls 1971).

When decisions are made in complex situations, one seldom has time to reconsider all relevant theoretical and normative factors. In particular, it is not possible to reconsider all ethical theories that back up reasonable claims, values, and principles. So one may be forced to consider various types of reasons that all appear suitable to the case and can be applied in a noncontradictory way, even though they are normally highlighted by conflicting theories. The various reasons may be incommensurable in the sense that there is no common denominator to measure them against each other, but this does not mean that they are incomparable (Bernstein 1983; Griffin 1986, chp. V).

It would be a mistake to believe that reasons only derive validity from general theories and lose all credibility if one discards underlying theories. If this were the case, theories would be like closed bubbles with impervious surfaces, and it would be impossible to argue across them. Theories are better understood as diverse ways of organising reasons, most of which appear in different shapes in alternative theories and, by and large, retain their relevance even if certain theoretical constructions break down. People's happiness does not stop being relevant just because one has dropped hedonistic utilitarianism as an all-encompassing theory.

A pluralist reflective equilibrium solution may seem unsatisfactory if one seeks a comprehensive theory fully equipped with a few foundational premises, from which one can deduce a consistent and well-considered set of values and principles that can be applied easily and coherently on all occasions. Reflective equilibrium works fine on a pluralist platform, however, with a differentiated mix of reasons, values, and obligations with a varied background. This platform may actually turn out to be less fragile than a platform designed from a single consistent, yet fallible theory, unless, of course, this theory itself turns out to be so complex and differentiated that it is hard to distinguish from pluralist approaches.

A recurring critique of virtue ethics is that it is not virtues but only arguments that one relies on when decisions are made. This is partly true, but arguments never turn up in easily recognisable preformed chunks that make it easy for anyone to apply and weigh them in specific situations. Patience, sensitivity, caring, and being scrupulous are necessary virtues if one wants to get the arguments right. Creativity and reflectivity are needed to refine reasons in order to restate and combine apparently contradictory claims. Without tolerance and openness one is likely to overlook important, but strangely expressed points. If a refined sense of justice is lacking, it is hard to believe that a variety of needs, wants and claims, which are not immediately commensurable, can be balanced in a proper way. Taste and humour bring more than mere superficial elegance and wit to solutions that may otherwise be dismissed.

However important individuals' virtues and weighing ability are, even the best judge must face his or her own limitations. Nobody can know all relevant arguments in a particular case. Nor can one single person be aware of all points of views, all needs, all wishes. Even the best reasons seldom lead smoothly into obvious conclusions. Too many 'burdens of judgment' (Rawls 1993) hinder different people from ending up with the very same conclusions in complex cases, no matter how reasonably they all proceed. Moreover, it may not be an easy task to find the best judge with moral integrity and the right combination of virtues. And even if it were possible to select a few persons, who are better than the rest, to evaluate reasons and weigh considerations, it would be extremely risky to entrust them with decision-making power in a broad variety of complex cases. Human beings are fragile creatures, and power corrupts all too easily if it is left without opposing forces. So we have to move on to a fourth step.

Step 4. Stakeholder dialogue

We have seen so far that there are a variety of ethical theories with diverse suggestions for rules and methods. Even though most people would agree that each of the theories represents important aspects and considerations, none of them seems able to beat the rest and be crowned as ultimate champion. Pluralism of theories as well as of considerations is difficult, however, and virtues are needed in order to be able to judge and weigh various kinds of deliberation. But if even the most virtuous person cannot be entrusted with full decision-making power, because he or she cannot know all relevant aspects of complex cases, how do we proceed?

The next step is conducted as a dialogue, where all stakeholders (and, if relevant, selected experts) are invited, first, to present arguments, viewpoints, needs, and aspirations that they believe to be relevant in the specific case, and second, to take part in a common evaluation process, where arguments and considerations are tried and weighed against each other in a common search for reflective equilibrium in a specific case. This exchange of arguments, commands, and requests expands the horizon from that of the singular decision maker, who was the focus in Step 3. It also brings much stronger feelings, engagement, and commitments into the debate than is possible in the more detached atmosphere of inner dialogues. There is an obvious advantage: people are more engaged and therefore also more observant in cases that mean a lot to them. However, this commitment can be a major weakness as well. In heated debates it is more difficult to keep one's cool. When strong feelings and personal interests are at stake, it becomes more difficult to make fair judgments of opponents' arguments.

A basic point of Jürgen Habermas' account of dialogue or discourse ethics (Habermas 1983) is that the completion of stakeholder dialogues legitimizes their outcome, whatever this happens to be, as long as certain basic rules are observed (cf. Alexy 1978). It is of primary importance that all partakers should participate on equal terms: everybody should be allowed to present their own points of view and bring attention to their own needs and wishes. Secondly, as all participants should only be convinced by arguments, they should try to reduce the influence of irrelevant matters such as personal interest, mutual attractions, impression of status, or fear of power. Everybody should avoid the use of force, fraud, and manipulation. Finally, everybody should strive to reach a common consensus. The participants should always aim for coherence, consistency, and correctness.

Public debates do not render inner dialogues superfluous, however, nor do they dispense with the need for the development of virtues among the participants. As long as heated feelings together with unavoidable inequalities and instances of force and fraud enter the discourse, the final results, if there are any, cannot carry as heavy a burden of proof as some discourse ethicists would like (Arler 1991; Scanlon 1998). It is undoubtedly an excellent idea to involve as many stakeholders as possible in decision-making processes. However, these processes can never be so clean in terms of equality, impartiality, and rationality that an achieved consensus among the attending participants would guarantee full legitimacy of the outcome. Reaching consensus would in itself be the exception rather than the rule in complex cases. A fifth step is needed in order to reach legitimate conclusions.

Step 5. Procedures

If consensus is difficult to reach in stakeholder dialogue, or if the consensus reached is unreliable due to asymmetric power relations, we will have to move to yet another level. In this final level, Step 5, formal procedures are introduced: negotiations, voting, polls, trials, and in some cases, even draws. Rawls has distinguished between three kinds of procedural justice (Rawls 1971, chp. 14). Perfect procedural justice occurs when there are independent criteria for a reasonable solution, and a specific procedure can give the desired outcome. This is seldom the case. Imperfect procedural justice occurs when an independent criterion exists, but it is impossible to design rules that guarantee correct results. This is the case in criminal trials. In pure procedural justice no independent criterion is available, but if the procedure is carried through properly, the outcome is fair. This is the case, for instance, with voting.

What can formal procedures do that could not be done on the first four levels? First of all, procedures can stop quarrels, at least temporarily, by specifying universally acceptable ways to reach decisions despite reasonable disagreement about substantial matters. When procedures have been designed in advance, in calm argument-driven sequences and through processes that are commonly accepted, they function as reliable backstops that can put an end to conflict-ridden decision-making processes.

It is worth remembering that the basic points introduced in each of the previous levels have not been redundant, but still do their job in this final round. First, if the procedures themselves were not constructed on the basis of points that emerge in theories applied to previous steps, they could never be accepted as backstops. Democratic procedures, for instance, build on ethical assumptions such as the right of individual citizens to participate equally in decision-making and to have their needs and aspirations taken into consideration. Similarly, law court procedures are based on the assumptions that all citizens are equally entitled to fair and impartial treatment, that arguments should carry weight independent of status and purchasing power, etc.

The main ethical content of the cases, which in the end have to be resolved through formal procedures, has already been uncovered in the first four steps. The consequences have been surveyed and analysed, questions of justice and distribution have been considered, involved parties have tried to weigh the different considerations in order to reach reflective equilibrium, discussions have taken place, and conflicts have in many cases been boiled down to reasonable disagreement. In standard sequences of decision-making, formal procedures are needed mainly in grey areas, where impartial evaluations of arguments can no longer clearly separate black areas of unjustifiable claims from white areas of inescapable truths.

Sometimes there is no settled final procedure that can end conflicts. This is the case, for instance, when there is reasonable disagreement about which of the existing procedures on different levels ought to be used (e.g., Arler 2012). When such cases occur in well-organized democratic societies, the courts usually have the formal competence to settle the dispute. In others cases, democratic assemblies can fill the gap and settle the conflict by passing a law.

When decisions are made through reasonable procedures, which are backed up by a large majority of citizens, their legitimacy is high. It is never complete, though. In almost all political cases at least one minority disagrees with the decision, and quite often this minority continues its efforts to change it even though the procedural setup behind the decision is respected. Civil disobedience only seldom occurs in democratic societies. When it does, it is because the result of certain procedures seems illegitimate and unacceptable to a group of people, measured by standards they believe everybody ought to accept, and it overrules the legitimacy springing from compliance with commonly accepted procedures.

These phenomena show that there is nothing final about the procedures in Step 5. It is always possible to return to one of the previous steps before moving upward again. In complex cases with significant public attention, no decision will be taken without procedures as a final step, even though all the important ingredients in the case may already be settled before the final confirmation.

> **Checklist of issues to be considered before decisions are made**
>
> 1 **Consequences**
>   Which consequences can be expected? Which consequences count and for whom? For how long? How should the various consequences be weighed? Which values are affected? Can common denominators be used? How can the best consequences be achieved?
> 2 **Justice and rights**
>   Who are the relevant stakeholders? Do all persons/animals/organisms count? Equally? Are all relevant stakeholders taken into account? Are relevant claims

A five-step model for ethically informed decision-making

on consideration respected? Are all stakeholders treated in a fair and just manner?

3 **Virtues, judgment, and reflective equilibrium**
   Have I found the right balance among different claims? Have I been sufficiently diligent, just, courageous, etc., in my judgment? Am I too superficial, too selfish, too cowardly, or too impatient? Do I listen to arguments, or do I only act out of habit?

4 **Stakeholder dialogue**
   Have all stakeholders been heard? Have all stakeholders been involved, and are their contributions taken sufficiently into account? Have groups of people or organisms that cannot participate in dialogues been properly represented by advocates?

5 **Procedures**
   Are decisions made through fair procedures? Are the decisions made in a democratic manner? What exactly does this mean? Do the procedures contain system-based flaws and inequalities?

Fig. 2. Checklist for decision-making

The role of theories

Let us return now to the original question: What can general ethical theories do for decision makers who are dealing with complex environmental issues? First of all, they can be helpful for anybody who tries to get an overview of the relevant ethical elements in a case. Checklists such as the one shown in the text box are informed by ethical theories and can be quite useful in complex cases with a number of considerations to take into account. This also means that items on the checklist can make decision makers aware of important issues they might have missed. Even the best decision makers will inevitably overlook certain elements, which some professional ethicists might have worked on and tried to bring to light in their theories. The debate on sustainability and sustainable development, for example, has certainly been informed by more or less specialised discussions on ethics.

Third, ethical theories may help decision makers to make their justifications both more coherent and more sensitive to differences. In the debates surrounding ethical theories, many differentiations are made and various suggestions for integration presented. This can obviously be helpful for observant decision makers, too. I write "may help" quite deliberately, because abstract debates about ethical theories can also be quite confusing and extremely time consuming if one is more interested in solving real world problems than in continuing to pursue nitty-gritty details.

Fourth, ethical theories have already been applied to the construction of methods and procedures that are used, for instance, in law, in economics, in public voting and election procedures, in parliamentary rules, or in court trials. These methods and procedures often become much more understandable once the ethical arguments behind them are presented as parts of more comprehensive theoretical constructions, and once their strengths and weaknesses become more apparent.

Ethical theories cannot in themselves determine the outcome of a conflict. Cases are usually too complex. A plurality of approaches and considerations that typically are highlighted by different theories is relevant in almost all interesting cases, and a reasonable equilibrium among the various claims and considerations can hardly be reached unless one is willing to involve more than one theoretical perspective.

It should also be remembered, however, that quite often disagreements are related more to the facts and interpretations involved in a case than to general ethical norms and values. Aristotle himself asserted that once an agreement about the factual elements in a case has been established, conflict will quickly disappear, because people seldom disagree on general principles and values (Aristotle 1968). He may have expressed this insight a bit too simplistically, but it is very important to remember that factual details become much more important when one is practising applied ethics rather than discussing ethical theory.

References

Alexy, R. 1978. Eine Theorie des praktischen Diskurses, in: Oelmüller W., ed. 1978, *Normenbegründung, Normendurchsetzung*, Paderborn: Ferdinand Schöningh.

Apel, K.-O. 1973. *Transformation der Philosophie*, bd. 2, Frankfurt a. M.: Suhrkamp.

Aristotle 1968. *Nicomachean Ethics*, London: Heinemann.

Arler, F. 1991. Diskursmoral, in: *Omkring dømmekraften*, ph.d.-thesis, Aarhus 1991, p. 178-227, (http://people.plan.aau.dk/~arler/manuskripter/Finn%20Arler%20ph%20d%20-afhandling.pdf).

Arler, F. 1996. Two Concepts of Justice," *Human Ecology Review* 3 (1), 1996, p. 63-76.

Arler, F. 2009, *Biodiversitet. Videnskab kultur etik*, vol. II, Aalborg: Aalborg University Press.

Arler, F. 2011. Landscape democracy in a globalizing world – the case of Tange Lake, in: *Landscape Research*, 36 4, 2011, p. 487-507.

Attfield, R. 1983/1991. *The Ethics of Environmental Concern*, Athens & London: The University of Georgia Press.

Barry, B. 1989. *Theories of Justice*, London: Harvester-Wheatsheaf.

Barry, B. 1995, *Justice as Impartiality*, Oxford: Oxford University Press.

Beitz, C.R. 1979, *Political Theory and International Relations*, Princeton: Princeton University Press.

Bentham, J. 1996. *An Introduction to the Principles of Morals and Legislation* (1789), Burns, J.H., Har, H.L.A. & Rose, F., eds., Oxford: Clarendon Press.

Bentham, J. 1887. *Theory of Legislation*, Dumont E. ed., London: Trübner & Company.

Bernstein, R.J. 1983. *Beyond Objectivism and Relativism: Science, Hermeneutics, and Praxis*, Philadelphia, PA: University of Pennsylvania Press.

Broome, J. 1999. *Ethics out of Economics*, Cambridge: Cambridge University Press.

Caney, S. 2005. *Justice Beyond Borders: A Global Political Theory*, Oxford: Oxford University Press.

Dworkin, R. 1977. *Taking Rights Seriously*, London: Duckworth.

Griffin, J. 1986. *Well-being. Its meaning, measurement, and moral importance*, Oxford: Clarendon Press.

Griffin, J. 2008. *On Human Rights*, Oxford: Oxford University Press.

Habermas, J. 1983. Diskursethik, in: Habermas, J. 1983, *Moralbewusstsein und kommunikatives Handeln*, Frankfurt am Main: Suhrkamp, p. 53-125.

Hare, R.M. 1981, *Moral thinking: its levels, method, and point*, Oxford: Clarendon Press.

Hume, D. 1966. *An Enquiry Concerning the Principles of Morals* (1751), La Salle, Illinois.

Jevons, W.S. 1888. *The Theory of Political Economy*, Third Edition, London: Macmillan and Co.

Kant, I. 1980. *Anthropologie in pragmatischer Hinsicht*, Hamburg: Felix Meiner Verlag.

Kymlicka, W. 2002. *Contemporary Political Philosophy. An Introduction.* Oxford: Oxford University Press.

Marshall, A. 1946. *Principles of Economics*, 1890, 1920^8, London: Macmillan.

Mill, J.S. 1957. *Utilitarianism*, London: Bobbs Merrill Co.

Miller, D. 1995. *On Nationality*. Oxford: Oxford University Press.

Miller, D. 2007. *National Responsibility and Global Justice*, Oxford: Oxford University Press.

Nord, E., N. Daniels, M. Kamlet 2009. QUALYs: Some Challenges, in: *Value in Health* **12** (Suppl. I), p. 10-15.

O'Neill, J. 1993. *Ecology, Policy and Politics. Human Well-Being and the Natural World*, London: Routledge.

Pareto, V. 1971. *Manual of Political Economy* (1909, 1927), London and Basingstoke: Mac-Millan.

Rawls, J. 1971. *A Theory of Justice*, Cambridge, Mass.: Harvard University Press.

Rawls, J. 1993. *Political Liberalism*, New York: Columbia University Press.

Rawls, J. 1993. *The Law of Peoples*, Cambridge: Harvard University Press.

Raz, J. 1986. *The Morality of Freedom*. London: Oxford University Press.

Regan, T. 1983. *The Case for Animal Rights*, Berkeley/Los Angeles: University of California Press.

Sandel, M. 2012. *What Money Can't Buy. The Moral Limits of Markets*, London: Allan Lane.

Scanlon, T. 1998. *What We Owe to Each Other*, Cambridge, Mass.: Belknap Press of Harvard University Press.

Sen, A. 1987. *On Ethics and Economics*, Oxford: Basil Blackwell.

Sidgwick, H. 1963. *The Methods of Ethics*, 7. ed., London: MacMillan & Co.
Singer, P. 1993. *Practical ethics*, Cambridge: Cambridge University Press.
Taylor, P. 1986. *Respect for Nature*, Princeton University Press.
Walzer, M. 1983. *Spheres of Justice*, New York: Basic Books.
Weinstein, M. C., G. Torrance A. McGuire 2009. QALYs: The Basics, in: *Value in Health* **12** (Suppl. I), 2009, p. 5-9.
Wellmer, A. 1986. *Ethik und Dialog*, Frankfurt a. M.: Suhrkamp.
Wenz, P. S. 1988. *Environmental Justice*, Albany: State University of New York Press.

Mogens Pahuus

Aspects of morality
Corresponding to aspects of actions and aspects of persons

In this article I will defend the view that there is an ontological foundation for morality, or rather that one can make distinctions among four ontological aspects of action and four corresponding aspects of the person, each of them connected to a certain type of moral consideration and concept. These four types of moral concepts are developed in each of the four main types of normative ethics: consequentialism/utilitarianism, Kantian deontological ethics, discourse-ethics/recognition-ethics, and, lastly, ontological ethics (ethics of caring). This theory of the connections between the four aspects of action/the person and four types of moral thinking explains why it is necessary in practical or applied ethics to take into account these four types of ethical considerations and concepts. Generally, a complex moral situation involves all four aspects of action/the person.

Four aspects of action and the corresponding four types of moral considerations

Insofar as you engage in goal-oriented actions, you pursue a goal that you consider a benefit or an advantage, but you also know that this pursuit may have harmful consequences. Therefore you try to behave in a way that maximizes the benefit and minimizes the harm. At the same time, you know that your action – consisting of an intervention in and alteration of the world – may affect other people and their chances of achieving their goals – and therefore it is natural to think in the same

Aspects of morality

way about other people. You wish to avoid harming them, avoid preventing them from achieving their goals. There is no necessity to think morally in relation to other people. But if one understands that other people can feel distress and pain in the same way as yourself, it is difficult to avoid seeing your own actions and the consequences of these in relation to other people in terms of benefit-harm. You are thinking according to a certain moral point of view.

Insofar as your goal-oriented actions have to be coordinated with the actions of other people, you cannot avoid thinking according to another moral point of view. When you make a promise ("I will do that tomorrow") or when you borrow something, you establish an obligation, a certain kind of "ought." To be aware of obligations is to think morally in a way other than you do when you think in terms of benefit/harm. Promising and borrowing is *eo ipso* establishing an obligation: to do tomorrow what you have promised – or to return what you have borrowed – after its use. The same is true for other types of cooperation.

Coordination can grow into cooperation, which is fundamentally, or rather minimally, mutual aid: If you help me, I will help you. So when one cooperates, one establishes equality. To cooperate is to say to each other: I will make no exception of myself. Similarly, when two persons communicate with each other in order to better understand a situation and their problems, they implicitly promise each other to tell the truth, to be honest, to seek mutual understanding and agreement – and not to act strategically.

But one can get even closer to other people in ways other than coordinating and cooperating with them. Face-to-face with another person I cannot help contacting the other or communicating with him – also without saying anything. And as long as I do this spontaneously, I deliver something of my life to him. If there is some spontaneity in the way I speak to him, I extend and deliver something of myself over to him. Therefore, the other is confronted with the choice: either he takes care of you or he is lets you down. Neutrality is not possible. Thinking in terms of what is best for the other insofar as you hold a part of his life in your hands is a fourth type of thinking morally. Here we talk about goodness (versus bad or evil) because a person who cares about the people with whom he comes into contact is a good person.

As to the assertion that the four types of action are necessary aspects of action in any type of society, I shall not say much. I agree with Habermas that there is a fundamental distinction between work (or goal-oriented action) and interaction – and then I distinguish between three different aspects of interaction. Of course interaction or social life differs very much in different societies, but I think one will always find the three elements I mention: coordination, cooperation, and the interdependence described by Løgstrup: entangledness.

The ethical theories have a tendency to establish one universal principle – or consideration. In my view they cover only one aspect of or type of action. It is not a universally valid principle that any act is good in so far as it creates as much happiness as possible for as many as possible or in so far as it maximizes the fulfillment of needs, but it is true, that you behave morally only if you consider the consequences for others of your interventions in the world. You only behave morally if you consider the consequences of your actions for all persons that are affected by your intervention. In the same way it is not universally true that any good action has to be done in respect to the categorical imperative, but it is true that when you coordinate with other people and cooperate with them, you obligate yourself in different ways. The idea of a communicating attitude (versus a strategic attitude) in discourse ethics and the idea of recognition of the other in recognition-ethics likewise are not the only supreme values in our lives, but they are valid as guiding ideas for our cooperation with others. And lastly it is not true that taking care of each other (love of neighbors or charity) is the center of ethics as maintained by K. E. Løgstrup and E. Levinas However, it is true that if a person (spontaneously) delivers himself to others or is delivered onto others – due to his distress or weakness – then goodness in the sense of spontaneous care is demanded by the situation.

The different aspects of morality are given as necessary concepts and considerations. But there is no given method of weighing them in a concrete situation. Here you have to make a judgment, both individually and collectively.

One can schematize what I just have explained in the following way:

Aspects of morality

Ontology	Ethics		
Aspects of the person Motivation/Identity	Types/aspects of action	Ethical concepts	Ethical theories
Basic needs/The mastering ego	Goal-oriented action	Benefit/good/advantage Harm/loss/damage	Teleological ethics Utilitarianism
Psychic-social needs/ The responsible ego	Interaction/Communication Coordination	Ethical duties Telling the truth/ Promising Borrowing/Contracting	Deontological e. Kantian ethics
Psychic-social needs The autonomous ego Dignity	Interaction/Communication Cooperation	Equality/Justice versus Injury	Deontological e. Discourse ethics Recognition e.
Urges/inclinations to self-realization The self The intrinsic worth of a human being	Interdependency The mutual relationship of being delivered-over-to Vulnerability/weakness/ distress	Trust/fidelity/sincerety Mercy/Lov Good versus evil	Caring ethics Nearness-ethics Løgstrup Levinas

Table 1. Judgments in terms of ontology and ethics

The central part of my model – the middle two rows – demonstrates the correspondence between aspects or types of action (the second row) and types of ethical concepts and considerations (the third row).

The phenomenon of ethics and resulting ethical considerations exist because we affect each other through our actions more or less directly. In the second row of the model are listed the actions that affect others indirectly: when you seek your own goals, you change the world and in this way your actions may have consequences for other persons and their chances of achieving their goals.

As you progress through the actions shown in the table, you reach ever closer relations. You are interacting and communicating with other people when you coordinate with them, but coordination – like promising or borrowing – is a rather formal, not very personal relation. You get closer to a person when you move from coordination to cooperation. Then he becomes a colleague or a comrade. But also this relation can be rather impersonal. You can get still closer to him – and that is the case in so far as you engage in a face-to-face-relation, where you behave spontaneously. In this case we become interdependent in the strongest sense of the word: we gain mutually something of the other person´s life.

In the third row I mention the ethical concepts that correspond to the different levels of action, or aspects of action. And in the fourth row I mention the normative ethical traditions or theories that build on (or focus on) a certain level or aspect of action. When you deal with a certain aspect of action, you have to call upon certain ethical concepts, and therefore a certain ethical theory becomes interesting or adequate.

If I am right in my assertion that these levels are at work in our other-related actions, then it is no wonder that we always have to think about ethical questions and difficulties in terms of a multitude of more or less conflicting ethical considerations. It is no wonder that we have to combine teleological, especially utilitarian, deontological and ontological ethical concepts and theories.

When issues in applied ethics are discussed you always find arguments pertaining to teleological traditions and deontological theories. Many moral philosophers have noticed this. But I think that mostly you find another type of moral consideration pertaining to ontological theories (the fourth level in my chart). (I borrow the term "ontological ethics" from Løgstrup). Some people feel that because these different ethical theories contradict each other (or are more or less irreconcilable), the use of different traditions in clarifying an issue in applied ethics is a kind of intellectual bankruptcy. But in my view human life demands the use of different types of ethical concepts, and therefore this combination of different ethical theories is what is needed intellectually.

Aspects of the person

In the first row of my chart I list the aspects of the person that correspond to the four levels of action. These aspects of the person are motivation and identity. One can distinguish between different types of motivation. I think one can argue that there is a fundamental difference between needs, on the one hand (traditionally divided into physical and psycho-social needs), and urges or inclinations to self-realization on the other side. I understand these urges as drives to use and develop your powers, talent, abilities. At the same time they are urges to make the world your own – to appropriate the world – in two ways: conquering the world and uniting with it. What is important is that these drives result in self-forgetful commitment to the world and to the others.

In a similar way, it is necessary to distinguish among the elements of personal identity. One important distinction is between the I – as Freud understands it (the reality-mastering instance in the person) – and the self – understood as the center of self-forgetful commitment to the world and other people. Finally, it is enlightening to distinguish among the elements of the I (the mastering I, the responsible I, and the autonomous I). The autonomous I is connected with dignity. The self is connected with the idea of the intrinsic worth of a person.

Illustrations

In the following section I will describe simple situations where the four levels of action and the four types of ethical concepts play a role. The first example is inspired by (but is not quite identical to) Sartre's famous tale about a student who sought his ethical advice. The second example is a situation in which doctors want to make an organ transplant.

The young man in Sartre's example wants to join the Free French forces because he thinks that fighting against the oppressors is the right and the good thing to do; combat will lead to the best consequences for him and his countrymen. He thinks morally in a teleological and utilitarian way, because he wants to act in a goal-directed way and sees the situation as one that can be changed through goal-directed action.

At the same time, the young man is aware of the fact that he has promised his father, who had died a few years earlier, to take care of his mother. He feels obligated to keep this promise. Here, he thinks deontologically.

But there are still other relevant ethical considerations. He also feels obliged to follow his friends, who have already joined the Free French forces. He feels that he will let down his comrades if he stays at home. He wants to risk his life as his comrades do. He wants to show solidarity, not to make an exception of himself. Here he also thinks in a deontological way, motivated by the obligations that are connected with cooperation with others and the equality that is so essential to cooperation.

Finally, he feels obligated in quite another sense. He is dear to his mother and she is dear to him, and therefore they are mutually dependent. They are self-delivering and hold much of each other's life in their hands. The young man feels a strong urge to care for his mother.

Now to the example of organ transplants. It is obvious that organ transplantation is a goal-directed activity and the goal is to make another person survive (longer than he would have otherwise). We carry out organ transplants because of teleological and utilitarian reasons. At the same time, we think consent is a necessary condition for using donor's organ(s). We may disagree about whether the consent has to be explicit or implicit (tacit) but we all think – and this is a deontological type of thinking -- that a person has a right to make decisions about his own body. The person should be autonomous, and as a consequence, a donor must give his informed consent for an organ transplant.

On the other hand, there are ethical considerations that speak against organ transplantation. We typically find two types of such considerations. The first are of a deontological type – maintaining that it is an offence against the dignity of a person (and therefore also the dignity of a breathing body) to use his organs. The other type of considerations concern the relatives; we hurt them when we force them to say good-bye forever to a son or a father who is still breathing. When one considers this morally wrong, one is thinking in terms of interdependence and caring.

	Sartre's example of the young man	Organ transplantation
Goal-oriented action/ Utilitarian ethics	Joining the Free French forces	Survival of another person
Coordination/ Deontological ethics	Keeping his promise to his father: to take care of his mother	The person has expressed his wish to be a donor.
Cooperation/ Discourse ethics	Following his friends: risking his life as they do	Offence against the dignity of a breathing body
Interdependency/ Caring ethics	Leaving his mother, who is dependent on him	Distressing the parents, who cannot say good-bye to him while he is still breathing

Table 2. Examples of ethical considerations

Considerations about "the good life"

When you hold part of another person's life in your hands, you have to think about what is best for the other person. You have to think about what makes a "good life." Here again I think that one can distinguish between a series of elements and ideas of the good life, each connected to a certain aspect of the person.

The person		The good life
Motivation	Identity	
Needs		Satisfaction of needs
	The mastering I	Cope with the situation
	The responsible I	Create and maintain your identity
	The autonomous I	Autonomy
Urges		Happiness
	The self	Self-realization

Table 3. The person and the good life

Thinking about different ideas of the good life is also relevant when there is a tension between taking care of other person and taking care of the values of one's own life. Here is where virtue-ethics tries to integrate the two areas. Virtue-ethics sees virtues as attitudes that simultaneously maintain and develop the community and the self-realization of the particular person.

Michael Kühler

The phenomenological trouble with moral dilemmas
Taking 'applied worries' seriously within theoretical ethics

Abstract

This paper is based on the view that theoretical ethics and applied ethics should be seen as mutually influential, i.e., that their plausible assumptions and conceptions should be harmonized or mutually incorporated in order to reach a coherent overall position. One of the main questions in this regard is whether the details of a situation are reflected adequately in moral reasoning and the judgment thus derived. Such worries are dubbed here as 'applied worries.' Taking the analysis of moral dilemmas as an example, the question is whether the familiar rejection of the possibility of 'real' moral dilemmas, featuring prominently in theoretical ethics, leaves enough conceptual room to incorporate the applied worry of so-called emotional moral remainders, i.e., regret or guilt feelings on the agent's part. I argue that the conception of *prima facie* moral ought, which is of prime importance when it comes to the question of how to incorporate the emotional moral remainder in this familiar view, remains unconvincing. As a consequence, there is too little conceptual room left to do justice to the diverse and intuitively plausible range of moral emotions involved in such situations. For this reason, I propose a genuinely normative approach to the analysis and acknowledgment of moral dilemmas. However, in the next step, I take on the opposite concept of applied worry, namely that feelings of guilt, which would imply guilt on the agent's part if they were adequate, should nevertheless be regarded as inappropriate because they are obviously unfair if the agent faces a moral dilemma through no fault of his own. In this respect, I argue that, due to the possibility of excuses, the normative approach also can do justice to this applied worry about fairness. Finally, I will argue that regret, when understood merely as the regret felt by a spectator, also proves to be an inadequate emotional moral remainder, and I will suggest that, instead, the notions of 'agent regret' and 'tragic remorse' account best for an agent's special, and sometimes even tragic, emotional predicament when faced with a moral dilemma.

Introduction

Concrete situations—real or fictional—and their details force us to rethink our ready-made moral judgments, especially when we try only to apply some general ethical view to the situation at hand. One of the main questions in this regard is whether the details of the situation are reflected adequately in moral reasoning and the judgment thus derived. Sometimes special or even completely new circumstances and features have to be taken into account; it often enough turns out to be an open question, at least for the time being, of how exactly these new circumstances and features have to be dealt with from a moral perspective. For this study, I dub such concrete concerns applied (ethical) worries. Such applied worries are thus at least *prima facie* capable of posing a challenge to certain positions of theoretical ethics whenever these positions, or the key assumptions on which they are based, cannot take such applied worries into account adequately—even to give sufficient reason to dismiss such worries as misguided. Therefore, it comes as no surprise that specialized forms of applied ethics have emerged that focus exclusively on certain selected practical contexts and their related applied worries. This, however, raises the question of the relationship in which applied ethics and theoretical ethics stand, or should stand, to one another.

I propose that there are three ways of conceiving the relationship between applied ethics and theoretical ethics. First, applied ethics could be seen as nothing more than the application of a given position in theoretical or normative ethics. However, such an approach has to cope with the problem of running the risk of implausibly neglecting, or at least underestimating, the special circumstances and problems posed by certain applied contexts.

Second, applied ethics could be seen as independent of theoretical ethics. If applied ethics were then able to solve all ethical problems adequately, theoretical ethics would appear to become superfluous, aside perhaps from metaethics. However, given that certain ethical problems located on a more theoretical level do not simply vanish, applied ethics would, as a consequence, have solved these problems within theoretical ethics as well. Hence, theoretical ethics would not have become superfluous at all, but have merely been taken over by applied ethics. It would be nothing more than a simple change of labels.

Third, applied ethics and theoretical ethics could be seen as mutually influential. Their respective assumptions and conceptions would have to be harmonized or mutually incorporated in order to be able to deal coherently with worries, on either side, that appear intuitively as sufficiently plausible and necessary for accommodation. Such attempts at construing a coherent combination of applied ethics and theoretical ethics would basically have to be understood as trying to reach some kind of "reflective equilibrium."[1] Moreover, the idea of a strict distinction between applied ethics and theoretical ethics would have to be regarded as misguided. Understood this way, applied ethics and theoretical ethics would not amount to independent ethical reasoning, but simply highlight different, albeit intimately connected, issues when trying to address certain ethical challenges in general.

This third option is the position I would like to advocate in this paper. Taking applied worries seriously within theoretical ethics simply amounts to the general challenge of developing a coherent comprehensive position that provides enough conceptual room to take into account adequately the respective worries from both perspectives. In the following pages, I will support this approach by way of example. I will address the question of how situations should be analyzed which, from the agent's point of view, appear to be moral dilemmas, i.e., the agent's apparent confrontation with a situation in which, for moral reasons, he ought to do (at least) two things, but cannot do both (or all of them).[2]

---

1   The term is borrowed from John Rawls. For his own conception of "reflective equilibrium" as justificatory basis of his theory of justice and of political liberalism, see Rawls 1971, ch. 1.4,, and Rawls 2001, §10.

2   Alternatively, the agent may be faced with a situation in which every possible course of action is apparently morally forbidden. Such situations have come to be known as prohibition or tragic dilemmas. For a general introduction to the debate on moral dilemmas and the various distinctions invoked, see McConnell 2010. See also Gowans 1987 and Mason 1996.

More specifically, I will be concerned with applied worry with regard to the ethical assessment of the so-called emotional moral remainder, i.e., regret or guilt feelings on the agent's part.[3]

First, I will sketch, from the perspective of theoretical ethics, the main argument underlying the opposition by many philosophers to the idea that 'real' moral dilemmas can exist (II). Next, I will show how these opponents of moral dilemmas nonetheless try to provide conceptual room in their position for an incorporation of the applied worry of an emotional moral remainder (III). However, I will also argue that the conception of *prima facie* moral ought, which carries the burden when it comes incorporating the emotional moral remainder, remains unconvincing (IV). As a consequence, there is too little conceptual room left to do justice to the diverse and intuitively plausible range of moral emotions involved in such situations. Thus, applied worry cannot be taken seriously enough from the perspective of theoretical ethics. This raises the questions of what kind of conceptual framework would be able to deal with the emotional moral remainder adequately and which kind of moral emotion has to be acknowledged accordingly. I will address these two crucial questions in a final step but first argue for a genuinely normative or moral approach when it comes to analyzing moral dilemmas (V). Such a genuinely normative conceptual framework will allow for an analysis of moral dilemmas that is able to incorporate the emotional moral remainder in sufficient detail. Second, I will take on the opposite applied worry, namely that feelings of guilt, which would imply actual guilt on the agent's part if they were considered adequate, should nevertheless be regarded as inadequate because they are obviously unfair if the agent faces a moral dilemma through no fault of his own. In this respect,

---

3   Accordingly, regarding the metaethical question of whether 'real' moral dilemmas exist at all, the so-called phenomenological argument was put forward in order to argue in favor of their existence. Basically, that argument states that moral dilemmas exist because agents experience regret or guilt feelings over an unfulfilled moral duty, and it is assumed that experiencing regret or guilt feelings is rational and adequate. See, for example, Bernard Williams' classical reference to regret in B. Williams 1965. However, the crucial assumption that regret or guilt feelings are rational and adequate is itself a matter of contention. The rationality or adequacy of regret or guilt feelings hinges on assessing the situation as morally dilemmatic in the first place. Moreover, it is arguable exactly what kind of moral emotion is at stake. For regret and guilt feelings apparently have different implications in regard to the moral assessment of the situation in question. Hence, the phenomenological argument proves to be unconvincing in this simple form.

I will argue that, due to the possibility of excuses, the normative approach can do justice to this applied worry about fairness as well (VI). Finally, I will argue that regret, when understood merely as the regret felt by a spectator, also proves to be an inadequate emotional moral remainder. I will suggest that, instead, agent regret and tragic remorse account best for an agent's special, and sometimes even tragic, emotional predicament when faced with a moral dilemma (VII).

Rejecting the possibility of 'real' moral dilemmas

The main argument against the possibility of 'real' moral dilemmas put forward in theoretical ethics is straightforward enough: if 'real' moral dilemmas existed, moral theory would be inconsistent and thus useless. While the details of the various forms of this argument draw heavily on deontic logic, the main line of thought is easy enough to grasp. Firstly, and for the sake of the argument, the existence of 'real' moral dilemmas is assumed, i.e., the proposition that an agent is morally obligated to do *a* as well as morally obligated to do *b*, but cannot do both *a* and *b*.[4]

1 $O(a) \,\&\, O(b) \,\&\, {-}C(a \,\&\, b)$ = definition of a moral dilemma (MD)[5]

Secondly, two principles of deontic logic are invoked that are assumed to be self-evident: "ought implies can," stating that, if you ought to do *a*, you can do *a*, on the one hand, and the so-called agglomeration principle, which states that, if you ought to do *a* and you ought to *b*, you ought to do both *a* and *b*, on the other hand.

2 $O(a) \rightarrow C(a)$ = "ought implies can"
3 $O(a) \,\&\, O(b) \rightarrow O(a \,\&\, b)$ = agglomeration principle

Taken together, these three premises inevitably lead to logical contradictions: the existence of a moral dilemma, as stated in the first premise,

---

4 The symbolizations of deontic logic used here are: "O" for "Ought" or "Obligation," "C" for "Can," "*a, b*, etc." for actions or states of affairs to be realized, "→" for the clause "if, then," "&" for the conjunction "and," and "−" for a negation.
5 An alternative definition of moral dilemmas should also be mentioned. It states that an agent is morally obligated to do A and is, at the same time, morally obligated to abstain from doing A: $O(a) \,\&\, O(-a)$.

includes the proposition that you cannot do both *a* and *b*. Yet, it also includes the two propositions that you are obligated to do each *a* and *b*, which, in combination with the third premise, i.e., the agglomeration principle, yields the conclusion that you ought to do both *a* and *b*. However, following the second premise, i.e., the principle "ought implies can," the conclusion has to be drawn that you can do both *a* and *b*, which logically contradicts the respective proposition in the first premise, which was the starting point of the argument and the main assumption of the definition of a moral dilemma in the first place: you cannot do both *a* and *b*.

4   O(a & b)   from 1) and 3)
5   C(a & b)   from 2) and 4)
6   –C(a & b) & C(a & b)   from 1) and 5): logical contradiction

Furthermore, another logical contradiction should be mentioned. For, using the proposition from the first premise that you cannot do both *a* and *b* as well as the contrapositive of the principle "ought implies can," it follows that it cannot be the case that you are obligated to do both *a* and *b*, which logically contradicts the definition of a moral dilemma together with the agglomeration principle, stating that you are obligated to do both *a* and *b*.

7   –O(a & b)   from 1) and 2), contrapositive
8   O(a & b) & –O(a & b)   from 4) and 7): logical contradiction

Assuming that the agglomeration principle and the principle "ought implies can" are valid,[6] or at least more plausible than accepting the

---

6   However, both principles face serious theoretical challenges, so their validity cannot simply be taken for granted. Bernard Williams, for example, questions in his seminal article the agglomeration principle on the basis that we are not, in all cases, obligated to do both *a* and *b* if we are obligated to do each *a* and *b*. See Williams 1965, 132ff. One of his examples is the case of a man promising two women—separately, of course—to marry them. Surely, it cannot be concluded that the man ought to marry both women at the same time. Furthermore, with regard to the principle "ought implies can," it is a matter of contention how it has to be understood exactly, e.g., as conceptual implication or as conversational implicature or even as moral principle. Moreover, the notions of "ought" and "can" are a matter of contention as well, leading to the question of what kind of "ought" (allegedly) implies what kind of "can." For an extensive discussion of the principle, see Kühler 2013a.

idea of 'real' moral dilemmas, many philosophers conclude that the assumption of 'real' moral dilemmas should be dropped in order to prevent moral theory from becoming inconsistent and thus useless.[7]

Yet, simply rejecting the possibility of 'real' moral dilemmas cannot be the whole story. For, we are obviously faced with conflicting moral obligations numerous times in everyday life. Given, for example, that we have a moral obligation to return borrowed money punctually, it is easy enough to imagine that, one day, I might face a situation in which I have borrowed some money from two of my friends, each of whom I have to pay back today. Yet, today I am unable to do so. All I can do is to repay one debt, but not both.

The rejection of the idea that I am faced with a 'real' moral dilemma, then, surely leaves open a number of questions. The most crucial are: first, given that I can, at least, repay one debt and actually do so, what does that mean for the other claim that I am obligated to repay the second debt today? Apparently, if I cannot be obligated to do something in a case where I cannot do it,[8] I can no longer be obligated to repay my second debt.[9] My initial respective moral obligation, giving rise to the moral dilemma in the first place, would seem to have simply disappeared.

Second, as a consequence, what kind of reaction on my part, especially concerning moral emotions, could still be justified as adequate with regard to the second debt left unreturned, if I am apparently no longer

---

7   Apart from the line of argument mentioned above, it has been argued that logical inconsistencies could even be derived without referring to "ought implies can" and the agglomeration principle. See on this note, for example, Brink 1994, 111ff., and De Haan 2001, 273ff. However, I have argued elsewhere that these arguments remain unconvincing, for they implicitly have to presuppose the principle "ought implies can." (cf. Kühler 2008a and Kühler 2013a, ch. 7). In any case, this issue does not play an important role for the purpose at hand. The crucial point here is simply the claim that, given certain deontic principles, the assumption of 'real' moral dilemmas leads to inconsistencies in moral theory and should therefore be abandoned.

8   As mentioned above, this results from the contrapositive of the principle "ought implies can," i.e., "cannot implies not-ought."

9   Usually, one would assume that I can at least no longer be obligated to repay my second debt today, but should repay my friend some time later when I have the necessary amount of money. However, it remains dubious and a matter of contention whether and how moral obligations can "survive" temporal inability on the addressee's part. My obligation was to repay my debt today, and not at a later time. Yet, according to the line of thought so far, the obligation to repay my debt today is no longer valid.

under an obligation to repay it? Given that I—the morally conscientious man I am—either regret or even feel guilty about not repaying a debt to a friend punctually, what is to be said about these moral emotions from the perspective of theoretical ethics? How can they be accounted for if their crucial intentional object, i.e., a moral obligation left unfulfilled, is forfeited? Or do they have to be dismissed as misguided? If so, can this consequence be regarded as plausible from the perspective of applied ethics, which would focus specifically on such crucial details and on a finely-grained analysis of the agent's emotional predicament?

Trying to acknowledge the emotional moral remainder while rejecting the possibility of 'real' moral dilemmas

Even opponents of 'real' moral dilemmas usually acknowledge the plausibility of an emotional moral remainder and also consider at least some of these moral emotions as morally adequate.[10] Consequently, they try to incorporate them into their analysis of such apparently dilemmatic situations. The key concept in this respect is the notion of "*prima facie* moral ought (or duty)"[11] in contrast to "actual moral duty."[12] The main distinction is this: in every situation, there can be only one actual moral duty that the agent is obligated to follow and that the agent also can follow. However, there can still be a number of *prima facie* moral duties that also apply to the situation at hand, as they pick out relevant and valid moral aspects. Hence, the term *prima facie* should not be understood as simply meaning "apparent" or "seeming." As with an actual moral duty, *prima facie* moral duties are 'real' moral duties, albeit not duties the agent should act upon. Accordingly, the deontic principles mentioned above, i.e., the agglomeration principle and the principle

---

10 Apart from the *emotional* moral remainder, other moral remainders also have to be accounted for. In the example mentioned above, one would think that at the very least I owe my friend an explanation for not repaying him.

11 For simplicity's sake, I use "duty," "ought," and "obligation" interchangeably here.

12 On this note, opponents of the concept of 'real' moral dilemmas follow the account of Sir William D. Ross. (cf. Ross 1930, ch. 2), where Ross also uses the phrase "duty *sans phrase*" for actual duty. For a helpful explanation, see, for example, Zimmerman 1996, 5f and especially chapter 5. For a critical view with respect to the topic at hand, see below (section IV) as well as Kühler 2008a and Kühler 2013a, esp. ch. 9.

"ought implies can," apply only to actual duties, but not to *prima facie* moral duties.

The relationship between an agent's actual moral duty in a given situation and the *prima facie* moral duties that apply to the situation is, then, as follows. First, every morally relevant aspect of the situation is taken into account and depicted as a respective *prima facie* moral duty. Secondly, these *prima facie* moral duties are weighed against each other, i.e., they are considered in respect to which of them, relative to all others, counts the most morally. If, for example, I am *prima facie* morally obligated to keep an appointment and also *prima facie* morally obligated to help the victim of car accident I happen to encounter, and if I cannot fulfill both duties, all things considered, my moral obligation to help the victim (usually) counts more than my obligation to keep my appointment. Hence, helping the victim becomes my actual moral duty—this is, what I ought to do—while my duty to keep my appointment is overridden and remains in its *prima facie* status. It will, for good moral reasons, not be fulfilled. A *prima facie* moral 'ought' thus does not imply 'can.'

Furthermore, given the case that two or more *prima facie* moral duties are symmetrical, i.e., equally strong, or incommensurable, i.e., cannot be measured against each other and thus also have to be taken as equally valid, the agglomeration princip does not apply. In such cases, it is argued that the agent's actual moral duty is now a disjunctive one, namely to fulfill one or the other of these *prima facie* moral duties. So understood, both *prima facie* moral duties are overridden by the disjunctive actual moral duty to do either a or b.[13]

9 $[o(a) \: \& \: o(b) \: \& \: -C(a \: \& \: b)] \rightarrow O(a \lor b)$[14] = symmetrical or incommensurable *prima facie* duties yield a disjunctive actual duty

---

[13] However, Walter Sinnott-Armstrong has argued that, all things considered, neither of the *prima facie* moral duties in question is overridden by a different *prima facie* moral duty. Instead, they are all not overridden, so that introducing the disjunctive actual moral duty has to be regarded as an extra move. See W. Sinnott-Armstrong 1996, 50f.

[14] Here, "o" stands for "*prima facie* moral ought" and "v" for the disjunction "or."

Consequently, when understood exclusively in terms of *prima facie* moral duties, moral dilemmas—or, to be more exact, moral conflicts that can be solved through disjunctive actual moral duty—are, indeed, possible because they no longer lead to a logical inconsistency in moral theory.

Following this line of thought, it is argued that *prima facie* moral duties that necessarily remain unfulfilled in cases of conflict, but which, nevertheless, remain 'real' moral duties, can also explain any moral remainder, thereby also serving as intentional objects of an emotional moral remainder.[15] Hence, it is quite possible to say that an agent regrets, or feels guilty about, one of his *prima facie* moral duties remaining unfulfilled, even if this is due to good moral reasons. Consequently, opponents of 'real' moral dilemmas seem to be able to do theoretical justice to the applied worry that apparently plausible emotional moral reactions by agents who face moral dilemmas[16] should be taken seriously and incorporated into the analysis of such situations.

However, not all emotional moral reactions are considered adequate. While regret is, indeed, seen as rational and adequate, guilt feelings are considered to be inadequate because, if they were seen as adequate, they would imply actual guilt on the agent's part. Yet, the agent cannot be judged as guilty for not fulfilling a *prima facie* moral duty which he explicitly ought not to fulfill due to its merely *prima facie* status. For that reason, while it is rational for me to regret not keeping my appointment, it would be irrational for me to feel guilty about it—presuming, of course, that I have fulfilled my actual moral duty to help the victim.[17]

All in all, everything seems to be in order, and the applied worry of taking seriously the emotional moral remainder of agents facing moral dilemmas or moral conflicts seems to be accounted for in theoretical ethics. The position sketched above even seems to present sufficient reason as to which moral emotion should be acknowledged as being adequate and which should be rejected as irrational. Where, then, is the flaw in this line of thinking?

---

15 On this note, see Brink 1994, 105 and 121f., fn. 17, who draws helpful distinctions among different intentional objects of regret, as well.

16 Or, once again more precisely, soluble moral conflicts.

17 With regard to the aforementioned example of my two debts, the adequacy of my moral emotion also hinges on the question of whether I was at (moral) fault in not having the necessary money today. I will come back to that later.

The impossibility of acknowledging the emotional moral remainder when rejecting the possibility of 'real' moral dilemmas

My main concern is with the notion of "*prima facie* moral ought (or duty)". First of all, the general concept of *moral ought* invoked in the argument above, especially with regard to the principles of deontic logic, i.e., the agglomeration principle and the principle "ought implies can," is based on a Kantian understanding of moral duty in the sense of practical necessity. Hence, if I am morally obligated to do *a*, doing *a* represents a practical necessity, i.e., I will (necessarily) do *a*—at least if I am a rational or morally conscientious person. So understood, this Kantian understanding of moral ought relies heavily on an analogy to modal necessity, which also explains why the principle "ought implies can" is seen as self-evident. For, if some event is necessarily bound to happen (because of modal necessity), it will actually happen, which, in turn, implies that its occurrence is possible. Similarly, if a moral duty represents a practical necessity, the (rational or moral) agent in question will actually act accordingly, which, indeed, implies that the agent can act accordingly. Such an understanding of moral ought also yields the validity of the agglomeration principle. For, if doing *a* and doing *b* is equally a matter of practical necessity, the agent in question will actually do both *a* and *b*.

Given the distinction between actual moral duties and *prima facie* moral duties, the above understanding of moral ought obviously applies only to actual moral duties, while *prima facie* moral duties cannot be a matter of practical necessity. This, however, raises the question of what kind of moral duty a *prima facie* moral duty can be if the crucial feature of the concept of moral ought, i.e., the notion of practical necessity, is explicitly abandoned. This holds especially for overridden *prima facie* moral duties, which the agent explicitly ought not to fulfill.[18] Does it really make sense to say that, while I have a '*real*,' but overridden *prima facie* moral duty to do *a*, I shall explicitly not act upon it? The problem becomes even more obvious when put this way: while I *prima facie*, yet '*really*' morally ought to do *a*, at the same time, I actually

---

18 Even in the case of the disjunctive actual moral duty to do either *a* or *b*, the individual *prima facie* moral duties to do each *a* and *b* are overridden. It is only the general content, i.e., *a* and *b*, that stays the same – barring the junction between the two. On this note, see again Sinnott-Armstrong 1996, 50f.

ought not to do *a* because the moral ought in question is overridden by a different one.

This whole idea strikes me to be just as inconsistent as the results of the initial argument presented by opponents of 'real' moral dilemmas. Therefore, if the general understanding of the concept of moral ought in the sense of practical necessity shall be kept, the notion of 'real' *prima facie* moral duties becomes unconvincing and has to be dropped. *Prima facie* moral duties would indeed be only apparent or seeming moral duties that (completely) disappear once the actual moral duty has been identified. This, however, has the consequence that it is no longer possible to refer to a 'real' moral obligation which is, nevertheless, overridden and thus necessarily remains unfulfilled in order to explain and justify further normative or evaluative judgments, i.e., any moral remainder, thus, of course, also including the emotional moral remainder. Hence, not only feelings of guilt, but also regret about a moral duty left unfulfilled, would have to regarded as irrational and inadequate. For there can no longer be any moral duty serving as an intentional object for such emotions. The critical result, therefore, is that the applied worry with regard to the emotional moral remainder cannot be taken seriously within such a theoretical conceptual framework.

A genuinely normative conceptual framework as an alternative

Nevertheless, the above result leaves open another option, namely to drop the general understanding of moral duties in the sense of practical necessity and thus the analogy to modal necessity. This way, the concept of moral ought would basically amount only to the normative claim that *a* and *b* should be done or realized by the agent in question. Hence, no further thesis would be implied with regard to the actual fulfillment of this claim.

This alternative conceptual framework makes use of a distinction between two opposing directions of fit, serving as a theoretical background assumption to explain the difference between descriptive statements and normative ones.[19] On the one hand, the main idea of descriptive state-

---

19   For an instructive overview, see Searle 2001, esp. ch. 2. See also the seminal passage in Anscombe (Anscombe 1963, 56), the discussions in Platts 1979, 256ff, Smith 1987, 50-58, Schueler 1991, Humberstone 1992, Zangwill 1998, Sobel/Copp 2001, and

ments is that they should depict truthfully some portion of the world, i.e., so to speak, "fit" the world. Accordingly, they are subject to a mind-to-world direction of fit. Hence, if there is a lack of conformity, i.e. if a descriptive statement does not depict the portion of the world in question accurately, this descriptive statement has to be considered as false, and it is the statement, not the world, that has to be changed in order to establish the claimed truth.

On the other hand, normative claims are thought of as not depicting truthfully some portion of the world. On the contrary, they convey some state of the world that is usually not the case (yet), but one that should be the case and be brought about. Normative claims thus primarily introduce a normative standard with respect to which the state of the world can be evaluated as being in accordance or not. Consequently, normative claims are subject not to a mind-to-world, but to an opposed world-to-mind direction of fit. Accordingly, if there is a lack of conformity, i.e., if a normative claim has not (yet) been met, this does not mean that the normative claim in question is false. It is not the normative claim that has to be changed, but the world must be changed to fit the normative standard. If that is not done or proves to be impossible, it is again not the normative claim but the world that remains, so to speak, "false" according to the normative standard.

Two general conclusions can be drawn at this point: first, it is not the theoretical, but rather the practical, sphere to which normative claims genuinely belong. In this respect, the analogy to the notion of necessity in modal logic mentioned above is misguided. Second, using the conceptual framework just described, it should become clear that, consequently, especially the principle "ought implies can" can no longer be regarded as self-evident. It is rather a matter of a genuine moral dispute whether addressees of normative claims should always be able to fulfill their obligations, which is indeed usually a good idea for reasons of fairness. However, given that the principle "ought implies can" loses its overall validity, it could very well be argued that, at least in case of moral dilemmas, the conflicting moral obligations should be regarded as staying in force in order to be able to do justice to the tragic predicament the agent finds

---

Milliken 2008. For a detailed discussion of the complex normative implications of directions of fit as they are being assumed here, i.e., of their comprised claims of what should be changed in order to establish "fitness," see Seebaß 1993, 86-143. For the following explanation, cf. also Kühler 2013b.

himself in, as well as to any moral remainder involved. Moreover, if the principle "ought implies can" is dropped, at least in case of moral dilemmas, moral theory is no longer in danger of becoming inconsistent when it includes an acceptance of the possibility of 'real' moral dilemmas. No normative conclusion can be drawn, at least that easily, from the fact that the agent in question cannot do both *a* and *b*.[20]

As plausible as these two conclusions may be on a general theoretical level—which is indeed the position I would favor as a starting point—this position now runs the risk of providing too much conceptual room for moral remainders. For, so understood, it seems that, if all moral obligations remain in full force, not only feelings of guilt on the agent's part, but also the agent's actual guilt for not fulfilling one of his moral obligations, would have to be accepted as rational and adequate. Surely, however, there is something wrong or unfair with the idea of an agent being guilty if he finds himself in a moral dilemma through no fault of his own. The pendulum of the applied worry of taking seriously the emotional moral remainder in moral dilemmas would thus swing in the opposite direction, again for intuitively plausible and good moral reasons. Therefore, the theoretical analysis just sketched has to provide some additional conceptual tools in order to address this last applied worry about a lack of fairness.

Taking the applied worry of the emotional moral remainder seriously: feelings of guilt, fairness, and the possibility of excuses

The first conceptual tool to be invoked for reasons of fairness within such a genuinely normative or moral discussion about the guilt or blameworthiness of agents facing moral dilemmas is the possibility of excuses.[21] The respective principle of fairness is this: no agent is to be considered guilty or blameworthy for not fulfilling one of his moral obligations if he is unable to fulfill it through no fault of his own. While this principle can

---

20 It should be noted that drawing such conclusions on a conceptual level raises concerns about a naturalistic fallacy as well. On this note, see Collingridge 1977, Pigden 1990, 2, and Statman 1995, 37. Cp. also Kühler 2008a and Kühler 2013a, ch. 5).

21 In this respect, see John L. Austin's seminal paper: Austin 1970. See also Suttle 1988 and 1994, ch. 5 and 6. Cf. also Kühler 2008b, Kühler 2013a ch. 11, and Kühler 2013b.

indeed be regarded as a variation of the principle "ought implies can," it does not refer to a conceptual implication but has to be understood as an explicitly normative or moral principle of fairness. Moreover, it does not concern the validity of moral obligations *per se*, but only the subsequent evaluation of the agent with regard to his possible guilt or blameworthiness. In this respect, a valid moral obligation is necessary in order to make sense of the idea of an excuse in the first place. For, if the agent were not under a valid moral obligation, there would be nothing to excuse. Instead, the agent would simply be morally justified in what he did. Hence, it has to be acknowledged that the agent did not fulfill one of his moral obligations. However, as he did so through no fault of his own or because he fulfilled a weightier or equally valid moral obligation instead, he is, for reasons of fairness, not to be considered as guilty or blameworthy. Accordingly, feelings of guilt can be judged as being inadequate.

Based on such an account, the examples mentioned above can be analyzed as follows: given that I have fulfilled my weightier moral obligation to help a victim of a car accident, with the result that I am no longer able to keep my appointment, it is, indeed, irrational for me to feel guilty about not keeping my appointment because I am excused and thus neither guilty nor blameworthy in this respect. Analogously, it is irrational for me to feel guilty about not paying back my second debt, at least as long as I am not at fault for my own inability. In contrast, had I had enough money the night before and decided to spend it on liquor, I would not face the situation through no fault of my own. Hence, the principle of fairness would not apply, and I would not be excused. This way, the normative approach proves to be quite able to take seriously the applied worry of a need for fairness when it comes to the question of the agent being guilty for not fulfilling one of his moral obligations and when it comes to judging the adequacy of his feelings of guilt.

Taking the applied worry of the emotional moral remainder seriously: 'agent regret' and 'tragic remorse'

Given that the genuinely normative framework introduced above is able to give a plausible answer to questions of fairness with regard to an agent's feelings of guilt, what are we to think of feelings of regret? It might be tempting to leave the story as it is at this point and just state that regret is the appropriate emotional moral remainder in cases where an agent faces a moral dilemma through no fault of his own. Yet, it should be noted that there are different kinds of regret that must be distinguished. Usually, regret amounts to the idea of spectator regret, i.e., the kind of regret one feels when one witnesses something (morally) bad happening. As Bernard Williams put it, the corresponding thought is simply: "how much better if it had been otherwise."[22]

However, in case of moral dilemmas, the agent is not just a mere witness to bad events unfolding. Instead, he is the one to make a decision and act. It is because of him that a morally bad event is bound to happen, namely, that one of his moral obligations remains unfulfilled. Accordingly, in the example of the car accident mentioned above, while it is, of course, the decision morally needed, it is still my decision to help the victim instead of keeping my appointment and, in the example of my debts, it is still my decision which of my two friends I pay back today. Hence, mere spectator regret cannot be the adequate emotional moral reaction if the agent's agential involvement shall be taken seriously.

The notion of regret to be invoked here is agent regret. This is the kind of regret an agent experiences if something (morally) bad happens because of him. However, in case of moral dilemmas it should not be understood as referring merely to the agent's causal involvement without him making any decision or taking action, as some authors note about this emotion.[23] Rather, it has to be understood as depicting explicitly the agential involvement mentioned above, i.e., the fact that it was the agent who made a decision and acted upon it—albeit, of course, within morally dilemmatic circumstances. Accordingly, I do not simply, i.e., as a mere spectator, regret the fact that a friend of mine does not get his money back, as had been promised. Rather, I regret that I am the one who decided not to pay him back and acted accordingly.

Furthermore, there may be cases of moral dilemmas in which even agent regret does not seem to be enough. Sometimes an agent might face a prohibition or tragic dilemma in which every possible course of action is morally forbidden or morally wrong in some crucial respect.[24] The para-

---

22 Williams 1981, 27.
23 On this note, see Rorty 1980, 493, Williams 1981, 28, Taylor 1985, 91, and Baron 1988, 260.
24 Much the same holds for dirty hands scenarios. On this note, see Michael Walzer's seminal paper: Walzer 1973 and Jean-Paul Sartre's play *Les mains sales*: Sartre 1948,

digmatic example of such a tragic dilemma is "Sophie's Choice."[25] The situation is this: in a Nazi concentration camp, Sophie is told to choose between her two children. Based on her choice, one will be taken to the gas chamber, while the other will be allowed to live. If she refuses to choose, both will be killed. Apparently, Sophie faces a situation in which all options available to her are morally forbidden or morally wrong. Accordingly, after finally and desperately pointing to her younger child to be taken to the gas chamber, she suffers enormous feelings of guilt, which eventually lead to her committing suicide.

Now, even if Sophie is not guilty and her feelings of guilt are thus not justified according to the principle of fairness mentioned above, her tragic decision seems to call for something more than agent regret. Choosing one of one's own children to die is not something merely to regret, even in the form of agent regret. The emotional moral remainder in such tragic dilemmas should rather depict the thought that the agent made, or had to make, a terrible immoral decision that will most probably haunt him for the rest of his life. The morally tragic aspect of the situation in comparison to the other examples mentioned is thus that, while, in the other examples, the agent can at least fulfill one of his moral obligations, in tragic dilemmas, he has to face, through no fault of his own, a situation of inescapable moral wrongdoing, i.e., he can only choose between immoral acts.[26]

Based on such considerations, Stephen De Wijze has suggested the notion of tragic remorse as adequate emotional moral response in cases of tragic dilemmas.[27] Tragic remorse thus depicts the fact that the agent repents of his actions, i.e., he feels remorse although he knows perfectly well that he did the best he could morally under tragic circumstances and is thus not to be blamed. The tragedy is that "the morally best" was not morally good at all, but merely the lesser evil.[28]

---

as well as Rynard/Shugarman 2000. For a current overview on the topic, see Coady 2009. Cf. also Kühler 2013a, ch. 13.

25 The example is based on William Styron's novel of the same name: Styron 1979. See especially Greenspan 1983, who was the first to mention this example as part of the philosophical debate on moral dilemmas.

26 On this note, see especially Gowans 1994, He focuses on such inescapable moral wrongdoing.

27 Cf. De Wijze 2004.

28 Even if one rejected the background assumption of a clear distinction between obligation dilemmas and prohibition or tragic dilemmas at this point, i.e., if one argued

Conclusion

If the general line of thought I have presented here is to be considered plausible, only a genuinely normative or moral approach to analyzing moral dilemmas proves to be able to provide enough conceptual room to incorporate the emotional moral remainder adequately and in sufficient detail. Accordingly, only a genuinely normative or moral approach is capable of taking seriously enough the applied worry about the emotional moral remainder of agents facing moral dilemmas so that a coherent comprehensive position can be formulated, incorporating convincingly the perspectives of both applied ethics and theoretical ethics in this context.

---

for the thesis that all dilemmas are either obligation dilemmas or prohibition dilemmas, the result would merely be that either agent regret or tragic remorse would always be appropriate. The main line of argument presented here would thus still remain intact.

References

Anscombe, G. E. M. 1963. *Intention, 2. Edition*, Cambridge: Harvard University Press.

Austin, John Longshaw 1970. A Plea for Excuses, in: Austin, John Longshaw 1970, *Philosophical Papers, 2. Edition*, London: Oxford University Press, p. 175-204.

Baron, Marcia 1988. Remorse and Agent-Regret, in: *Midwest Studies in Philosophy* 13, p. 259-281.

Brink, David O. 1994. Moral Conflict and Its Structure, in: Mason, Homer E. (ed.) 1996, *Moral Dilemmas and Moral Theory*, New York: Oxford University Press, p. 102-126.

Coady, C. A. J. (Tony) 2009. The Problem of Dirty Hands, in: Zalta, Edward N. ed. 2009, *The Stanford Encyclopedia of Philosophy (Fall 2009 Edition)*, URL=http://plato.stanford.edu/archives/fall2009/entries/dirty-hands/.

Collingridge, David G. 1977. 'Ought-Implies-Can' and Hume's Rule, in: *Philosophy* 52, p. 348-351.

De Haan, Jurriaan 2001. The Definition of Moral Dilemmas: A Logical Problem, in: *Ethical Theory and Moral Practice* 4, p. 267-284.

De Wijze, Stephen 2004. Tragic-Remorse – The Anguish of Dirty Hands, in: *Ethical Theory and Moral Practice* 7, p. 453-471.

Gowans, Christopher W., ed. 1987. *Moral Dilemmas*, New York: Oxford University Press.

Gowans, Christopher W. 1994. *Innocence Lost. An Examination of Inescapable Moral Wrongdoing*, New York: Oxford University Press.

Greenspan, Patricia S. 1983. Moral Dilemmas and Guilt, in: *Philosophical Studies* 43, p. 117-125.

Humberstone, I. L. 1992. "Direction of fit," in: *Mind* 101, 59-83.

Kühler, Michael 2008a. Moralische Dilemmata, die Gefahr moraltheoretischer Inkonsistenz und der zugrunde gelegte Pflichtbegriff, in: *Zeitschrift für philosophische Forschung* 62, p. 516-536.

Kühler, Michael 2008b. Sollen impliziert Können – begrifflich?, in: Fürst, Martina/Gombocz, Wolfgang/Hiebaum, Christian eds. 2008, *Analysen, Argumente, Ansätze. Beiträge zum 8. Internationalen Kongress der Österreichischen Gesellschaft für Philosophie in Graz*, Frankfurt am Main: Ontos, 2008, p. 363-370.

Kühler, Michael 2013a. *Sollen ohne Können? Über Sinn und Geltung nicht erfüllbarer Sollensansprüche*, Münster: Mentis, forthcoming.

Kühler, Michael 2013b. Who Am I to Uphold Unrealizable Normative Claims?, in: Kühler, Michael/Jelinek, Nadja, eds. 2013, *Autonomy and the Self*, Dordrecht: Springer, p. 191-209.

Mason, Homer E., ed. 1996. *Moral Dilemmas and Moral Theory*, New York: Oxford University Press.

McConnell, Terrance Callihan 2010. Moral Dilemmas, in: Zalta, Edward N. (ed.): *The Stanford Encyclopedia of Philosophy (Summer 2010 Edition)*, URL=http://plato.stanford.edu/archives/sum2010/entries/moral-dilemmas/.

Milliken, John 2008. In a Fitter Direction: Moving Beyond the Direction of Fit Picture of Belief and Desire, in: *Ethical Theory and Moral Practice* 11, p. 563–571.

Pigden, Charles 1990. Ought-Implies-Can: Erasmus Luther and R.M. Hare, in: *Sophia* 29, p. 2-30.

Platts, Mark 1979. *Ways of Meaning, 2. Edition*, Cambridge: MIT Press, 1. Edition: London: Routledge & Paul, 1979.

Rawls, John 1971. *A Theory of Justice*, Cambridge, Mass.: Belknap Press of Harvard University Press.

Rawls, John 2001. *Justice as Fairness. A Restatement*, Cambridge: Belknap Press.

Rorty, Amélie O. 1980. Agent Regret, in: Rorty, Amélie O. ed. 1980, *Explaining Emotions*, Berkeley: University of California Press, p. 489-506.

Ross, William David 1930. *The Right and the Good*, Oxford: Clarendon Press.

Rynard, Paul/Shugarman, David P. eds., 2000. *Cruelty and Deception: The Controversy Over Dirty Hands in Politics*, Peterborough: Broadview Press.

Sartre, Jean-Paul 1948. *Les mains sales*, Paris: Gallimard.

Schueler, G. F. 1991. Pro-Attitudes and Direction of Fit, in: *Mind* 100, p. 277-281.

Searle, John 2001. *Rationality in Action*, Cambridge: Bradford Book, MIT Press.

Seebaß, Gottfried 1993. *Wollen*, Frankfurt am Main: Klostermann.

Sinnott-Armstrong, Walter 1996. Moral Dilemmas and Rights, in: Mason, Homer E., ed. 1996, *Moral Dilemmas and Moral Theory*, New York: Oxford University Press, p. 48-65.

Smith, Michael 1987. The Humean Theory of Motivation, in: *Mind* 96, p. 36-61.
Sobel, David/Copp, David 2001. Against Direction of Fit Accounts of Belief and Desire, in: *Analysis* 61, p. 44-53.
Statman, Daniel 1995. *Moral Dilemmas*, Amsterdam: Rodopi.
Styron, William 1979. *Sophie's Choice*, New York: Random House.
Suttle, Bruce 1988. Duties and Excusing Conditions, in: Lee, S. H., ed. 1988, *Inquiries into Values: The Inaugural Session of the International Society for Value Inquiry*, Lewiston: Edwin Mellen Press, p. 119-129.
Taylor, Gabriele 1985. *Pride, Shame, and Guilt. Emotions of self-assessment*, Oxford: Clarendon Press.
Wallace, R. Jay 1994. *Responsibility and the Moral Sentiments*, Cambridge: Harvard University Press.
Walzer, Michael 1973. Political Action: The Problem of Dirty Hands, in: *Philosophy and Public Affairs* 2, p. 160-180.
Williams, Bernard 1965. Ethical Consistency, in: Gowans, Christopher W., ed. 1987, *Moral Dilemmas*, New York: Oxford University Press, p. 115-137.
Williams, Bernard 1981. Moral Luck, in: Williams, Bernard 1981, *Moral Luck*, Cambridge: Cambridge University Press, p. 20-39.
Zangwill, Nick 1998. Direction of Fit and Normative Functionalism, in: *Philosophical Studies* 91, p. 173–203.
Zimmerman, Michael J. 1996. *The Concept of Moral Obligation*, Cambridge: Cambridge University Press.

Ole Riis

Ethical theory and popular ethics

Relations between ethical theory and popular ethics

Ethical theory refers to academic discourses on normative reasoning, or the philosophical justification for ethical directives. Popular ethics refers to people's moral reasoning, or the logic by which they justify social practices as moral. Popular ethics thus resembles the underlying principles that people use when they judge some aspect of their society to be just or unjust (Miller, 1999). There is, of course, a connection between ethical theory and popular ethics. Ethical theory is historically inspired by popular ethics, and popular ethics is influenced by ethical theory. This essay aims to describe popular ethics in the Nordic countries around the year 2000, and discuss its challenges for ethical theory.

In principle, ethical theory and popular ethics can be related in four ways. First, ethical theory can be primary and popular ethics can be derived from it. One hypothesis says that popular ethics forms a simplified version of ethical theory; another hypothesis says that popular ethics is based on an outdated version of contemporary ethical theory. Ethical theory is historically assigned a primary status in hegemonic cultures, such as medieval, Christian Europe or the Confucian Chinese Empire, or present-day Iran. In hegemonic cultures, ethical theory represents not only an academic discourse but also a moral perspective that is confirmed and prescribed by political authorities. Deviations from the ethical standards are subject to sanctions. This perspective may be legitimized by claims that ethical rules are determined by a sacred tradition or divinely ordained.

Second, popular ethics can be primary and ethical theory derived from it. This may be the case when ethical theories aim to elaborate and clarify views that are supported by common ethics. A more populistic version holds that ethical theory affirms and supports popular ethics. This relationship would predominate in social situations where the institutional status of intellectuals is weak. In historical situations where established institutions have been undermined, due to internal or external crises, ethical theory is under pressure to be reformulated according to popular demands. This may be legitimized by claims that norms are socially constructed conventions.

Thirdly, it is possible that ethical theory and popular ethics are disconnected. In this case, ethical theory is based on a segregated institution that has little affiliation with popular ethics, and popular ethics follows its own pragmatic reasoning. This may be the case in societies that allow academic institutions to pursue their own, internal agendas. Historically, monastic ethical theories can be seen as such insulated discourses, which have little regard for moral concerns of everyday life in secular society. This relationship may be legitimized by claims that ethical theory refers to purely mental states that can be polluted by the menial material concerns of everyday life.

Finally, in the fourth case, there may be a dialectical relationship between ethical theory and popular ethics. This constitutes the 'normal' case. Ethical theories are inspired by social discourses that arise from popular ethics, and they refer back to popular ethical discourses. Thus, we may trace a dual inspiration in both ethical theory and popular ethics. Popular ethics adopts points of view that have been proposed by ethical theory, and ethical theory adresses topics that have arisen in popular ethics. Such a dialectical stance may be legitimized by the claim that there is a natural ethical capacity in humankind on which ethical theory may reflect and aid its development.

Such a dialectical connection is implied in the plea by Molewijk et al. for an 'integrated empirical ethics' (2004), which assumes that ethics and the social sciences are mutually constitutive. This paper is based on the same assumption, adding that the empirical data refer to social practices. Thus integrated ethics does not only refer to research problems but points further to the reasoning behind ethical practices.

The relationship between ethical theory and popular ethics is complicated since neither forms a unity. Certain types of ethical theory may define some types of popular ethics for instance in the context of authoritarian subcultures. Certain types of popular ethics may have a strong impact on ethical theory. Thus, the emergence of new social movements has a strong impact on public discourse.

This approach opens for consideration whether ethical theory is connected with popular ethics in our own, contemporary society. In order to illustrate this question, I will refer back to survey studies on popular ethics from the 1990s and their reception by ethical theorists. I will not attempt to bring the discussion up to date. Such an updating is hardly needed when the discussion concerns long-term trends.

Popular ethics: Private and public morality

It is seldom that surveys investigate moral reasoning. Questions have to be easy to answer for all types of respondents. Therefore, the items typically refer to a moral position on an issue. This was, for instance, the case with the European Values Survey (EVS) which includes a series of items (questions with possible answers) about moral issues. The questions refer to the degree of acceptance of breaking a moral norm, such as tax fraud, divorce, etc. One of the main conclusions drawn from the EVS data on morality in the Nordic countries indicated that moral attitudes did not follow one dimension. Respondents were not completely tolerant or restrictive. Their attitudes varied according to the topic, and the topics formed – at least – two dimensions. It is of course a gross simplification to 'measure' moral attitudes by referring to terms that can raise many associations among the respondents. For instance, divorce may refer to many ways in which and many reasons for which a marriage is ended. It may therefore be questioned whether the items contain several dimensions. However, this source of error is diminished as several items are combined into one scale. Thus, whereas each of the items relating to private morality may be questioned, the combined scale can be interpreted theoretically in a meaningful way.

One cluster of topics is formed by issues such as infidelity, abortion, homosexuality, and divorce. Responses to each of these clusters of topics were closely related. If you knew a person's response to one topic, you were able to predict attitudes toward the other topics. These topics focus on moral issues that are related to a certain sphere of social life, which we often label as 'the private sphere'. The issues refer to intimate inter-personal relationships, which are regulated by informal standards rather than formal rules. In past ages, such issues were regulated by religious authorities, but today they are subject to public discussions in the media and private decisions among couples. A special type of social relationship is involved in these issues, namely those that involve intimate partnerships, institutionalized through family types. Among most Nordic people, attitudes on these topics can be described as relatively they generally pardon transgressions. This does not imply a libertarian attitude where 'anything goes'. Instead it indicates a general hesitation to condemn such transgressions because there may be mitigating circumstances. Some diversity was found among Nordic respondents. Statistical analyses indicated that attitudes on moral issues relating to the private sphere varied with social position. Permissiveness was lower at the periphery, among those with only basic education, among the older generations, in low-income categories, and was lower among men than women.

A second cluster of topics is formed by issues such as cheating on social benefits or tax fraud, not paying for public transportation, bribery etc. These topics all refer to cheating the public system in many ways. Transgressions are generally not regarded as heroic acts of civil disobedience against a suppressive state but as sabotage of a public system that aims to provide safety, security, and welfare for all its citizens. Actions in the public sphere are mostly regulated by formal rules. The restrictive answers to the public topics stood in contrast to permissiveness on the private topics. Furthermore, there was much less variation regarding public topics. Such transgressions were generally regarded as unacceptable. This homogeneous tendency implied that it was not possible to identify patterns of variation that were sociologically meaningful.

The distinction between public and private norms (Riis in Bexell 1998 p. 39) is made problematic by Rawls' ethical theory that distinguishes between an overlapping consensus and rational doctrines. However, the distinction makes sense when it is interpreted as moral reflections that refer to justification of premises and consequences relating to the social structure versus premises and consequences that refer primarily to an individual life.

Whatever the reason, it is worth reflecting on the moral mapping. It seems reasonable to form distinctions among different types of moral challenges, rather than to present uniform guidelines that must apply to all types of moral problems. It may be reasonable to follow moral rules on some problems, to regard the context of others, to look at motives in some cases and consequences in others. Whereas some moral philosophers may regard such shifts as contradictory, they can be quite sensible. Peoples' practical morality can based on sound reasoning although it is not stated in an intellectual language, but instead practiced in the challenges of everyday life.

These findings indicate that modern Nordic people form a mental mapping of moral topics. One reason for the distinction between moral attitudes in the private and the public sphere may be that the consequences have a different extension. Moral deviations in the private sphere may threaten the family unit, but hardly the institution of the family. Moral deviations in the public sphere may not threaten the local community or a transportation firm, but deviations eventually undermine the welfare state and the efficient infrastructure of modern society. Furthermore, motives for deviating from private norms and public standards are probably very different. Whereas deviations from private morality are probably motivated by psychological conditions that are difficult to control, deviations from public standards are probably motivated by egotism. We do not know the reasons behind the answers in this survey.

Popular ethics: Moral judgments

The study on Religious and Moral Pluralism in Western Europe (RAMP) was from its inception designed to supplement the European Values Study (EVS), especially regarding items on religion and morality. Instead of asking about moral attitudes, RAMP asked about moral reasons and ethical justifications. The questionnaire was designed from scratch by an international team in which I participated as the Nordic representative. The European RAMP project became the empirical source material for a NORFACE-financed project on folk-churches and religious pluralism in the Nordic countries, a study in which I also participated. The findings from the RAMP study were presented mainly through articles in *Research in the Social Scientific Study of Religion,* 13 (2002) and 14 (2003). The Nordic study was published more widely. Findings relating to the sociology of religion were presented in a volume edited by Gustafsson and Pettersson (2001) while the findings that related to ethics were presented in a volume edited by Østnor (2001). The Nordic findings were commented in a cultural analytical perspective in a volume edited by Henriksen and Krogseth (2001).

Developing the items on morality was hard work. Members of the team asked some professors on ethics – such as those at the University of Aarhus – to propose questions on ethics. However, these items were rather abstract and our pretest respondents had difficulties with relating to them. The research team held high professional standards and therefore aimed at measuring by using scales rather than single items. A research group at ZUMA, Cologne, performed extensive pretests with various moral items. However, most had to be discarded, either because people could not respond to them or because the answers did not form a pattern we could interpret. Although it was not too difficult to develop questions about moral attitudes, it was more problematic to form questions about moral reasoning.

The eventual RAMP questionnaire contained several series of moral questions. Among the topics are: bribes, tax fraud, abortion, homosexual rights, euthanasia, gender equality, and nepotism. Many of the moral questions referred to attitudes, where people were asked to judge whether a certain action could be justified. However, the theme of justification was expanded in a few issues that presented conditions for the action and then asked whether the action could be justified under the specific conditions. Thus, tax fraud, death penalty, and abortion were addressed by statements about various reasons for these acts. We were able to form the items into unidimensional scales which showed that the responses formed a consistent pattern. Each respondent has of course her or his specific moral position. However, when these responses are combined, a clear pattern emerges. This may be seen as an outcome of a general popular discourse on morality. People are not unilaterally for or against tax fraud, the death penalty or abortion. Their attitude depends on conditions, motives, reasons, and consequences. A few are against such acts under all conditions. But when mitigating circumstances are provided, most people take a more nuanced stand. These nuances form a consistent pattern, which we can observe statistically in the form of a scale. We were also able to trace the relationship between how respondents positioned themselves on each scale and their sociological characteristics. There is no need to go into detail here about the findings. The major point is that popular morality does not present a haphazard picture but forms a meaningful pattern, which results from an ongoing popular discourse on morality.

The RAMP study contains several topics that are relevant for illustrating popular morality and have not been addressed by other studies. While the data may be somewhat outdated after thirteen years, they still point to basic patterns that are probably quite stable unless a major event takes place that questions assumptions about social trust.

One of the characteristic features of the RAMP questionnaire was that it allowed nuanced answers, often on a scale of 1 to 7. A description of the responses raises two central questions. These are: at which point do responses converge and how much do responses diverge from that point? For reasons of simplicity these questions are answered by the mean and standard deviation, but the measurement is not strictly speaking an interval scale. On issues where responses are greatly skewed, the proportion of extreme answers is also noticed. Results are stated for the combined and weighted Nordic data file. There are national variations on some topics, but these are not central here.

One of the issues of ethical discourse relates to the weight of general moral rules versus the circumstances of a given case. This issue was also addressed by the RAMP study in a particular question. The answer was requsted on a scale ranging from 1 to 7, where 1 indicates that the case depends only on circumstances and 7 that the rules apply at all times. At first, the responses may be seen as diffuse, since many respondents chose a middle position and the standard deviation is quite large. However, this can also be read as a mature reflection on the problem. Moderation due to circumstances does not necessarily indicate casuistry or utilitarianism. It may express a morally qualified reflection that considers whether and to which extent the moral maxims apply in concrete cases. The influence of circumstances will be further illuminated as we focus on specific moral problems.

Table 1: The moral foundation: principles or circumstances:

	Mean	Standard deviation
	3.8	2.0

"Some people think that what is good and what is bad or evil depends entirely upon the circumstances. Other people think that rules about what is good or bad apply at all times. What is closest to your opinion?" On a scale of 1-7 -1 'depends on circumstances' and 7 'apply at all times'.

We will first consider a central topic regarding public morality, namely tax evasion. Taxes are relatively high in the Nordic countries, as they provide the means for financing public welfare. Simultaneously, many people think that tax evasion is becoming more common, although it is not, as a rule, accepted. However, some reasons are regarded as more acceptable than others. Unfair tax laws are more accepted than general cheating or high taxes. Responses to these reasons form a single dimension, which is open to different interpretations. One plausible interpretation is that support for the tax system is supposed to be mutual. Citizens are supposed to contribute by paying their fair share, so self-centered reasons for tax evasion are not accepted. But if the government does not economize and secure fairness, some persons regard tax evasion as more justified. These data indicate an implicit social contract between the taxpaying citizens and the government, which supports the Nordic welfare model. Attitudes to tax evasion formed a unidimensional scale according to factor analysis. As responses are skewed on all these items, correlations will be based on relatively few deviant answers.

Table 2: Reasons for tax evasion

Tax evasion is more justifiable…	Mean	Standard deviation	Percent that strongly disagrees
the more everyone is cheating anyway	2.0	1.6	61
the higher the taxes are	2.3	1.8	53
the more the government is wasting our money	2.9	2.0	41
the more unfair the tax laws are	3.1	2.1	36

1: Strongly agree; 7: strongly disagree

A central topic regarding private morality concerns abortion. This does not indicate that abortion is, by definition, an entirely private matter.

But the EVS study indicated that attitudes to abortion were related to a set of moral items that referred to the private sphere in social life. Regarding this topic, it was only possible to give a positive or negative response to the stated reason.

Table 3: Reasons for accepting an abortion

Percent agreeing that "It should be possible for a woman to have an abortion for the following reason"	
If her health is seriously endangered by the pregnancy	96
If she became pregnant as the result of rape	95
If there is a serious defect in the baby	91
If she does not want to have more children	67
If the family does not think it can afford more children	50
If she does not want to have a baby at that time	47
If she does not want to marry the father of the child	46

In general, Nordic people are tolerant regarding abortion. This was already noticed by the EVS which had a single question on abortion. However, the RAMP study indicates that this toleration does not indicate a moral permissiveness. Some reasons for abortion are more acceptable than others, and these reasons form a clear pattern. Thus, while there is an almost universal acceptance of reasons that point to a *force majeure* or health risk, fewer accept reasons that point to egotistic convenience. Attitudes to abortion formed a unidimensional Guttman-scale, as indicated above.

These findings raise questions regarding international surveys based on a simple question about accepting or rejecting abortion such as the World Values Survey. Responses to general questions are influenced by the local, contextual grounds for obtaining an abortion. Many respondents who at first reject abortion on principle take a more moderate position when they are confronted with real, mitigating circumstances. It is very likely that moral views on abortion become even more understanding, the closer the respondents are to the people involved.

Furthermore, RAMP included items that addressed moral dilemmas, such as access to an operation, the choice of an employee, or euthanasia. An effort was made to present a moral choice that could illuminate the moral dimension identified by Kohlberg and Habermas. However, this did not succeed in practice, perhaps because the dilemma was too simple or because people did not follow that moral logic.

Moral sources

RAMP also included items about the sources of ethical justification. People are probably not very aware of the actual sources of their moral views. A typical answer, such as 'my conscience' does not indicate on what that conscience is based. Nevertheless, responses indicate which moral sources Nordic people recognize, and how these sources may be related. Again, the questions were presented in terms of scales which made it possible to grade degrees of importance.

Thus, the respondents were asked how much importance they gave to their conscience, the opinions others, their upbringing, the law, their reli-

Table 7. The moral foundation: sources of the morality

	Mean	Standard deviation
My conscience	6.0	1.2
What others will think of me	3.2	1.7
My upbringing	5.4	1.5
The law	5.4	1.5
My religion	3.3	2.1
What makes other people happy or unhappy	5.1	1.5
What makes me happy or unhappy	5.3	1.5

"If you need to decide what is right or wrong and good or bad, how strongly are you influenced by the following? On a scale of 1-7. 1: not at all influenced; 7: strongly influenced.

gion, what makes other people happy or unhappy, and what make the respondents themselves happy or unhappy. It was obvious that people did not see these sources as mutually exclusive. Therefore, questions were presented as scaled items that allowed for nuance and combinations. Most respondents in the Nordic countries said that they simultaneously considered the happiness of others as well as their own. This approach makes the analysis much more complicated, but it also allows us to obtain a more nuanced and realistic image of how people think about moral questions. We may have ended with a scattered image of individuals who have very different and inconsistent moral opinions, but the answers actually formed patterns that could be interpreted in a meaningful manner.

Most people refer to their conscience, but this does not tell much about its foundation. Relatively few refer to other people's opinion or to their own religion. Relatively many point to their upbringing or the law, or to what makes other people or themselves happy or unhappy. However, these responses form two distinct parts. People who point to their upbringing also tend to point to the law, and people who decide what makes other people happy also consider what makes themselves happy.

Analysis of the RAMP data (Pettersson in Gustafsson & Pettersson, 2000, Halman and Pettersson 2002) identifies two major dimensions in moral attitudes, namely a 'tradition-oriented rule morality' based on a combination of one's upbringing and the law, and a 'consequence-oriented happiness morality' based on concerns for happiness for both oneself and for others. The former corresponds with a deontological approach while the latter corresponds with a consequentialist approach. Pettersson identifies sociological characteristics: A 'tradition-oriented rule morality' is more prevalent among the older, those with less formal education, and religiously active persons, while a 'consequence-oriented happiness morality' is more prevalent among the young, those with more formal education, and religious skeptics. This follows our general stereotypes. However, gender presents an interesting factor since women score higher simultaneously on both types of moral attitudes. This may indicate that women are more morally concerned than men.

It is the covariatiations that are important, rather than the attitudes to single isuues. The scales indicate that moral responses to a topic form a relatively consistent pattern. The next question is whether people connect moral topics. One possibility is that people are morally strict or permissive on all topics. This means that some people are morally strict whatever the topic while others are morally permissive. This hypothesis is not supported by the data. People may be consistently strict on one set of topics and consistently permissive on another. This point can be illustrated by considering attitudes about tax evasion, abortion and suicide. While attitudes about tax evasion and abortion were measured by scales, attitudes about suicide were identified by a single, graded question.

The correlation between tax fraud and abortion was very low and slightly negative ($r = -0.05$) These topics are, for the most part separated in respondents' moral views; there is a slight indication that some people who accept tax fraud for some reason tend to reject the reasons for abortion. The correlation between tax fraud and suicide is not significant, hence we cannot identify any correspondence in the responses to these topics. However, the correlation between abortion and suicide is positive and quite high ($r = +0.27$). Thus, people who accept several reasons for abortion also tend to accept suicide. This correlation shows that people form patterns of moral topics, and hold similar attitudes to the topical set. Moral attitudes to a public topic such as tax fraud are thus distinct from moral attitudes to personal topics such as abortion or suicide. Furthermore, people refer to different moral sources when they evaluate such topics. Persons who are most permissive on a moral topic are characterized by the moral sources that they reject rather than by the ones they think are important. People who tend to accept reasons for tax fraud simultaneously tend to reject the law as a main source of morality ($r=-0.126$). Also those who accept abortion are less prone to point to the law as a moral source, but this tendency is much weaker ($r = -0.08$). People who tend to accept suicide tend to reject religion as a main source of morality ($r = -0.171$).

The critique of surveys on popular morality

Surveys are designed to give a quantified overview of the distribution of responses to standardized questions at a certain point of time. Several objections can be raised to this approach. The questions may be invalid because people do not understand them in the intended way. Also, the design of the survey does not allow for direct causal or motivational inferences. It can only point to covariations between responses and background variables. Surveys can only illustrate responses, but not the way in which people actually act in moral dilemmas. Finally, the approach is behavioristic, but it necessitates hermeneutic assumptions about how people understand the questions.

The Finnish professor Tage Kurtén has criticized the questions for being rationalistic, pointing especially to the one on tax fraud (Østnor 2001). However, the wording of the question does not point to a decision on whether to perform tax fraud but to reasons for a normative judgment. We may guess how the question was interpreted by the respondents. However, instead of projecting our own interpretation onto other people, we may actually ask respondents how they interpret the question. Professors of ethics probably read such questions in a manner that is quite different from the interpretations of laypersons. Professors of ethics are intellectually trained to trace the subtle assumptions behind moral questions, whereas laypersons normally grasp them as pragmatic challenges.

The above-mentioned sociological distinction between moral problems relating to public and private concerns was also taken up by Jaana Hallamaa in her reading of the RAMP data (Østnor 2001). She distinguishes between moral dilemmas that relate to social structures and those that relate to individuals. Respondents were generally unanimous in rejecting tax fraud and nepotism. Moral deviation on these issues may threaten the basic structure of the welfare society, its solidarity of financing, and the principle of equal justice. However, there is more variation with regard to evaluating reasons for abortion or euthanasia. These issues are not just a private matter; they also involve society, and they are regulated by laws. The dilemmas do not necessarily relate to oneself, but rather to an understanding of another person in a moral dilemma. Hallamaa's interpretation is in accord with my own. She therefore concludes that two types of moral pluralism are involved, one that may threaten the basic structure of society or the overarching consensus that maintains trust and mutual respect and another that relates to tolerating a diversity of values and norms in society.

The above-mentioned reservations about survey data do not indicate that the data should be discarded. Surveys can provide an overview that allows us to go into depth with specific case studies. In order to obtain a more complete sociological description of popular morality, surveys need to be supplemented by in-depth interviews on people's reflections, focus interviews on group dynamics of ethical decisions, and observations of moral actions. Differences in the epistemological assumptions behind the singular methods are not a hindrance to combining the types of knowledge obtained from all the studies. This combined knowledge depends on a meta-epistemology; but we perform that operation routinely in our everyday life, and also when we consider how to produce validated knowledge about popular ethics. This is a complex topic, where several types of knowledge are relevant: At the agency level this calls for information about what people think and do; at the intersubjective level about how people discuss ethics and form shared norms or form sanctions for trespassing norms; and at the structural level, this calls for information about the recognized and unrecognized potentials for and restraints on ethical decisions.

Re-reading the RAMP data, I would like to point out that some expected patterns were not found. On some topics, no specific pattern of response has been identified. It is quite possible that the analytical approaches neglected some angles. However, it is more likely that people are uncertain about the topics. The topics refer to moral dilemmas, and the lack of a pattern in the responses indicate that people are ambiguous, uncertain, unclarified. The RAMP study posed an ethical question about a hospital that must choose only one out of three patients for a vital heart operation due to limited resources. Responses were quite ambiguous and did not point to a clear rule. This does not indicate a lack of moral capacity. It follows from the dilemma itself and indicates that answers are based on serious thought.

Studies on popular ethics, like RAMP, indicates that moral arguments are influenced by a combination of moral principles, by respondens' interpretation of the concrete problem, and their classification of the concrete problem within a general framework of views on human relations. People seem unable or unwilling to pursue the logic of one ethical theory deductively. However, this does not imply a casuistic *ad hoc* bricolage. The moral attitude to a specific problem seems to depend on a classification of its type, which points to the principles that apply. This line of argument corresponds to jurisprudence, where the first concern is to specify the problem. This leads to identify those parts of jurisprudence that are relevant to consider. Popular ethics seems to follow a similar type of reasoning, which is abductive rather than deductive. This is not illogical.

Popular moral reasoning involves a constellation of several considerations. First and foremost it involves an identification of the moral issue –referring a concrete case to a typology that, in turn, refers to relevant prior experiences and evaluations. Popular moral discourse is concerned with definitions of the issue. For example, a statement can according to the situation be classified as a case of 'lying' or 'politeness', a case of 'cheating' or 'solving', etc. One way of typologizing a case is by its social character, which is the constellation of people involved in the case and the way in which moral actions affect the situation. By typologizing the case, it becomes possible to evaluate potential outcomes of different moral actions. It also becomes possible to identify those dimensions of benefits and liabilities that are relevant for evaluating possible moral actions. As the case is associated with a type of cases, it is possible to point to general rules for evaluating it, whether precedents, procedures, moral discourses or formal regulations. Thus, popular moral reasoning routinely performs judgments that are parallel to those made by courts of justice. People may ponder about their moral judgments, and discuss them with other people they consider significant. Everyday social life is saturated with such moral discourses. Their discourse is reflected culturally by television programmes that address moral issues in various settings, such as presenting moral dilemmas as entertaining drama.

Relating popular morality and moral theory

Thorleif Pettersson has proposed an empirical approach inspired by David Miller's suggestion to be sensitive to popular opinion while being attentive to the social contexts in which principles of justice are applied. Pettersson's model studies respondents' views of concrete moral problems as being influenced by moral principles as well as their views on human relations (Gustafsson and Pettersson 2000 p. 206).

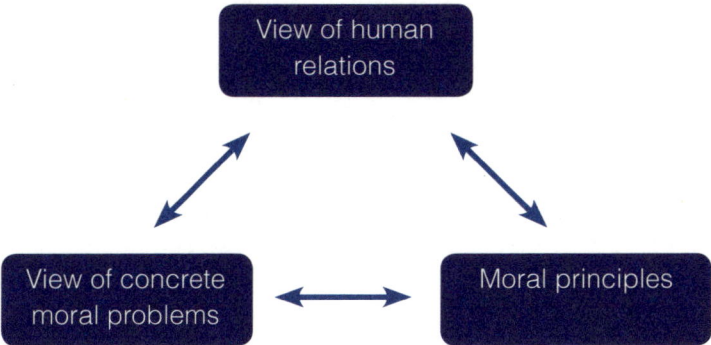

Fig. 1. Pettersson's model of popular moral reasoning.

Pettersson's model includes a sociological component, namely the general view of human relations. The general view of human conditions can be rendered in terms of philosophical anthropology, or of political ideologies. People seem to make systematic distinctions about ethical questions according to human relations. Pettersson illustrates this by referring to mutual or free relations between free agents and hierarchical relations. We may pursue his line of reasoning by pointing out that it is possible and relevant to distinguish among types of social problems, according to how agents are involved in them. Moral and ethical concerns about an agent's responsibility in the situation depend on the capacities and liabilities of agency in the specific context. This involves whether the action has consequences for the agent, a close group, a wider community, or humanity at large.

The moral principles are contextualized as they refer to human relations, and the views on human relations can become activated as they refer to moral principles. The model allows for feedback among the components. New challenges resulting from concrete moral challenges can lead us to review both our understanding of human relations and to reformulate our moral principles.

Modern society is generally regarded as characterized by an increasing individualization that may lead to utilitarian egotism. However, these tendencies can be tempered by 'reflexivity'. Its sociological usage is inspired by G. H. Mead, "the turning-back of the experience of the individual upon himself which enables an individual to 'take the attitude of the other toward himself'" (1967, p. 134). Thereby the individual is able to consciously adjust himself to the social process. In modern sociology, reflexivity refers both to a social consciousness among the human agents and to a structure that gives options and responsibilities to citizens. Giddens, for instance, talks about reflexivity as "the monitored character of the ongoing flow of social life" (1986, p. 3), while U. Beck proposes a distinction between reflection and reflexivity: Reflexive modernization implies self-confrontation with the effects of risk society though not necessarily what may later become the object of public, political or scientific reflection. (1994, p. 6). The term is used by several other sociologists, such as Bourdieu and Gouldner, with some variations.

Reflexivity may also characterize moral issues. Habermas refers to a normative reflexivity, where agents evaluate moral actions according to universal ethical principles. He refers to L. Kohlberg's theory about moral stages, which ends with "The universal ethical principle orientation" where the basic principles of justice are "the equality of human rights and respect for the dignity of human beings as individuals" (1990, p. 124). Habermas proposes a 'discourse ethics' – where the generalizability of interests is the result of an 'intersubjectively mounted public discourse' between equal partners and is thus free from the influence of authorities. This position overlaps modern versions of Kantian contractarianism, i.e. the writing of J. Rawls. His version of ethics focuses on the rightness rather than the goodness of actions and it is based on principles of equality and voluntarism combined with a sense of communitarianism. According to Rawls, problems of justice cannot be resolved by individual decisions but only through a sort of social contract, in which the participants agree on the basic institutions of society and procedures of solving disagreements. A full agreement is hardly possible though a 'reflexive equilibrium' can be reached through a voluntary discourse, when there is agreement about democratic procedures.

Concluding remarks

There is a field of discourse possible between ethical theory and popular ethics. Without such a discourse, ethical theory might ultimately become nothing more than abstract ideas without practical relevance, while popular ethics might become pragmatic postures without serious reflections. The solution is neither to initiate a popular education in ethical theory nor to let popular ethics determine ethical theory. The goal is rather to advance the ways in which considerations about ethical theory could become guidelines for ethical practices and, further, could be illuminated by investigating how people relate to ethical problems in their daily lives.

Among the many reasons for this gap between ethical theory and popular ethics, there is one worth considering in the light of popular moral reasoning: Ethical theories are proposed in discourses at a high level of abstraction, while popular moral reasoning belongs to discourses that relate to concrete cases. Moral challenges in everyday life consist of cases with many aspects and mitigating circumstances. Ethical theories are abstracted from such concrete cases by forming ideal types that clarify the issue by eliminating complicating factors. Such an abstraction and reduction is necessary to present the problem with a degree of clarity that allows for a unequivocal, rational response. However, this also distances the argument from the muddled, concrete moral problems encountered in everyday life.

Our survey data indicate that most people are quite reflected about ethical problems. They distinguish between different classes of situations that call for certain moral rules and seem able to make reasonable judgments. This does not imply that ethical theory has to absorb and affirm popular morality. Ethical theory could be a critic and qualifier for popular ethical discourses. However, in order to fulfill this critical function, ethical theory has to advance toward the level of concreteness that characterizes popular moral discourse. An intellectual critique that reveals the internal contradictions of popular ethical discourse merely affirms that the practical challenges are complex; an abstract critique that refers to unrealistic, idealized preconditions can be easily dismissed. There is an ongoing popular moral discourse, both in private circles and in public that indicates an interest in utilizing ethical theory in order to clarify how to approach concrete, complex problems encountered in contemporary society.

References

Beck, Ulrich et al. 1994. *Reflexive Modernization*. Cambridge: Cambridge University Press.
Botvar, Pål Kjetil 2001. Sin egen lykkemorals smed? Individualiseringens følger for religion og moral i vestlige samfundd. In: *Pluralisme og Identitet*, eds. Jan Olav Henriksen og Otto, 319-53. Oslo: Gyldendahl Akademisk.
Dobbelaere, Karel and Ole Riis 2003. Religious and Moral Pluralism. Theories, research questions and design. *Research in the Social Scientific Study of Religion*, Brill 13, 159-72.
Østnor, Lars ed. 2001. Etisk pluralism i Norden, Kristiansand: Høyskoleforlaget.
Gustafsson Göran and Pettersson Thorleif eds. 2000. *Folkkyrkor och religiös pluralism – den nordiska modellen*, Stockholm: Verbum.
Giddens, Anthony, 1986. *The Constitution of Society*, Cambridge: Polity Press.
Halman, Loek and Pettersson, Thorleif 2002. Moral pluralism in contemporary religion. Evidence from the project Religious and moral pluralism. *Research in the Social Scientific Study of Religion*, Brill, 13 173-205.
Habermas, Jürgen 1990. *Moral Consciousness and Communicative Action*, Cambridge: Polity Press.
Mead, George Herbert. 1967. *Mind, Self & Society.* London: University of Chicago Press.
Miller, David. 1999. *Principles of Social Justice*. Cambridge: Harvard University Press.
Molewijk, Bert et al. 2004, Empirical data and moral theory. A plea for integrated ethics, *Medicine, Health Care and Philosophy,* 7 p. 55-69.
Pettersson, Thorleif and Riis, Ole 2002. Social capital and its impact on moral and political values. In: Bexell Göran and Andersson Dan Erik eds. 2002. *Universal Ethics*, The Hague: Martinus Nijhoff Publishers, p. 197-222.
Riis, Ole. 2011. Normativity in empirical social studies. In: Henriksen, Jan-Olav ed. 2011. *Difficult Normativity*, Frankfurt am Main: Peter Lang, p.109-30.
Riis, Ole. 2004, Religiøs og moralsk pluralisme i Norden. In: *Det unika Norden,* vol 4, p. 23-40.

Jörg Zeller

The missing link between theoretical and applied ethics

Abstract

The challenge of ethics asserts itself in the space between theoretical reasoning, sensual experiencing, emotional feeling, and practical/poietical acting. We know there is – if not in theory then in practice – a dichotomy between theoretical and applied ethics. Of course, the theory-practice gap in moral reasoning has been noticed not least by Aristotle and Kant. Both (among others) also tried to bridge the gap. In my paper I seek to investigate what we can learn from these trials. I will do it on the assumption that the theory-application gap in ethics is the result of a too restrictive approach to ethics and morals.

Tertium datur between theoretical and applied ethics

In my opinion, the distinction between theoretical and applied ethics is misleading. I will argue that ethics is neither a theoretical nor an applied discipline but a third entity. In ethical concerns we have apparently to face a '*tertium datur*' between thinking and doing[1]. From an ontological

---

1   That the principle of bivalence, i.e. the principle of the excluded middle, is not necessarily a principle of practical reasoning. For example, Aristotle's understanding of virtue as the middle ground between exaggeration and scarcity. Giddens 1984 introduces the concept of practical consciousness in his structuration theory of societal constitution. It is different from discursive consciousness, i.e., from what actors are able to realize and discursively communicate about the conditions of their action. This makes practical consciousness a kind of tacit knowledge. The difference between practical and discursive consciousness is, however, according to Giddens

point of view reason is not an object or a quality or relation but an action mode. Practical reason handles actions, theoretical reason handles facts. The latter constructs concepts out of experiences, propositions out of concepts, and arguments out of propositions. The former, practical, reason constitutes intentions out of motives and desires, decisions out of intentions and factual knowledge, and performances out of decisions and bodily motor functions. 'To construct' means, in general, to make something become or work from something else. Accordingly, my approach to ethics is constructive.

According to Singer applied ethics is "the application of ethical reasoning to specific issues or areas of practical concern" (Singer 1991 p. 1 xiii). To make sense of this explanation one has to presuppose that ethical theory exists in advance of its application to reality. This priority can be understood temporally or logically. Temporally it would imply that nobody would be able to act morally before having constructed or learned an ethical theory. It is very unlikely that we learn to act morally in this way, because what then would be the prior condition of being able to construct or learn an ethical theory?

Does it help then if the priority of theory in moral affairs is logical? I don't think so. Broadly understood, logic is about conceptualizing our experiences – or more precisely constructing concepts, propositions and inferences out of experiences. If this means that we can't act without having conceived what it is to act, then we again are in trouble with the question of what our ability to think is based on. This asserts itself *a fortiori* when we realize that thinking itself is a kind of activity. If it weren't then thinking would be the same as unintentional experiencing – an uncontrollable part of the consciousness stream.

To differentiate between thinking and doing and thus between theoretical and applied or practical approaches to our experience of reality makes sense only if we assume that thinking and doing are only two implemen-

---

    not as clear-cut, as one might think "I do not intend the distinction between discursive and practical consciousness be a rigid and impermeable one". On the other hand, there is a barrier between the discursive and the unconscious consciousness. The latter is the result of repressive powers that bar the actor from realizing the conditions of his/her action. Against this background, the practical consciousness appears to be the homeland of morals. This, however, is not where Giddens himself places morality. According to him, it dwells in the discursive consciousness or its personification as *I,* ibid p. 8). In my opinion the region of discursiveness, i.e., of verbalizing and logical reasoning, is better consined to ethics.

tation modes of the same thing. I will call this third entity that connects and mediates thinking and doing actorship, the power of acting.

If ethics is reasoning about what is good or valuable in not only different real-life situations but in the totality of real, human life, i.e. in what existentialists mean by 'existence' then the space in which ethics originates and operates is the totality of consciousness. The tradition of moral reflection like the tradition of most other branches of philosophical reflection has been dominated by interchanging efforts of reductionism. Either moral acting was believed to be reducible to thinking alone (idealism, Platonism) – thus excluding that sensual, emotional, or practical experience should play a role in moral affairs or the principle and origin of moral acting was reduced to sensual and/or emotional experience (hedonism). Or eventually moral acting was assumed to be reducible to what turns out to be practical and useful (utilitarianism, pragmatism).

Nonreductionist ontology of ethics

To sketch the basis of a non-reductionist approach to ethics I take as my point of departure Nørreklit's 2004/2012 theory of reality construction. If reality is understood as an integration of four dimensions – fact, possibility, value and meaning – then ethics can be taken as the motivating end of our individual and collective reality construction. Generally, ethics is about why we do what we do, i.e. about the reason behind our acting. We do what we do on the background of what we know, feel and wish about the world – understood as the totality of what there is and happens, the totality of facts. But the factual world is not identical with the real world, the world in which living beings not only react to and experience what happens but intentionally act on and change the world according to their needs and desires. The world in which ethics is possible and makes sense is a world not only of actual and possible facts but also of values and meanings. It is a world not only of facts and events but also of living and mental beings, artifacts and histories. Its dynamic is not reducible to effective causes but has to be enlarged to an Aristotelian style manifold causality involving animal and human actors producing technical, artistic and epistemic things (Rheinberger 2001) and social institutions, thereby realizing conditions of life as the foundation and driving force to unfold their existence in personal and social histories.

The world as totality of facts has no meaning, no value and thus no Morale. Of course, it doesn't make sense at all to reduce ethics to experiential facts. But I doubt that the naturalistic fallacy (Moore 1996) and the immorality of the world can be "healed" by moral intuition if intuition is understood as a faculty additional to sensual and emotional experience and by thought processes that are not ingrained in the overall fabric of reality and mind. The key concept in the ontology of ethics is actorship.

By unfolding this concept, ethics, I hope, will be understandable as something that lies between theory (thinking, reasoning) and practice (doing, realizing). Let me start by making clear clear what ethics is not about. Ethics is not about thinking about the right thing to do in a given situation. Ethical behavior is not only theoretical behavior. Nor does ethics concern doing the right thing in the right situation without thinking about why I should do it, or why my action is the right one for the actual situation, or why the situation is the right one for my act. In my opinion, the differentiation between theoretical and applied ethics is based on a misunderstanding of what ethics is about. But why do I stress this?

If 'behaving morally' means 'doing right' or 'doing the good' then it is impossible to behave in the right way only theoretically. We have to do what we think is good to find out if it is really good. The practical reasonable is constrained to contingency. It is, however, also impossible to behave merely practically right or good without having considered why doing so is right or good or for whom and under which circumstances. If thinking and doing are two different faculties of the human mind, then behaving ethically presupposes a third faculty that links thinking and doing. Here I will be bold and suggest a name for this hybrid mediating faculty: actorship. Misunderstandings of this concept can be averted if we recognize that thinking is a kind of action and doing is a kind of thinking.

But why should we do this? I want to show that the dichotomy between thinking and doing — and I think it is a real one — opens a gap between what we should do and what we really do, a gap between ethics as the theoretical foundation and morals as the practical application of what we think is meaningful and good. This gap concerns that which we call free will on the one hand and that which we call responsibility in form of social obliging customs, rules and norms on the other.

Jörg Zeller

Phronesis and pure reason

If we believe with Kant that freedom – having a choice between possible action alternatives – is the *conditio sine qua non* of practical reason, i.e. of the possibility that practice can be reasonable and the reasonable can be practiced, then you can't behave ethically without thinking about why you mean that you decide the right thing to do in the actual situation with reference to those facts and living beings that have to bear the consequences of your doing. Conversely, you can't behave ethically without daring to act, to make real what you think is the right thing to do in the actual situation and with reference to those facts and living beings that have to bear the consequences of your doing. One cannot refrain from thinking about the maning of what I do. The situation is quite the contrary according to Hannah Arendt 1998. She believed that wickedness is a failure of thinking, or, as I would put it, a failure of medidating the freedom of thinking with the responsibility of doing. The foundation of responsibility is the fact that we are not alone but respond all the time to a universe of everything else. Wickedness is thus the result of a false reality construction.

If acting in the suggested sense is the cornerstone of moral behavior, then it has to be a faculty of sentient beings that combines the freedom of thinking whatever one can imagine as possible with the responsibility of doing. As already indicated, 'responsibility' should be understood in a factual instead of an axiological way. Actions have factual consequences and this makes the actor responsible for what he or she does. To find a less controversial expression of what I mean by 'actorship' let's turn to Aristotle's concept of *phronesis*. Aristotle differentiates between five kinds of knowledge: *techne, episteme, phronesis,* wisdom and mindfulness (cf. Aristotle 1991, p. 234).

Phronesis is neither *episteme* nor *techne* (ibidem, p. 236). It is something other than *episteme* – theoretical knowledge – because it is not about unchangeable laws and rules but about changeable things constrained to contingency. *Phronesis* is not like *techne* – knowledge about how to produce things – because it is not productive or in Greek *poietic* practice. Instead, *phronesis* is behavioral or – as I prefer to call it – moral practice. The difference between technical and moral practice is according to Aristotle that the former has its end in something other and the later has an end in itself. Moral practice is thus doing what we do in a good way. This is the best we can do and if we do so we achieve a good life. Acting on the basis of *phronesis* is thus the same as doing what you do in a virtuous or excellent way. *Phronesis* and virtue/arete are two twigs of the same plant. However, apart from being different from theoretical and technical knowledge, *phronesis* is akin to them. It is, as Aristotle (Nikomachean Ethics 1140 b 20) puts it, "a necessarily with good reasons combined active behavior regarding human goods" (Aristotle 1991, p. 237).

No doubt, *phronesis* is Aristotle's version of practical reason. The interesting part of this version is that Greek philosophers, including Aristotle, also differentiated between two senses of 'practical' in an instrumentalist and moral sense. *Poiesis*, the Greek noun for producing desirable goods, achieves artistic or technical goals in order to reach ends outside themselves. *Poiesis* serves as an instrument or medium for satisfying desires. *Praxis*, the Greek noun for realizing ends in themselves, has in my opinion to be understood as a kind of second order practice, or the way in which we try to realize the supreme meaning of our life. The Greeks called this meaning the good life and the mental condition of realizing a good life was called *eudaimonia*, being in good spirit.

However, if the good life is not only the result of good luck and thus independent of moral behavior, then any theory of what I call actorship has to address the problem of freedom. For Kant 1788/2003, freedom is critical to our understanding of ethics. Without free will we are not responsible for the consequences of our actions, and without responsibility free will is in danger of becoming immoral. The whole problem of ethics unfolds then within the temporal distance between activating and realizing the will. In this interval the moral drama of desire, motivation, reasoning, decision, performance, result and the consequence of what I call action takes places. It is a drama[2] because we can't know but only reasonably guess at the result and consequences of our action. To act implies the possibility of failing. As actors we always risk making the wrong decision. This characterizes the peculiarity of practical reason, the faculty of acting which is peculiar of living and especially of sentient beings.

But what do reason and reasoning actually mean? Through Kant's eyes let's take a look at the concept of practical reason.

---

2 The primary meaning of the Greek word 'drama' is 'action' The drama performed on stage makes a spectacle for the spectators. The stage is a place where human action can be made exemplary and considered by everyone who sees it. The drama as spectacle is the display of moral stuff, of something the spectators should think about in relation to their own moral challenges.

Jörg Zeller

Practical reason

According to Kant 1788/2003, practical reason is not about how objects can be thought of but about how the will can be determined to realize an object that can be thought about (cf. Kant 2003, p. 19). The will is understood as the faculty to produce object-corresponding ideas (*Vorstellungen*) or at least to decide to do so (p. 18). Unlike theoretical reason that determines objects, practical reason determines the will to act. Theoretical reason is thus – translated into the theory of reality construction (Nørreklit 2004/2012) – about real or possible facts, while practical reason is about real or possible actions. Freedom, i.e. free will, is according to Kant a special kind of causality, namely unconditioned causality. By determining the will, practical reason transduces (Zeller 2011) ideas into facts. In contrast, theoretical reason transduces facts into ideas. Practical reason studies the laws of the free will (cf. Kant 2003, p. 20). Reason as such (*Vernunft*) – practical or theoretical – is the ability to justify or constitute either facts (theoretical) or actions (practical). To understand why Kant believes that reason – the operation mode of conceptualizing our experience of the world – can as practical reason be made real, we have to clarify that theoretical and practical reasoning are only two manifestations of the same faculty of constructing reality. (Remember the integration of the four-dimensional ontology of facts, possibilities, meanings and values that construct reality out of what there is and what happens).

Kant 2003 differentiates between practical laws (action rules for all rational beings) and practical maxims (subjective action rules). This can be used to specify the difference between ethics and morals. Morality is governed by maxims, i.e., subjectively desire-oriented action rules. In contrast, ethics is (or should be?) about practical laws, i.e. what is reasonable for every rational being to do. According to Kant practical reason deals with the faculty of desire. It determines which desires exercised by which subjects are rational and which are not. This is critical for the differentiation of maxims and laws and thus for the differentiation of morals into applied ethics and pure ethics. Ethics is about actorship, i.e., about the faculty of forming or constructing a reality on the basis of experiencing the world and inferring practical possibilities. In this sense, ethics is a formal theory or logic of the faculty of acting and not a logic of action. If this difference makes sense, then the difference between theoretical and applied ethics also makes sense. We have a pure but empty faculty of construction on the one hand and materially loaded constructions of epistemic world views and technical, artistic or political reality forms on the other.

The difference between (unconditioned) moral laws and (conditioned, hypothetical) moral maxims is decisive regarding the question if absolute moral laws can be established – i.e. moral laws that are independent of special kinds of moral subjects (and their abilities to realize these laws). Kant 2003 calls these laws categorical. They determine an actor's will regardless of his/her ability to realize the desired end (cf. ibidem, p. 25). Moral laws are categorical imperatives of the will in general -i.e. the faculty of unconditioned practical causality. One example from Kant is the imperative never to give a false categorical promise. But how can he prove this? It is easy to present situations – e.g. when it could save a life to give a false promise – in which it would be immoral to obey this imperative. However, what about this promise, made in all sincerity: If you don't stop bothering me, I will kill you?

Conclusion

Why was it so critical for Kant to devise and present a formal foundation for ethics? Reason – i.e. justifying or giving reasons for something – is about the form and not the content of thinking and doing. If thinking then is not only a human but a general faculty of all beings that are physically equipped with the ability to form concepts and propositions and to infer conclusions from premises, then practical reason as the faculty of determining the will and perform actions would be the same for all beings equipped with this ability. Against this background, one could argue that the promise to do (p) and at the same time not to intend to do (p) is a contradiction in itself, i.e. a promise that is not a promise. If a promise itself is understood as a kind of action – some philosophers would say a speech act – then a promise that isn't a promise is a practical contradiction. As in the case with theoretical contradictions, practical actions have consequences. If both p and not p is the case, anything whatsoever can be the case. If, for example, actor a both loves and doesn't love actor b she causes great emotional confusion for b. If I intend to sail – i.e. to utilize the wind as driving force of a boat – but at the same time interfere with the wind driving the boat, then I practically contradict my intention to sail. My sailing wouldn't really be sailing.

If understood in this way, practical reason is not identical to ethics. Practical contradictions are not necessarily immoral and practical tautologies or valid practical inferences are not necessarily morally correct.

This makes me suspect that pure practical reason – i.e. reason for an action that is not confined to a particular subject and object of desire in particular circumstances – is ethically useless.

Kant's effort to find a transcendental foundation for ethics is rooted in his conviction or credo that reason, although theoretically confined by experience, is practically real or realizable. Perhaps he believes this because, ultimately, he believes in a divine creator of a world in which some of its living and sentient beings, as developed through evolution, are able to make the world meaningful and valuable. I agree in part with the factual existence of living and sentient beings capable of realizing meaningful and valuable things, institutions, and actions. I am, however, skeptical about the idea of an unconstrained rationality as expressed in a formal categorical imperative with universal moral laws satisfying it. I understand that this is a consequence of Kant's program of transcendentalism. The problem is that a transcendental justification of our factual and practical faculty of reasoning does not completely explain what knowledge and ethics is about.

When I compare the Kantian and the Aristotelian approaches bridging the gap between the freedom of theoretical and the constraining contingency of practical reasoning, I prefer the Aristotelian one.

If ethics is concerned with the ways in which living and sentient beings can transform or transduce the factual world into a meaningful and valuable reality, what is needed is a faculty that is able to integrate all dimensions of being conscious: experiencing, thinking, feeling, and acting. I call this faculty 'actionship' and I think Aristotle's *phronesis* is a good representative of it.

References

Arendt, H. 1998. *Om vold, tænkning og moral,* Frederiksberg: Det lille Forlag.
Aristotle 1991. *Die Nikomachische Ethik,* München: Deutscher Taschenbuch Verlag.
A Companion to Ethics 1991. Ed. P. Singer. Oxford: Blackwell.
Giddens, A. 1984/2011. *The Constitution of Society,* Cambridge/Malden: Polity Press.
Kant, I. 2003. *Kritik der praktischen Vernunft,* Hamburg: Felix Meiner Verlag.
Moore, G.E. 1996. *Principia ehica,* Stuttgart: Philipp Reclam jun.
Nørreklit, L. 2004. Hvad er virkelighed?, In: Christensen, J ed., 2004. *Vidensgrundlag for handlen,* Aalborg: Aalborg Universitetsforlag, p. 25-59.
Nørreklit, L. 2012. Filosofi i praksis. In: Reinbacher, G.S. & Zeller, J. eds. 2012. *Filosofiens anvendelighed,* Aalborg: Aalborg Universitetsforlag, p. 9-49.
Rheinberger, H-J. 2001, *Experimentalsysteme und epistemische Dinge.* Göttingen: Wallstein Verlag.
Zeller, J. 2011, *Information, Medie, Kommunikation.* Aalborg: Aalborg Universitetsforlag.

Anne Gerdes

Ethical Issues in Human Robot interaction

Abstract

In this paper I will reflect upon the ethical implications of human-robot interaction. Issues are discussed in relation to two scenarios: (1) In focusing on robots with intelligent behavior, but without consciousness, attention is focused on the obstacles to forming trustful relations. Here, it is illustrated that human-robot interaction will lack the kind of commitment, that stems from the fact that life is interpersonal, implying that trust is fundamental to human relationships. (2) In focusing on the possibility of developing machine consciousness, issues of our responsibility as creators of robots are discussed, as well as issues dealing with the kind of relationships we might form with such robots. Here, we are faced with a God-like responsibility and ethical obligations towards a creature, who will possibly develop a mind of its own, that might become radically different from the human mind.

Keywords: Human-robot relations, ethics, trust, artificial intelligence, AI, consciousness, (anti)physicalism, behaviorism

Introduction

Since being challenged to further activity, being set greater obstacles to overcome, is the sum and substance of our lives as teleological beings, developing robots – setting ourselves further technological-cultural goals – is not an inhuman or antihuman enterprise. It is simply part and parcel of the life of a species that first began cultivation the land, devising tools and machines, and cultivation – culturally developing – members of the species itself. Machines and artifacts are an inevitable part of human culture. Moral robots are merely a part that still lies in the future (Versenyi 1974, p. 259).

With the recent development of increasingly human-like robots, which of course still are nothing but "stupid machines", we might expect that in the near future, such surprisingly human-like geminoids will be able to simulate intelligent behavior, when acting within restricted contexts.

From a philosophical viewpoint we may still argue about the status of intelligence. But, in real life, people will start to form relationships with robots, whether they are truly intelligent or not. The fact that they look like us, combined with their growing ability to behave in an intelligent manner, will cause new forms of friending and bonding in human-robot interaction. We interact already with quite advanced artificial companions, primitive robot toys, and robots for therapeutic purposes. Here, we are aware that these robots are nothing but machines. Still, the fact that we are highly meaning-seeking and interpretative beings, causes us to anthropomorphisize robots and intuitively interpret them as fellows. As summarized in a phrase by Turkle, robots press our "Darwian buttons" and we respond with care even to simple, designed robot-expressions of emotions (Turkle 2011, p. 8; Benford and Malatre 2007, p. 165).

Furthermore, since the 1950s[1], the classical mind-body problem has been reframed to account for the possibility or unfeasibility of robot and machine consciousness (Wisdom et al. 1952; Scriven 1953; Mackay 1956; Ziff 1959; Lacey 1960; Culbertson 1963; Putnam 1964). Hence, from a cognitive perspective on AI, it could be argued that human and robot coexist in a natural continuum, whereby some kind of robot evolution is realizable and will bring about robots with minds of their own. In this case, we are dealing with a conscious robot with free will, intentions, goals, self-interest, that is, a moral agent with a justified claim for rights. If robots have this status, we are committed to treat them as moral beings.

The purpose of this paper is to reflect upon ethical implications of relationships within these two contexts. In particular issues are discussed from these two perspectives:

---

1 Historically, AI as a research field was initiated at the Dartmouth Conference in 1956. Turing wrote his famous article *Computing Machinery and Intelligence* six years earlier (Turing 1950).

(1) In focusing on the possibility of developing robots with intelligent behavior but without consciousness, I will focus on obstacles establishing trusting relationsships in human-robot interaction. (2) In focusing on the possibility of developing intelligent robots with a mental life of their own, issues of our responsibility as creators of robots will be discussed, as well as issues dealing with the kind of relationships we might establish with such robots.[2]

Perspectives on an artificial intelligence

In what follows, I will discuss two well-known views on strong artificial intelligence. These two positions raise both similar and different ethical issues about the character of human-robot interaction.

Thus, within a behaviorist framework, we might be concerned with the idea of artificial intelligence from a perspective of pure performance. In the strong classical sense of logical behaviorism, mental events are logical constructions from behavior events, whereas the weaker version maintains that there exist entailments between mind-statement and behavior statements (Putnam 1965, p. 25,). The behaviorist perspective focuses on appearance, in holding a definition of intelligence in which intelligence equals intelligent behavior. Consequently, it is not considered meaningful to maintain a distinction between real human intelligence and artificial intelligence, if the latter is indistinguishable from human behavior. This idea is encapsulated in the famous Turing test (1950), which has not yet been passed by any machine. Turing reminds us that when we form judgments about whether or not another person thinks, we only have access to their outward behavior. Therefore, according to Turing, the interesting question is not whether a computer can think, but instead to treat the computer as a 'black box' and ask what kind of behavior a computer has to present in order for us to declare it intelligent.

On the other hand, the 'materialist' approach toward artificial intelligence would disagree with Touring's behaviouristic 'black box' assumption, maintaining that it is a poor solution to offer an explanation in which you deal with the problem of consciousness by denying its existence. In this framework it is assumed that consciousness is a valid con-

---

2   There are, of course, relevant ethical related issues regarding agency and responsibility in a legal context, which I do not touch upon. These issues are discussed in an excellent paper by Ugo Pagallo 2011.

cept; we do have a mind, but this does not imply a mind-body problem, as dualists hold, since withholding a reductive materialist theory of mind "we can give a complete account of man in purely physico-chemical terms"(Armstrong 1980, p. 191). Thus, according to 'physicalism', mental states are nothing but bio-physical entities, enabling us to explain consciousness reductively by means of objective neuroscience and bio-physical events in the brain. As such, we are (nothing but) machines ourselves, or as stated by Marvin Minsky: "The brain is just a computer made out of meat!" (Minsky 1988).

The ethical implications of these two positions for artificial intelligence – the behaviorist and physicalist – will be discussed below from a phenomenological approach. Thus, one might ask what kind of ethical issues we are faced with if robots in the future come to behave like us, or be like us, or rather (maybe) not be like us at all?

Ethical issues in relation to a behaviorist approach toward AI: the "as if" scenario

With a behaviorist framework, what characterizes human-robot interactions? Here, we are dealing with a "look-alike setting", in which mental states are considered unnecessary for the creation of artificial intelligence. The robot's behavior is all that counts. This carries over to the field of machine ethics. When we allocate more responsibility to robots, we need to ensure that they perform adequate actions when interacting with humans and other machines or robots. Thus, responsibility and accountability go hand in hand.

Modeling the richness of human moral decision-making is the main target of machine ethics. In seeking to design artificial moral agency, the challenge of developing robots with an ethical dimension is typically met by distinguishing a continuum of different levels of morality. It runs from operational ethical machines, which are comparable to computer systems or robots with ethical dimensions fully controlled by the built in design[3] to variations of functional morality, with gradually increasing built-in abilities for displaying autonomy and ethical sensitivity to values and towards the surroundings. This level is comparable to systems capable of ethical reasoning due to algorithms that model moral theories such as deontic logic. Finally, full-blown responsible moral

---

3   For instance, a simple control-system in a credit card system that blocks purchases when faced with user patterns suggesting fraud (Wallach and Allan 2009, p. 29).

agents are characterized by having the same ability for ethical decision-making in real life settings as humans have. Put differently, the same distinction is reflected in James Moor's article "Four kinds of ethical Robot" (Moor 2011), in which he concludes that we still haven't created sophisticated robots with algorithms for making ethical decisions even within well-defined domains. Nevertheless, we need to be concerned about robot ethics where robots can exercise moral reasoning within gradually more unpredictable domains (what Moor calls explicit ethical agents). On the other hand, according to Moor, we need not deal with issues on the level of so-called full ethical agents, i.e. robots comparable to human agents with features such as free will, consciousness and intentionality. Although I agree with Moor that robots with mental states are still a goal for the future, we might gain insight from framing a discussion about our humanity and its unique characteristics within the context of artificial intelligence from a physicalist stance. (I will attempt to do this in the following section). For the moment, however, let's pursue the idea of how ethics might be programmed into robots. Anderson, Anderson and Armen 2004 suggest modeling ethical reasoning by a combination of act utilitarianism, which allows for cost-benefit calculations of pleasures and displeasures in the outcome of a given action. Furthermore, they apply Ross' theory of duty-based actions, relying on *prima facia* duties: fidelity, reparation, gratitude, justice, beneficence, non-malefience and self-improvement. And finally, here is Rawls' concept of "reflective equilibrium" that weighs relevant *prima facia* duties against each other:

> Instead of computing a single value based only on pleasure/displeasure, we must compute the sum of up to seven values, depending on the number of Ross' duties relevant to the particular action. The value for each such duty could be computed as with Hedonistic Act Utilitarianism, as the product of Intensity, Duration, and Probability. (Anderson, Anderson & Armen 2004, sec. 3).

This kind of machine ethical reasoning should not be confused with ethical autonomous decision-making. Thus, according to McDermott, ethical decision-making involves a conflict between self-interest and ethics, whereas challenges regarding ethical reasoning concern how to formalize human reasoning processes, which may be considered computationally complex, but not fundamentally different from other kinds of reasoning processes (McDermott 2008, p. 2). In order to be a genuine ethical decision-maker one must have free will to sometimes choose to act in one's self-interest even though it runs counter to moral prescriptions.

> There is nothing particularly ethical about adding up utilities or weighing pros and cons, until the decision maker feels the urge not to follow the ethical course of action it arrives at. (McDermott 2008, p. 6).

Correspondingly, we may point to an asymmetric relationship between the robot and ourselves, in which case the robot only behaves like us, implying that even though interaction is smooth, the robot is simply a machine good at producing certain kind of behavior, without any intention behind it. Or, as Searle says in his famous arguments against the idea of artificial intelligence: "Simulation is not duplication and syntax is not semantics" (Searle 1995, p. 75; Searle 1980.[4])

Hence, the connection between my experiences of the world and my mind is not one of simple cause and effect. I am able to reflect upon my experiences of the world, and I'm aware that this is the case. The robot reacts to the outer world, not because it wants to, but because its programming causes it to do so (Putnam 1964 p. 672[5]). As such, intelligence and abilities for moral reasoning have to be understood as rooted in the unified whole of human life and experience:

---

4   Here, Searle 1980 presents his famous Chinese argument to demonstrate the fallibility of the Turing Test. Searle encourages us to join a simple thought experiment, the "Chinese room argument" in which we have to imagine that Searle is like a computer, sitting in a room manipulating meaningless symbols, rules and computational operations, which enables him to produce nice sentences in Chinese without having the slightest idea about the content of these utterances. Nevertheless, from the outside he appears to understand Chinese. As such, artificial intelligence boils down to producing behavior without any sense behind it.

5   Here, Putnam refers to an argument in an unpublished paper by Baier given at Albert Einstein College of Medicine in 1962. In this article, Putnam's concern is not how to speak about machines but rather how we should speak about humans. Thus "clarity with respect to the "borderline case" of robots, if it can be achieved, will carry with it clarity with respect to the "central area" of talk about feelings, thoughts, consciousness, life, etc." (Putnam 1964, p. 669). Putnam argues for the possibility of robot consciousness as something that calls for a decision rather than a discovery.

> If one thinks of the importance of the sensory-motor skills in the development of our ability to recognize and cope with objects, or the role of needs and desires in structuring all social situations, or finally of the whole cultural background of human self-interpretation in our simply knowing how to pick out and use chairs, the idea that we can simply ignore this know-how while formalizing our intellectual understanding as a complex system of facts and rules is highly implausible. (Dreyfus 1992, p. 63).

Still, within a scenario in which robots gradually become more and more sophisticated at simulating human behavior, there is a need to explore what is ethically at stake in human relationships and to discuss whether this can be challenged by, improved by or simply carried over to human-robot interaction. Thus, it is generally acknowledged that trust is vital for the flourishing of human life, and a precondition of any cultural ordering[6]. According to the moral philosophy of Løgstrup 1997, our fundamental human condition is rooted in the fact that life is interpersonal; we are mutually dependent on each other. Consequently, openness, in the sense of trusting, i.e., daring to risk ourselves in coming forward to meet the other, is a definitive feature of human co-existence and inherent in all communication. When we place trust in others, it involves genuine risk-taking since we surrender ourselves to the other. Thus, the mutual dependence, from which the ethical in human life springs, can only be comprehended in understanding what is at stake in a given context between two given persons. In speaking from an existential phenomenological position, Løgstrup holds that moral knowledge is not comparable to some kind of static intuition of values, but deals instead with existing individuals, who participate in real conflicts of the real world of values. When faced with 'the ethical demand', we have the power to choose between either rejecting the other or entering into a relationship by listening carefully to what we encounter in the situation:

> If one takes seriously the ethical fact that human nature is an ordered nature and its orders are orders for our life with and against each other, so that we are forced in responsible relations.

---

6   See, for example, (Løgstrup 1946, 1995, 1997), (Rawls 1999, p. 433), (Fukuyama 2003, p. 126).

> Then, whether he likes it or not, the individual is placed in the choice for or against the other (or the others). And here the law is not a formal principle, it is rather material; it is the law of responsibility saying that the neighbor is to be served. (Løgstrup 1947, p. 154) (Translation by Anne Gerdes.)

The structure of all human encounters or any kind of approach presupposes a fundamental trust that the other will meet your request and carries within it a risk that you will be met with rejection or carelessness. Thus, we are obliged to act out of consideration for the best of the other. Løgstrup is not addressing the kind of universality that we find in Kant's categorical imperative (Kant 1974, A54); instead, Løgstrup says that we find ourselves situated in a given context with a particular person in a specific situation. What is ethically important is, so to speak, consideration for the other in a particular situation and not consideration for ethical or moral demands as something abstract, which allows us to put our moral dispositions to the test (Fink 2005, p. 99).

But in dealing with human-robot interaction, we are not faced with having to surrender ourselves to the social robot. Even though the robot acts in a human-like way and displays emotions, there is nothing at stake besides "as-if" behavior caused by programmed internal states and executed to ensure adequate adaption to the surroundings. I know that this is the case about our relationship: the robot simulates, and I invest without cost. This does not necessarily imply that I will be unable to respond emotionally to the robot, on the contrary, several studies observe that we anthropomorphize artifacts with even the slightest human features and that we nurture them (Wilks 2010; Levy 2008; Turkle, 201). This theme is also taken up in science fiction, especially in Spielberg's movie "*AI*":

> Programmed to give and elicit love and affection, David is soon calling Monica 'Mommy' and, bereft of her only natural child, she accepts and warms to the artificial boy. (Clocksin 2003, p. 1738).

Yet, when her real son returns, 'mommy' abandons the robot boy David in a forest.

As such, our interaction with robots can be characterized as risk-free and without demand, and we might even come to favor this kind of risk-free relationship with fellows. Sherry Turkle has coined the term robotic moment to account for the moment when we turn to robot relationships rather than human ones. In her book, *Alone Together*, her techno-anthropological studies have led her to the conclusion that: "We fear the risks and disappointments of relationships with our fellow humans; we expect more from technology and less from each other" (Turkle 2011, p. xii).

Ethical issues from a position of physicalism: the "consciousness-robot scenario"

> There is nothing in the little we know to suggest that machine consciousness is an impossibility. (Copeland, 1993, p. 164).

In addressing AI with reference to a physicalist model of the mind, matters appear differently. Here, we assume that our mental states on all levels equal biophysical events, which can be described and eventually represented in machine-readable form. In turn, this makes us capable of developing a robot or sketching a design from which machine consciousness could emerge. In Copeland's reformulation of Descartes, this becomes "I think, therefore I am a machine" (Copeland, 1993, p. 249). However, in order to frame the discussion adequately, let us first look at the disagreements between physicalists and antiphysicalists. Thus, in his famous antiphysicalist article "What is It Like to Be a Bat?"(1974), Nagel gives a serious critique of physicalism arguing that reductive approaches to the mind fail to appreciate the fundamental nature of consciousness. He maintains that objective neuroscience is unable to account for the raw sensation of experience, i.e., *qualia*, implying that in interacting with external objects, our sensory episodes are accompanied by subjective inner experiences. Hence, there is something it is like to be a consciousness organism; I see colours, I hear the sound of music, I smell flowers, I taste a lemon, and all of these experiences feel a certain way to me. They have a quality of experience, and one got to experience them to know what they are like. Consequently, even supposing we uncovered everything there is to know about the neuro-physiological functioning of bats, who perceive the world by sonar, we would not be in a position to establish what it is like to be a bat since we cannot capture the subjective character of bat-qualia in a form comprehensible to humans, who are incapable of having those experiences (Nagel 1974, p. 449). The same goes for the famous colour-blind neuro-scientist Mary, presented in Jackson's argument against physicalism (Jackson 1986). Here, Mary has learned all the brain science in the world, including all there is to know about colour vision. Still, physicalism omits something, since she doesn't know what it is like to actually see red because she hasn't had any conscious experience of red. Finally, she gets an operation that cures her colour blindness and she bursts out: "Aha, that's it. That's what it is like to see red!" This argument suggests that there is more to consciousness than a physical process in the brain. You can know all there is to know about physical processes in the brain and still not know all there is to know about consciousness. Cahlmers (1995, 1996, 2010) has framed the discussion in terms of "the easy problem" of consciousness, referring to the fact that we already know about the part of consciousness dealing with our ability to categorize, discriminate, and react adequately to environmental stimuli. Additionally, we discover more and more about brain processes, neural circuits and the algorithms of the brain, and we will probably end up knowing all there is to know about the complexity of the brain. But, "the hard problem" of consciousness is the problem of experience, i.e., to learn why all that processing accompanies my consciousness experience. Why does it feel like something from the inside? Here, according to Chalmers, neural circuits omit that. As such, **mental** *qualia* escape reduction to biophysical matters, and in modern dualism, property dualists hold that the mind has two fundamentally different types of properties, bio-physical and *qualia*:

> It is inevitable that increasingly sophisticated reductive explanations of consciousness will be put forward, but these will only produce increasingly sophisticated explanations of cognitive functions. Even such "revolutionary" developments as the invocation of connectionist networks, nonlinear dynamics, artificial life, and quantum mechanics will provide only more powerful functional explanations. This may make for some very interesting cognitive science, but the mystery of consciousness will not be removed (Chalmers 1996, p. 121).

On the other hand physicalists assume that consciousness can be reductively explained. As such, *qualia* can be fully accounted for with reference to biophysical events in the brain:

> I believe it was Einstein who once advised us that science could not give us the taste of the soup. Could such a wise man have been wrong? Yes, if he is taken to have been trying to remind us of the qualia that hide forever from objective science in the subjective inner sancta of our minds. There are no such things (Dennett 1988 p. 48).

Likewise, and in response to Nagel, Copeland argues that physicalists don't disagree with the point that we cannot imagine what it is like to be a bat. However, physicalist theories deal with the nature of *qualia* and not with the power of our imagination. Copeland sums up neurophysological discoveries regarding variations of taste sensitivity among rats, cats and humans:

> ..These are speculations about rat qualia and cat qualia: a small discovery concerning the neurophysiology of taste has given us a minutely better imaginative grasp of how things might be for rats and cats. Admittedly, the comparative taste of saccharin versus sugar is a very small stitch in the total fabric of experience – but if a modest neurophysiological discovery like this one can give a tiny nudge to the imagination, who can tell how the neurophysiological advances of the next four or five centuries might affect our ability to imagine the lot of a cat, rat, or bat? (Copeland 1993, p. 176).

Hence, according to Copeland, from the poverty of our ability to imagine something, it does not follow that bats aren't purely biophysical entities in nature. He emphasizes that nobody knows the truth about *qualia* but even though anti-physicalism turns out to be true, it may still be possible to have robot-*qualia*: if non-physical properties can spring from a natural brain then why not from an artificial brain as well? (Copeland 1993, p. 179).

Let's assume that consciousness can be explained in terms of a physicalist framework. Eventually we shall be faced with a robot, which could experience *qualia*. It might turn out to be the case that the robot would have a mind different from the human mind. In this scenario, the phenomenological objections of the last section of this article do not count, because, in this case, robots and human beings are on equal footing.

Setting aside the possibility that physicalists might someday devise an artificial intelligence with a mind of its own, then the phenomenological approach would suffer severe problems. However, for the sake of argument, I shall maintain a phenomenological perspective in my exploration of ethical issues.

Well aware that the robot might develop a mind radically different from ours, we would still have to address initial design issues. For example, should we set out to create a robot capable of feeling pain either in the shape of a fully pre-programmed intelligence or an emerging intelligence, capable of self-adaptation? Normally, we consider it morally wrong to cause somebody pain. Yet, we might argue that lack of ability to feel pain would reduce the quality of life considerably for the robot and perhaps even make the robot unable to act emphatic towards others. As human beings we use different kinds of enhancers to improve our life, so why not set out to design a robot who would be placed into a permanent state of happiness? One objection could be that the lack of challenge would probably make the robot unable to fulfill its potential. But, we would not be able to take that for granted, since we might not recognize the kind of psychological developmental path the robot would follow. Future generations of robots might even be sophisticated to the point where their capacity for self-construction would imply that we were no longer to be involved in the process of their creation; they would know more of themselves and their needs than we could possibly know. As such, robots might evolve into rational beings entirely different from us and demand ethical rights of their own, which would be incomprehensible to us.

However, if the robot could still be said to be rational in nature, then according to Kant, we would have to treat the robot as morally equal to us, since what provides us with absolute value is the fact that we are possessed of reason and, through free will, are able to determine our actions in agreement with the ideas of laws. It is rationality that forms the basis of moral obligation towards other creatures and further implies that we are to be considered as ends in ourselves. Rational nature is an end in itself and, as such, independent of any particular kind of embodiment (human or robot bodies count equally). To be a moral agent, embodiment doesn't matter since taking embodiment into account would be to rely on empirical criteria rather than rational criteria in establishing our moral attitudes (Versenyi 1974, p. 252).

Within this context, we are faced with a God-like responsibility and ethical obligations towards a creature, which possibly will turn out to be beyond our imagination.

Conclusion

This paper has dealt with ethical implications related to human-robot interaction according to two scenarios of artificial intelligence, of which the first is already in progress. The scenario is probably not realizable until a time in the distant future (if ever).

Thus, we are approaching a time in which human-like robots – capable of intelligent behavior within more or less restricted contexts – will be able to provide us with reliable companionship. But here we are dealing with risk-free relations without demands. Human-robot interaction will lack the kind of basic commitment, which stems from the fact that life is interpersonal. We live in a state of surrender to each other, implying that trust is a fundamental human condition that we cannot escape. Placing trust in others thus involves genuine risk-taking, in the form of surrendering-ourselves-to-others. This is the fundamental root of all interpersonal interaction, which a human-robot relationship will not have.

In the second scenario, the focus is on the possibility of developing robots with a conscious mind. Here, we find ourselves faced with a God-like responsibility in deciding what kind of design we should implement. Furthermore, we might be unable to understand the robot, since it might turn out to develop a mind radically different from the human mind and maybe even demand ethical rights of its own; these rights could turn out to be incomprehensible to us.

In both scenarios, our relationships with the robot would be radically different from what we have been familiar to date, that which we have appreciated and and by which we have been challenged. New experiences and ways of being together will arise from human-robot interaction. We might even pass beyond something that we treasure about human companionship without even discovering that we have passed a borderline. In speaking of technology in a different sense specifically addressing enhancement and cyborg technology, Fukuyama puts it this way:

> - the deepest fear that people express about technology…is a fear that, in the end, biotechnology will cause us in some way to lose our humanity – Worse yet, we might make this change without recognizing that we had lost something of great value. We might thus emerge on the other side of a great divide between human and post human history and not even see that the watershed had been breached because we lost sight of what that essence was (Fukuyama 2003, p. 101).

Here, Fukuyama speaks of a subtle, yet dramatic change, which we may undergo when altering our human body and biology by means of medical and technological enhancement. Nevertheless, his concerns can equally well be extend to human-robot interaction in the existential sense that we might end up losing sight of what constitutes human communication and fellowship.

References

Anderson, M., Anderson, L. S., and Armen, C. 2004. *Towards Machine Ethics.* http://www.aaai.org/Papers/Workshops/2004/WS-04-02/WS04-02-008.pdf (Accessed March 20 2013).

Armstrong, D. M. 1980. *The Nature of Mind and Other Essays,* Brisbane: University of Queensland Press.

Benford, G. and E. Malartre 2007. *Beyond Human – Living with Robots and Cyborgs.* New York: A Forge Book.

Chalmers, D. J. 1995. Facing up to the problem of consciousness. In: *Journal of Consciousness Studies* (2):3 p. 200-19.

Chalmers, D. J.1996. *The Conscious Mind – In Search of a Fundamental Theory.* New York: Oxford University Press.

Chalmers, D.J.2010. *The Character of Consciousness,* New York: Oxford University Press.

Copeland, J. 1993, *Artificial Intelligence,* Oxford: Blackwell Publishing.

Clocksin, W. F. 2003. Artificial intelligence and the future. In: *Philosophical Transactions: Mathematical, Physical and Engineering Sciences* (36) 1 1721-48, No 1809. Online: "Information, Knowledge and Technology" (Aug. 15, 2003) http://www.jstor.org/stable/3559219 (Accessed March 20, 2013).

Culbertson, J. T. 1963. *The Mind of Robots,* Illnois: University of Illnois Press.

Dennett, D. C., and Q. Quining 1988. Qualia. In: *Consciousness in Modern Science,* eds. A. Marcel and E. Bisiach. Oxford: Oxford University Press. http://www.cogprints.org/254/1/quinqual.htm (Accessed March 20, 2013).

Dreyfus, H. L. 1992. *What Computers Still Can't Do,* Cambridge MA: MIT Press.

Dreyfus, H. L., and S.E. Dreyfus 1986. *Mind over Machine,* London: Macmillan.

Fink, H. 2005, Etikkonceptionen i Den etiske fordring. In: *Slagmark,* 42 p. 89-101.

Fukuyama, F. 2003. *Our Posthuman Future – Consequences of the Biotechnology Revolution,* New York: Picador.

Jackson, F. C. 1986. What Mary didn't know. In: *The Journal of Philosophy,* 83 p. 291-95.

Kant, I. 1974. *Kritik der Praktischen Vernuft,* Frankfurt am Main: Surhkamp Verlag.

Lacey, A. R. 1960. Men and Robots. In: *The philosophical Quarterly*, Vol. 10 No. 38 (January, 1960), p. 61 - 72.

Levy, D. 2008. *Love and Sex with Robots.* London: Duckworth.

Løgstrup, K. E. 1947. Antropologien i Kants Etik. In: *Festskrift til Jens Nørregaard*, 146-57. København: Gads Forlag.

Løgstrup, K.E. 1997. *The Ethical Demand.* Notre Dame: University of Notre Dame Press.

Mackay, D. M. 1956. The epistemological problem for automata. In: *Automata Studies*, 235-51. Princeton: Princeton University Press.

McDermott, D. 2008. Why ethics is a high hurdle for AI. In: *North American Conference on Computers and Philosophy (NA-CAP)*, Bloomington, Indiana, July 2008. http://www.cs.yale.edu/homes/dvm/papers/ethical-machine.pdf (Accessed March 20, 2013).

Minsky, M. 1988. *The Society of Mind.* New York: Simon and Schuster.

Moor, J. 2006. The Nature, Importance, and Difficulty of Machine Ethics. In: *IEEE Intlligent Systems* 21 (4) p. 18-21.

Nagel, T. 1974. What is it like to be a bat? In: *The Philosophical Review* Vol 83 p 435-50, No 4 (Oct 1974), Duke University Press.

Natural language Processing 8: Close Engagements with Artificial Companions – Key social, psychological, ethical and design issues. 2010. Ed. Y. Wilks. Amsterdam: John Benjamins Publishing Company.

Pagallo, U. 2010. The human master with a modern slave? Some remarks on robotics, ethics, and the law. In: *Proceedings of the 11th International ETHICOMP Conference, University of Rovira i Virgili, Tarragona*, p. 397-410.

Putnam, H. 1964. Robots: Machines or artificially created life? In: *The Journal of Philosophy*, Vol 62: 1 p. 668-91. . No. 21, American Philosophical Association. Eastern Division Sixty-First Annual Meeting (Nov. 12, 1964, http://www.jstor.org/stable/2023045 (Accessed March 20, 2013).

Putnam, H. 1965. Brains and behaviour. In: *Analytical Philosophy, Vol 2, ed. R. J.* p. 24-36.

Rawls, J. 1999. *A Theory of Justice.* Rev. ed. Oxford: Oxford University Press.

Scriven, M. 1953. The mechanical concept of mind. *Mind* 62 XII, 246, p. 230-40.

Searle, J. R. 1980. Minds, brains and programs. In *Behavioral and Brain Sciences*, vol. 3, p. 417-24. Cambridge: Cambridge University Press.

Searle, J. R. 1995. How artificial intelligence fails. In: *The world & I. Currents in Modern Thought – Artificial Intelligence: Oxymoron or New Frontier.* July p. 285-295.

Turing, A. 1950. Computing machinery and intelligence. In: *Mind,* 59 p. 433-60.

Turkle, S. 2011. *Alone Together – Why We Expect More From Technology and Less From Each Other.* New York: Basic Books.

Versenyi, L. 1974. Can robots be moral? In: *Ethics,* Vol. 84, no. 3 (April), p. 248-59.

Wallach, W., and C. Allan 2009. Moral Machines – Teaching Robots Right from Wrong. Published by Oxford Scholarship Online: January 2009, Print ISBN-13: 978-0-19-537404-9.

Wisdom, J. O., R.T. Spilsbury, and D.M. Mackay 1952. Symposium: Mentality in Machines. In: *Proceedings of the Aristotelian Society* (supp) Vol. 26 p. 1-86. Online at, http://www.jstor.org/stable/4106628?origin=JSTOR-pdf. (Accessed 20 March 2013).

Ziff, P. 1959. The feelings of robots. In: *Analysis* Vol. 19 No. 3 (January) p. 64 – 68.

Lennart Nørreklit

Applied ethics and practice ontology

Introduction

If ethics is not related to our activities and practice, if it is only speculation, then it is irrelevant. There is only one way to connect it to practice, to the things that are and what we do, and that is through ontology. One can apply it through an ontology. Thus it is necessary to have answers to arguments that deny that it is logically possible to relate ethics and ontology, such as Hume's is-ought guillotine[1] and Moore's open-question argument.[2] This article outlines an ontology emanating from the need for ethics to be applicable.

Ethics is about how we treat each other, our concern for the wellbeing and happiness of our fellow human beings, current as well as future generations. Ethics permeates everything we do, and it tells the story of who we are. It is not concerned only with exceptional situations, in which there are special ethical conflicts. We are always concerned with handling people, whether relatives or foreigners, or with handling the world people live in, whereby we influence their living conditions. We are always ethical actors on the scene, whether we act or not. We may pretend we are not, but we are.

We want not only the respect and love of our friends and recognition from society, but we also need to be acceptable to ourselves. And that is complicated because we know what we have done over time.

---

[1] Hume, D. 1739: *A Treatise on Human Nature*, Bok III, Part I, Section I.
[2] Moore, G. E. 1903.*Principia Etica* , §13.

Applied ethics and practice ontology

We have a comprehensive though not always conscious memory of our deeds. If we embark on a path that is not ethical, not based on care and concern, but on egoistical desires or anxieties that make us exploit or trick others, then we create a story about ourselves as paltry persons. We cannot escape that story, no matter how rich and famous we may become. We did something that was not good although we knew what goodness is; that it is the measure – even our own measure – because we possess the concept of goodness. We may think we can hide and escape judgment, but that is impossible because it is within us. We may deceive others as to who we are, but in order to deceive ourselves we must do things to ourselves that hurt us and deprive us of happiness. On the other hand, it takes courage to stick to ethics. It also takes moderation, consideration and wise guidance on how to approach life. But ethics are rewarded.

Here is a summary of some of the ethical statements outlined:

- Ethical principles presuppose ontological interpretation to be applicable.
- Goodness presupposes reasons.
- The good person pursues the good life of others.
- Reasons relate to the overarching value of a loving approach to life.

Ethics and Ontology

While theoretical ethics addresses abstract normative principles, applied ethics must connect them to the practical world. There must be guidelines for this connection. Such guidelines are ontological interpretations of the concepts that define the ethical principles. If there is no ontological interpretation of these concepts, then the normative principles cannot be applied in a nonarbitrary manner, i.e., they cannot be applied ethically. The good and right cannot be reduced to something arbitrary.

Suppose we want to apply a principle or rule of ethics, PE, to a certain problem. PE is expressed as a general statement about what is good and what should be done. For PE to make practical sense its command to do something good must be directed to somebody, who has the duty to perform it. Otherwise it can have no effect. In other words, there must be an ethical actor, the benefactor. Further the ethical recipients, the beneficiaries (or, eventually, the malefactors, if they are to be punished), must be defined. This reasoning demonstrates that an ontological interpretation is a condition for applying an ethical rule or principle in a nonsubjective manner. Such determination is an 'ontological interpretation in use' of the ethical rule or principle.

Additionally, the ontological demand involves an epistemological claim. What is needed is an ontology used in practice, i.e., the ontological distinctions must be recognizable so that they can be applied. It must be possible in a practical sense to distinguish between ethical actors and non-actors and to distinguish between ethical recipients and non-recipients. Let us assume that ethical actors are only mentally healthy adults. This determination must be practically applicable, i.e., we must be able to delimit the group of adults and the group of the mentally healthy. Similarly, "you must not harm or kill the other" is a generally accepted ethical command attempting to protect the ethical recipient. However, does this apply also to murderers, to attackers, or to enemy soldiers? It is necessary to identify the recipient of the principle in a nonarbitrary manner. Thus the concept of ontology shall here be used broadly to include also the epistemology necessary to make its distinctions applicable in practice. The objection might be raised that it is unproblematic to whom the principles apply, and who the responsible actors and beneficiaries are. Practice shows that this is not true. The importance of clarifying the ontological determination of the ethical actor and recipient is illustrated in the ethical discussion in modern society. For example, consider the discussions of abortion and of organ transplants. The arguments are outlined in a utilitarian and in duty ethic perspective. The debate concerns possible changes in practical ontology from one based on the concept of life to one based on the concept of consciousness.

The utilitarian principle claims that the moral goal is the greatest possible happiness for most people. But we must ask: who is the moral actor that upholds the principle, and who are the beneficiaries, whose happiness is to be calculated. That this is not trivial was seen already when J.S. Mill claimed, concerning the beneficiary that 'an unhappy Socrates is better than a happy pig'.[3] Let us now consider the contemporary issue of free abortion. The problem with the utilitarian calculus

---

3   Mill, J. S. 1863 *Utilitarianism*, Parker, Sun, and Bourn, Online at §14, internet ed.

is that of determining whose happiness is to be included. Are we to include only persons who have been born, or should the unborn child, the fetus, also be included? If the first is true, then abortion is no ethical problem for the utilitarian thinker, because nobody is deprived of happiness by an abortion. If the second view is true, then the happiness of the fetus must be taken into account and there can be no free abortion real, existing. The calculus of happiness presupposes a decision about whether there should be free abortion or not. The calculus applies to real, existing persons, people that do not exist cannot be deprived of happiness, so they need not be included in the calculus. Thus, if a fetus is not an existing person, then it is not included in the calculus and abortion can be free. But if a fetus is a real existing person then abortion cannot be free because the happiness of the fetus must be included in the calculus. This debate surely focuses on the ontological status of the fetus. People opposing free abortion argue that the fetus has the same or a similar ontological status as a person who has been born, and that this should be respected. The fetus has the same right to happiness as other people. People arguing for legalized abortion emphasize the difference between persons and a fetus, especially a young fetus. Some countries have formulated a compromise; for example, an abortion is free up to week 11 of pregnancy but no later. During the growth of the fetus its brain activities develop and consciousness may start to emerge, as indicated by rapid eye movements as if it were dreaming. While it is unlikely that the few cells of the early fetus should have consciousness, it may be assumed that we should admit the older fetus as a person with some form of mental activity. Thus one might interpret an 11 week rule as an implicit reference to a change in ontological status in that the fetus changes from being a group of cells to becoming a being with early elements of consciousness.

Delimiting the beneficiaries of the ethical principle makes little practical sense if there are no ethical actors. If nobody could perform a safe abortion, abortion should be outlawed on that ground. The deciding person is the pregnant woman, but she cannot perform the abortion herself. Another actor is needed. Can this be demanded of any qualified doctor? Or must the doctor decide for herself whether she does it or not? The doctor has taken the Hippocratic Oath which is an element of duty ethics. If the fetus is not ontologically a person, then abortion does not violate the Hippocratic Oath. But if the fetus has the same status as the born child then the doctor is bound by the Hippocratic Oath to help it and not to kill and destroy it.

Now consider the case of organ transplant. For successful organ transplantation to be possible the organs must be living healthy tissue not in any state of decay after the heart has stopped, i.e., death. Thus they must be removed from a donor before she is dead. This means that the doctor should actually kill a patient in order to obtain a usable organ. Obviously this violates duty ethics, which forbids murder. Thus many people that could have been helped by organs taken from people that could not survive injuries or disease could not be helped. This problem has somehow been solved by a change in the criterion of what constitutes death. In the past, death occurred when the heart stopped beating; today, death occurs when the brain stops functioning. In the latter case, the body and most of its organs can be alive and healthy although the person is technically dead because her brain is dead. In this case, good organs can be harvested from a brain-dead person without violating the commandment not to commit murder. As long as the body is alive and the heart and lungs provide the system with oxygen, the organs stay fresh and usable. Once the brain is dead, the person cannot regain consciousness, memories, feelings, thoughts, and so on. The ontology of the living person has changed from a living body to a living body with consciousness. From a utilitarian perspective the ontological change is very helpful: the criterion of brain death excludes the brain-dead person from the happiness calculus. The puzzle of how to consider the happiness of a brain-dead person has been solved.

Concerning both abortion and organ transplantation, the debates and changes in practice relate to the brain as the enabling presence of human consciousness. The operationalization of consciousness as a brain function would become irrelevant if brain dead people started to talk and function as normal people. That would stop the use of the criterion of brain death.

Modern society seems to be refining its ethics by indicating that ethical beneficiaries are beings with consciousness. This is an ontological change in relation to earlier practices. This change has been made possible through technological medical developments that enabled us to apply more sophisticated principles. Historically practical ontological changes were slow and thus ontological discussions less relevant. The pace of modern development has uncovered their importance to ethics.

Applied ethics and practice ontology

The ethical actor: Action control versus actor control

The answer to the question "What should I do?" depends on the ontology in use, where the concept of consciousness is to be connected to the person, the ethical actor and the beneficiary. Consciousness is not a free-floating thing in our universe, but a part of living people that enables them to cope with life. The ontology of life was not eliminated, only narrowed by adding consciousness. The question: "What should I do?" presupposes that the person has alternative courses of action and therefore a conscious choice. An ethical actor is not an acting machine, but a living person whose actions are controlled consciously.

Without an ethical actor there can be no ethical action, no recipient, and no ethical meaning. Ethics, which eliminates the actor, destroys itself. Thus, the 'consciousness that chooses' and the 'consciousness that controls' the action cannot be separated. They belong to the same person making her an actor. An actor cannot say, "I did it consciously, but I am not responsible, because somebody else made the decision I should do it." If action were determined independently of the acting person, it would eliminate her status as responsible ethical actor.

This is, however, what many forms of 'distant' action control try to do either by general rules or principles or by managerial practice. This happens also in ethics. The utilitarian calculus of happiness and the commandments of duty ethics determine the action to be taken. Thus they determine the ethical action disregarding the sovereignty of the actor. Disposition ethics (e.g., virtue ethics), on the other hand, address the person, her intentionality and character, and reference to consequences and duty commandments only assists the person.

Consider the fragment:

A: "What should I do?"
B: "You should do S."
A: "But S is not a good thing. S is something bad and evil."
B: "That does not matter. You should do S."

A's initial question might be a search for help making a decision. *A*'s objection to *B*'s suggestion shows that she intends to be in conscious control of her actions, which *B* flatly rejects as unwarranted despite *A*'s reasons. *B* does not accept that *A* is in control of her own action. She even disregards *A*'s concern for the good. She undermines *A* as an ethical actor. This is unethical no matter whether *B*'s suggestion actually is the best thing to do. *B*'s behavior is especially bad if she has power over *A*. Ethically *B* must help *A* to make good decisions, but not command and take control over her action.

Ethical rules and norms as well as leadership should inspire the actor to improve her actions, not take direct control over her actions. To improve our decisions, we use principles from different forms of ethics. Principles that concern which actions to perform can be misused as if they were commandments. They can seduce those in authority to issue commands in the name of ethics in order to control an actor's actions. This then nullifies the person as actor, depriving her of the sovereign control of her actions. This also abuses ethical principles. Ethics cannot eliminate the ethical actor. An ethical actor is in conscious command of her actions. The development of applied ontology underscores this focus on consciousness. Commanding a person eliminates her free will and makes her act according to external commands or norms. A person may seek 'protection' from responsibility in this way, but there is no escape from ethical responsibility. There are many ways to gain control over a person's action – for example, threatening, confusing, or seducing – thus eliminating her as ethical actor. Social control is filled with methods designed to control the actions of other people. Even when social laws command people to act in an unethical way, this should not eliminate the ethical actor who should then use civil disobedience.

Ethics is an appeal to the person to do good and right things despite the problems that doing so might cause. Ethics lives and breathes through the sovereignty of the actor. The idea that ethics can legitimize bypassing the actor and control her actions conflicts with the spirit of ethics although there may be cases where elements of such courses of action are necessary for the greater good. The purpose of ethics is not to oppress people by means of ethics. On the contrary, ethical principles and reflections address and help the actor. It is not a military that controls and commands her actions. That would eliminate the ethical actor and, thus ethics.

This concern for the ethical actor fits disposition ethics as for instance virtue ethics. In contrast, consequence ethics and duty ethics may be abused in order to suppress the actor. The ethical good person is defined not through her actions but through her dispositions, i.e. her endeavors and intentions to perform good actions. The actions are still part of the evidence for her intentions; nevertheless, it is the intentions that are subject to ethic cultivating and judgment. It is unethical for a party to take direct control over the actions of another person; that would be to treat her like a slave[4]. (Exceptions are teaching or other situations where guidance is necessary.) Ethical principles for good action are important because the actor in control may be in doubt about what she should do in situations with poor information or conflicting concerns. Ethical principles or rules should not take over this control unless called for and accepted by the actor herself. We find this prevalent in training and learning situations.

A condition for ethics in practice is that the acting person is allowed to be in control of her actions. Thus ethics relates people who create the foundation to a community. When reducing or eliminating ethical actorship, the society loses its character of community. This imposes ethical duties on management and leadership in organizations. Managerial perspectives often attempt direct action-control, not respecting the actor's own conscious control. Such leadership using commands and specifying and registering actions may remind one of programming mindless robots. Such a mind-set may remind one of a cold, sometimes more fascist, culture rather than an ethical one.

Self-preservation of ethics would suggest that the ontology of the beneficiary also be molded as an ethical actor. Let us assume that the recipient is a conscious being capable of being happy. Suppose happiness is a state of the brain that can be achieved by drugs. This leads to a vision of the utilitarian goal as a society of happily drugged people passively enjoying their happiness.[5] In this awful vision self-preservation of ethical actorship is lost. As a minimum, the ethical perspective must protect the conditions for ethics. Thus beneficiaries should become ethical actors, if possible. The sick shall become healthy, the fetus a responsible adult etc. If the goal is happiness as produced by substances in the brain, then the beneficiary's actorship is irrelevant.

Recognition of and respect for a person involves respect for the person as actor choosing according to her knowledge and values. These values

---

4   According to Kant, only the will can be good, by following reason. Thus he appears to support the principle of actor control. Nevertheless, the categorical imperative is very much understood as a form of action control used to subjugate the actor under the rule of duty.

5   Compare, for example, Huxley, A., *Brave New World*, London 1932.

are the personal values of the actor, not social values such as wealth and profit, beauty, fame, and power though they may motivate the actor. The social values are objectified means by which to achieve personal values. A part of recognition of the person is attributing fairly her performance to her, so that she can feel justified that she has accomplished things and contributed to society. It is an ethical duty of leadership to ensure that actors are recognized for their accomplishments and not, for instance, to attribute their accomplishments to their superiors or the friends of the managers etc.

Self and agent

Modern business is commonly managed by so called agents as analyzed in the agency theory. An agent acts on behalf of a different person or group, so-called principals, who hire the agent. The purpose of the agent's work is defined by the principal, but the conscious act is that of the agent. The agent is controlled by a contract that defines the goals of and rewards given to the agent according to her performance in achieving the goals. In this way the goal of the principal also becomes the goal of the agent. This plays an important role in modern management. The theory analyzes the economic consequences of various types of contracts. Here the relationship of trust and cooperation of the ethical community is replaced by contractual relation. It is believed that contractual goal setting is efficient and that the legal system warrants credibility.

However, ethics cannot be replaced by legal control. Legal control is itself organized work. Thus either it is based on legalistic principles, e.g., the egoistic agency contract, or it presupposes nonlegalistic, ethical control. If it is based only on legalistic control, then there is an infinite regress because legalistic control is itself work, that must be legalistically controlled etc. ad infinitum. Consequently, a nonlegalistic form of control is necessary. This control must be ethical and nonegoistic because otherwise trust in cooperation is not possible. Legality cannot replace ethics; it can only supplement it.

The concept of an actor is very different from that of an agent. The concept of an agent is in contrast to the concept of a self. A person as actor acts on behalf of herself. A person as agent acts on behalf of another person, another self, the principal, whom the agent represents.⁶ Both agent and principal are assumed to be selfish, egoistical, i.e. not ethical. Nevertheless, the agent is supposed to set her own self aside in favor of the self of the principal as the source of the goals that guid her actions. The agent is therefore a hybrid type of person. The selfish motivation of a person to work as an agent is the rewards she achieves by fulfilling the contract. The motivation of the principal is the fulfillment of the contractual goals. The contract is the assumed guarantee that the agent does not use her superior knowledge to her own advantage at the expense of the principal.

A special model for the agent is the secret agent, the spy, i.e., a person who appears to be acting according to the presented self, but who secretly represents somebody else whose interests are pursued without others knowing. Although agency theory concerns other contexts there is in practice still an element of secrecy. The contracts that drive managerial agents are little known to employees and other stakeholders whose interests may not be protected under the contract. Such elements of secrecy and eventual bias drive an agent to promote the interests included in the contract at the expense of the interests of other stakeholders. Secret management contracts easily make the working environment incomprehensible to employees, because the motives of managerial behavior are hidden. Thus one can outline an ethical difference between a manager as actor whose task it is to lead a company to success addressing all stakeholders and a manager as agent who is driven by specific contractual goals concerning for example, turn-over, market share or similar factors. The actor-manager is presumed to balance the interests of the stakeholders while the agent-manager is presumed to exploit stakeholders to achieve the specified contractual rewards.

All work addresses the interests of people other than only the worker. The relationship between self-interest and concern for others lies in the ethical nature of the actor. The ethical actor wants to do something good, i.e. take care of the concerns of other people. This is part of what it is to be an actor. However, in the role as agent representing a different self, the ethical sovereignty of the actor is subjugated. A hint of something schizophrenic takes place. The actor makes herself an instrument

---

6   The Oxford philosopher J. MacMurray uses the term "agent" as I use "actor" (See his 1957. *The Self as Agent*. Oxford: Oxford University Press). His usage blurs the essential distinction between agents and actors.

to exploit the other stakeholders in order to serve the principal and herself. The agent as a secret egoistic actor almost must exploit the contract that defines her agency. Thus, the agent is presumed not to be an ethical but an egoistic actor.

Further, the principals must normally be represented by agents in the formulation of contracts. Thus in practice the contracts can only be made between agents. One agent is elected to represent the principals, and other agents are hired by the elected agent to act on behalf of the principals. Thus the use of the theory facilitates the development of strong agent networks that exploit other stakeholders. Agent networks replace class structures and ethical communities.

Goodness: The basic norm

The perspective that an underlying intent of ethical action is to enable the beneficiary to be an ethical actor provides a minimalistic guideline for choosing ontology and ethical principles. However, as a reason for choice is unsatisfactory. We need the choices to be legitimized as good. We should choose the best ontology, and the best ontology depends on the conditions at hand. Before the development of modern technology the ontology in use focused on the notion of life. Improved technology enabled us to use a better ontology by focusing on consciousness and brain function. Thus, ethics guides the choice of ontology although the use of ontology is to enable the use of ethics.

Goodness thus appears to be the basic concept for normative judgment. There are many normative concepts besides goodness. Concepts such as right, duty, virtue, even apparently descriptive concepts such as happiness all point to ethical principles and traditions. One must decide which normative concept and which ethical principle to use. One must choose that which the best in the situation.

Goodness is the overall ethical principle. The other ethical principles are not absolute but subject to assessment. One may argue for the advantages of hedonism and utilitarianism, of duty ethics or virtue ethics by demonstrating that one is better than the others in a given situation. Overall they supplement each other in practice. There are many situations in which we need guidance from concepts such as duty, prudence, or virtue because one does not in the situation know what, in general, is the good or best thing to do.

A problem in determining good action is the unpredictability of things. It is unpredictable to the actor how people react to her actions, which makes consequence calculation impossible. Here good virtue ethics and duty ethics reduce that problem because such *habita* establish an element of predictability in behavior making consequences more calculable. Thus, paradoxically, consequentialism, such as utilitarianism, only works in practice in an environment of duty and virtue ethics. In a purely consequential ethics environment on the contrary, it is impossible to calculate consequences because nobody knows how other people react. They must also calculate the consequences of their actions, which they cannot do either because they depend on how other people act, etc. Consequentialism presupposes established rule systems, i.e., duty ethics, that enable the calculation of consequences. In a society where there is no such ethics the consequences can be calculated in a very limited time perspective only.

It is generally assumed that social laws are within the range of ethics, and also that it is ethically good to keep the laws. This is not always the case. Again it must be the reference to goodness that justifies legal righteousness not vice versa. In practice it is sometimes the case that following the rules and doing the right things creates bad results. Doing the good thing and doing the right thing can diverge. One may be forced to violate the rules in order to do the good thing. Thus we need to insist that goodness is the primary normative concept: righteousness and rules must be brought into accord with the principle of goodness. The question of goodness cannot be bent to be brought into accord with a concept of legality and righteousness. In democracies laws are claimed good because they are democratic. But even that which is democratic has to be assessed in terms of whether it is good. Things are not good automatically if they are democratic. There are conditions that must be met in order for a democracy to be good, conditions such as tolerance, knowledge, etc.

The form of assessment

The problem with the concept of goodness is that it is elusive. Nobody knows what goodness is. We are confronted with a gulf between "is" and "ought" since we do not know what goodness is. Thus it cannot be of any use. The open-question argument demonstrates that no factual definition of goodness is possible because it always makes sense to ask whether the defining characteristic is good or not. Thus it seems logically impossible to know what goodness is. My interpretation of this argument is that goodness is a formal concept. Therefore, the open-question argument cannot have an answer. The concept of goodness formats the structure of assessment. It is not a material concept with a special object: 'the good', or 'goodness itself', or 'the intuitive quality of goodness'. The fact that one can ask about anything, whether it is good or not, means, that goodness is a formal concept. It enables us to expand the horizon of assessment and reflection in any direction. It is never a forbidden issue. The concept of goodness creates an open horizon, an open mind.

Attempts to define the good are instances of the naming type of fallacy, which Wittgenstein describes.[7] Ontology of the good cannot be found because there is no such ontology.

The notion of goodness is used to structure assessments and comparisons. It calls for borders between that which is good and acceptable and that which is bad and evil. It can be qualified: good, better, best; and bad, worse, worst. Most comparative concepts compare only certain types of things. There are no such restrictions concerning goodness – cf. for instance: the best innovation, the most efficient production, the best character, the most beautiful appearance etc.

There are no limits to the use of the concept of goodness. The question "Is it good?" can be raised about anything: the reason, the ethics, and the argument. For instance one may ask if an apple is good and expect an answer explaining why it is or is not a good apple. Conversely, the question "Is the stone good?" makes little sense. However, if we use stones for a purpose, then suddenly the question does make sense. As soon as we have a perspective, we can establish comparison with respect to goodness. The perspective is delimited in the ontology of life, consciousness and actorship. Goodness creates a polarized good/bad relation-structure that can be used to create evaluations and norms. Goodness is not a perspective but presupposes a goal or value as a perspective of its assessments. When the apple is good for somebody it may be because it is healthy or because it tastes good. These are two different perspectives of goodness.

Further, we must distinguish whether something is good in itself for the person or as a means. Often the good thing is not only good for somebody

---

7   Wittgenstein, L. 1953, *Philosophical Investigation*, §1. Oxford: Basil Blackwell.

it is good to something that is good *for* somebody. If it is good by being good to something, then goodness is instrumental. Otherwise, it is good in itself. Instrumental goodness presupposes goodness in itself. In practice, however, instrumental values may be given precedence and displace the values in themselves. For instance, high gross national product (GNP) per capita is the goal of most governments in developed countries. Most other goals are considered subordinate to this one. Thus economic growth is treated as a goal in itself. This, however, is a dangerous globalized illusion. Economics is obviously not a value in itself. It is an instrumental value and as such, should be considered a cost to be kept as low as possible in relation to its ability to produce the desired values.

Modern society assesses everything. Everywhere we see questionnaires asking whether the service, the product, the work was good on a scale from, say, 1 to 5. Such subjective assessments address what people say they like are often used as measurement of goodness. But that may be misleading. Goodness and liking are not the same. That somebody likes something is no proof that it is good. People may like poor things and dislike good things. Thus one must question even whether a usage of goodness is good. One may ask: "Is this usage of comparison a good practice? Or is it becoming pathological?" Sometimes it stresses people and makes them afraid and unhappy for no reason. Some get poor marks only because they are different and innovative.

Thus goodness is an assessment concept essential to controlling practice. Our work ethics wants practice to be good; all human and technological processes and products should be good. This also applies to new practices. The notion of goodness drives development and quality in practice. In ethics the idea of goodness is driving man to perform well not because of some profit but because he wants to do good things. Goodness is a motivator in itself. This constituting force in work and performance should not be corrupted by other motives such as profit and reward.

Competition

Goodness involves two formal forms of assessment. The fundamental assessment is to establish whether something is good or not. If it is good then it is all right and worthy of recognition. If it is not good, then it does not pass. To be good is to meet a minimum standard. A comparative assessment on the other hand establishes the best, the one that surpasses all others. There is even an absolute comparative form: to be the best possible. In a population many people, perhaps all can be good. But only one or a small group can be the best. In a society where the fundamental assessment rules most people, perhaps all can be good and therefore worthy of recognition. In a society where comparative assessment rules only a few members pass, all the others fail.

Ethics of goodness calls for norms for goodness where everybody has a chance of recognition. Ethics of comparative assessment focuses on comparison and competition and recognizes only the best. Ethics based on ideas of maximization are of the comparative type in which that which is good but not the best, is not good enough. A utilitarian principle that demands the greatest possible happiness and its cost benefit maximization equivalent belong to this type. It is however almost always impossible to determine what creates the best possible results. And the very ethical credo that only the best counts creates automatically a majority of unhappy losers, which is counterproductive and thus unethical even according to this credo. An ethics where the norm is the best cannot create the best or, possibly, even a good society.

Thus one must settle for an ethics of goodness. However, this ethics seems at odds with free competition across market economies. When free competition is the driver, then the winner takes all, the others lose. This is the ethics of comparison; only the best is good enough. She is the winner. Thus market economy sets higher performance demands than the ethics of goodness. Therefore many good people and good practices may lose. Thus social practices, driven by the credo of the best, are at odds with ethics of goodness, because it destroys good people. The benefit of it – in utilitarian cost-benefit terms – is that it appears to increase technological and economic development. However, ethics might suggest that better leadership can create the same or even much better results because the desire to do something good is the real driver. To be the best means that the perspective of comparison is already given thus to be the best cannot be really innovative. The real driver of development appears to be the motive to create something that is as good as possible; and this can be truly creative and new. Thus the good may outperform the best.

Competition is part of development and learning when it takes care not to create losers. It must apply a fundamental assessment so that both losers and winners can gain recognition and continue to develop.

However, market forces have little room for a loser. Once tolerance and equality were essential, but in high-level competition they mean little.

The dilemma between the basic ethics of goodness and the credo of the best is recognizable in the works of the father of modern economics Adam Smith. He was professor of ethics advocating sympathy as the natural tendency to care about the wellbeing of others,[8] while in economics he advocated free market competition.[9] His moral theory advocates sympathy and goodness not only toward the best, but to all good people. His economic philosophy on the other hand is that free competition increases welfare and is therefore apparently also good. However, the negative side of competition must be included: competition lets only the best win and eliminates the others. Thus in the cradle of modern economics as given birth by Adam Smith, the conflict between the logic of ethics of goodness and the logic of the economics of the best appear as conflicting perspectives. While modern society politically advocates the principle of tolerance and respect for the individual, economics installs a comparative principle that is for winners only. The struggle between social and liberal politics continuously looks for solutions to this problem.

Goodness presupposes reasons

When we choose something because it is good or the best, then we give a formal justification for our choice. This justification can therefore always be challenged by the question "Why is it good/the best?" This asks for a reason why it is good, not for a cause. Causes make things happen. Reasons explain why we want them to happen. The concept of goodness demands a reason. The question "Why is it good?" is always appropriate. One cannot claim that something is good without being willing to provide a reason why it is or why one believes it to be good. Thus there is a conceptual relation between goodness and reason. Goodness provides formal reasons for choosing and acting only by presupposing specific or concrete reasons. The normative concept of goodness is linked to the world by means of reason. Goodness provides a normative status to the condi-

---

8   Smith, A. 1790. *The Theory of Moral Sentiments*, London: A. Millar.
9   Smith, A. 1776. *An Inquiry into the Nature and Causes of the Wealth of Nations.* London: W. Strahan.

tion that is presented as a reason. The reasons seem to be instruments linking the formal status of goodness to an ontological foundation.

Let me illuminate this thesis by trying to reject it. Consider a dialogue fragment in which *A* tries to reject the thesis by claiming that an object, O, is good without any reason, while *B* tries to support the thesis:

A: "O is good".
B: "Why is O good?"
A: "I don't know why."
B: "If you don't know why it is good, then how can you know it is?"
A: "I don't know. But it is good, I know that."

A behaves in a ridiculous manner. In the following versions of the dialogue, *B* tries to help *A* to make sense anyway by suggesting reasons that transcend the range of ordinary rationality:

(1) *B*: "You believe that God makes O good?"
    A: "No, I do not know what God does."

(2) *B*: "You believe that O is good, because some authorities you respect claim that it is so?"
    A: "No. Opinions of authorities make no difference whether O is good or not."

(3) *B*: "You believe that O is good because you say it is good?"
    A: "No, O is good – no matter whether or not I say so."

In this scenario, *A*'s suggestions would make *B*'s claim circular. But it does not work. Now let *B* address *A*'s state of mind:

(4) B: "O is good because you believe that O is good?"
    A: "No, I don't think that my belief that O is good makes it good."

(5) B: "You believe that O is good because you feel, sense, hope that it is good?"
    A: "No O is good – no matter what I feel or hope."

(6) B: "You believe that O is good because you know it is good?"
A: "No. – Of course, since I know it is good, then it is good; but that is not the reason why it is good. But I can't tell you the reason because there is none."

Here, *B*'s attempt is also absurd.

B finally tries to give excuses to which *A* could resort:

(7) B: "You remember that O is good, but you have forgotten the reason why it is good?"
A: "No, I have forgotten nothing. There is just no reason why it is good."

It is obvious that if *A*'s claim, O is good, is not based on any possible reason, then the claim is unacceptable. *B*'s attempts to help *A* by transcending rationality make *A* appear even more irrational. Thus we must uphold the thesis and demand both rationality and reason.

Now imagine that *A* is in fact a moral philosopher. In the first scenario, *A* is an intuitionist:

A: "You see the thing, O, is red – there is no reason why it is red, it simply is red. Similarly there is no reason why O is good, it simply is good."
B: "But you have a reason to claim that O is red because you see that it is red. You don't see that O is good. What should goodness look like?"

B rejects *A*'s intuitivist attempt. Now imagine that *A* is a non-naturalist moral philosopher in a wider sense and uses Moore's open-question argument:

A: "There are no moral properties. Goodness cannot be defined, because we can ask: "Is it good?" of any characteristic. Thus there can be no answer to your question about why it is good! Suppose I would answer: 'O is good because of property P.' Then you would ask once more: 'Why is P good?' and so forth. Thus it is impossible to answer your question! Your first question presupposes that goodness is a sort of property, which your second question proves that it cannot be."

A uses the open question argument to prove that *B*'s call for a reason is absurd. Nevertheless, intuitively, understanding language, *A*'s claim still appears unacceptable. We still expect that *A* must have a reason for claiming O to be good; without it her claim is not legitimate. One can imagine many types of reasons for being good: O is healthy, has high quality, is beautiful, interesting, friendly etc. We may even allow for uncertainty as to precisely which of these characteristics apply – but it is not acceptable to claim that there is no reason whatsoever that O is good.

More importantly: *A*'s counterargument, her final use of the open-question argument, is fallacious because to give a reason why O is good is not to identify the reason with goodness. If A says O is good because of P, that does not identify P with goodness. A similar example: "I like her because she is brave" does not mean that her bravery is identical with my liking.

Let us examine the following. "The reason why O is good is P." Here is a similar example: "The apple is good because it contains vitamins." To understand this on a deeper level, we ask again, as *A* did: "Why does P make O good?" This is similar to: "Why do vitamins make the apple good?" An answer might be "P makes O good because of Q." Compare this to "Vitamins make the apple good because they make it healthy." We see that now the answer refers to causes or condition: vitamins cause or are a condition for health. Thus vitamins are values instrumental to achieving the value of health. The question changed character. The second question did not ask for a reason but for a cause or condition.

When however asking about why health is good, we are not at ease because health is a basic value. It is a condition for living and thus for any possible value to the person. The perspective of assessment would not exist without the person. A person who asks why health is good seems to be in trouble with her life or not to understand life and health. A utilitarian might consider health an instrumental value as a condition for happiness. This would re-invite the open-question argument: "Why is happiness good?" Mostly people would presumably like to be healthy because they can live and do things they like to do rather than because it makes them happy.

In practice basic values are interconnected to some extent. For instance, some might say, "Happiness is good because it makes people nice and gentle." Similarly: "Beauty, which is a value in itself, produces happiness"; and "Happiness makes people beautiful and healthy." All of these statements concern causalities and conditions. Thus the question of why basic values are good does not vindicate *A*'s position, that goodness does not demand a reason, because here we address causes and conditions or the very existence of the perspective.

Let us say that reason is the capability to operate with reasons. The relationship between goodness and reason is the basis for justification and therefore the basis to practice. The primary norm, the norm of norms, which installs reason, is that goodness demands a reason. Without this ethics in practice does not exist. Respecting the call for reason is the foundation for a civilized society.

A's position is unacceptable. Rejection of the obligation to provide credible reasons destroys the ethical character of cooperation whether in management, politics, social work or education. Taking care to provide convincing and trustworthy reasons for one's decision influences practice. Without such care decisions may be feeble. When a reflective language meets practice this is an issue.

Subjectivity and reason

As mentioned earlier, goodness presupposes a perspective. For something to be more or less good, it must be so to someone. Happiness is good because it is good for a person. It makes no sense to consider happiness as good in itself without any person. When something is called good in itself, it does not mean that it is a goodness existing independently in the universe. It means that for the person the goodness is not a means to some other good.

This implies that the reason that something is more or less good must relate it to the person for whom it is good. Real reasons are not objective reasons existing in the world around us that may be found in a book, told by an authority, a history or something similar. No matter what is to be found in history, books, or authorities, these statements are not a reason for a person unless the person consciously or intuitively adapts it as such. Reasons are personal. They affect us because they connect the world to our values and feelings. Reasons to choose and act are reasons for an actor, a person.

When somebody wants to persuade others to do something, then she needs a reason that is accepted by the others. Thus reasons also interconnect actors and relate them as actors to the environment. Tolerance and respect are the acceptance of the principle that every person has her own reasons as living actor and that cooperation is based on a reasoning in which these individual reasons are coordinated.

The good life and the good person

There can be several reasons that a certain thing is good and/or bad. And there are a number of possible lines of action, several of which can be good for different reasons. Thus there still remains the question of how to choose among the good reasons for good lines of action. To enable choice and avoid arbitrariness, an overarching unifying perspective is needed. With it, one creates priorities among the alternatives. Without an overarching perspective one may waver and shift incoherently between the possible good practices.

The child develops through its many spontaneous decisions about daily life. Parents and guardians make overarching decisions structuring the child's life. The child does not need an overarching perspective. When it becomes an adult she must take responsibility for her life and make the overarching decisions to structure it. Nobody else can do it. Others may give advice, but the adult is in charge. The adult needs an overarching perspective to create a way of living and organizing life coherently. Through this perspective she sets her values, feelings, reasons; controls her actions, creates her personal identity and forms herself as a person with a certain life, developing her relations and goals. These actions determine who we are and what we want to do in life.

By making the life the overarching perspective, the role of reasons and actions is to create a good life. The overarching reason that organizes daily reasons is to contribute to a good life. Thus to get hold on the reasons the person must face the question: What is the good life? And the place to look for an answer is in the related why-question: "What is the reason to live?" What happens beyond life, if anything, people cannot know, so no credible reason applies.

Some think that this question is unanswerable or meaningless. That is wrong. Consider an existentialist arguing that there is a fundamental existential choice through which a person chooses and becomes herself. And this choice can have no reason because all reason presupposes that choice. Thus it is neither a good nor a bad choice. However, such choice is no real choice. Consider the beginning of Hamlet's famous soliloquy: "To be or not to be, that is the question.."[10] From an existential viewpoint this might be a decision with no reason. However, for Hamlet it is the motivation to reason. He seems to consider the reasons for the one and the other alternative to find out which is better. Further, consider Caesar's decision to cross the river Rubicon with his army. He threw the dice and claimed "*Iacta est alea*" (the dice are thrown). But this is hardly a reason. Is Caesar really making an important decision without any reason – similar to the existential choice? He is not. We must assume that Caesar has considered the alternatives carefully, analyzing reasons for and against his action. But he found the reasons inconclusive. Both alternatives were open. Then he settled the matter arbitrarily by throwing the dice.

Besides the question of the good life and a reason to live there is another even more important overarching consideration: that of being a good person. If a person strives for a good life only, she is controlled by an egoistic motive. This downgrades her morally. To this criticism adherents of moral egoism say that the wish for the wellbeing of others is part of the good life. This may be true. But this defense makes the good life of others an instrument to achieve the good life, which further strengthens criticism of egoism. It is ethically improper to consider the lives of others as the means to one's own good life. Their lives are goals in themselves. In practice a person often sacrifices important things, even risks her life and health, in order to help others. That is not aiming at the good life; that is taking responsibility as a moral person.

Our self-assessment follows us all the time, consciously aware of what we do. Imagine the self-respect of a person who is concerned with achieving a good life and imagine a person who is concerned with the wellbeing of others. The former is concerned with obtaining and having something, the latter with doing and giving something. The goal of "having a good life" creates a deficit of meaning that prevents one from

---

10 Shakespeare, W., 1623. *Hamlet*, first folio text 3,1.

feeling good about herself and obtaining a good life. The commitment to act as a good person, on the other hand at least enables the person not to despise herself.

The person that just wants to get something – a good job, friends, children – lacks something: herself. She needs to do something with her life, contributing values. Such values are not her good life; they are gifts to people and the world, no matter whether she knows it or survives it. To achieve a good life, she must not try to achieve it but try to be a good person. The good person is an ethical actor. She can be trusted to protect good values in her world. She acts based on empathy and good personal values.

The same applies to social practice. There must be an idea, a mission that operates as a motivating and organizing reason to drive the organization and make a difference.

Reasons to live: I love therefore I am.

Is there a reason to live? The question is neither unanswerable, nonsensical nor beyond reason. It has obvious positive as well as negative answers. We start with the positive answers. Here is basic reason to live:

1   "I live because I love life. I love to live."

or in a weaker form:

1*   "I live because I like to live/enjoy living."

Liking/loving to live is a reason to live. A good life is driven by loving or at least liking life. There are many variations. Instead of loving life, one can for instance consider "loving to be in this world" or "loving to exist". These distinctions are important in some situations. The positions 1 and 1* do not give every person a reason to live. The reason is conditional: if a person likes or loves life, then she has a reason to live. Not all persons like or love or even like life, and they do not have this reason to live. Thus negative answers are possible:

2   "I do not like to live. I do not have a reason to live."

Not loving life does not exclude other possible reasons to live. The statement 1 is an inference, the statement 2 is not. However, the shift from "not liking to live" to "not having a reason to live" is reasonable. A person who does not like life, is in trouble.

People may of course live a fine life without believing they have a reason to live. Some philosophers point out that they have problems with the meaning of life, only if they think about it. Still, mostly they like their life thus, unknowingly, they do have a reason to live. Objections such as one cannot ask for a reason to live, because that would be a categorical mistake, make no sense. The question on the other hand makes sense. Many people have pondered it, and it has a range of possible answers. There are situations in life which people feel confronted with such questions. It is the basis of maturity, because it makes the person take responsibility for her life. Recall Hamlet: "To be, or not to be, that is the question". Shakespeare does not let Hamlet make a famous categorical mistake. The question is the very start of Hamlet's important reflection about the course of his life or death.

Liking and loving differ in depth and strength, but both provide reasons to live. Love drives life by creating long-term endeavors. Love provides reasons to organize a course of action. Love structures life through commitments. Love gives meaning and history. Love creates the overarching perspective. Liking does no such thing. Liking relates to life here and now. Liking and loving can be at odds; it is possible to like things that one does not love and vice versa. Loving is more involving than liking. It is a reason for the actor to live a life until the end. Liking is a motive of a receiving person, a beneficiary. It is a reason to live here and now. Liking depends on the ability to adapt.

Positive reasons alternative to love and liking are for instance care, empathy or sympathy. Although important none of these traits provide a reason to live. Let us take as an example caring: "I live because I care to live/for life" This appears to be a causal statement that I stayed alive because I took care or cared, and not a reason to live. If caring is to express a reason, one should like to know why she cares in order to understand it to be a reason to live. If she cares because it is her job, then the question is, whether she likes her job or not. If she does not like or want to care then caring is no reason for her to live, i.e., the reason hinges on her likings not on her care. It is not so with love; love is a reason whether she likes it or not. She may hate that she loves, but as long as she loves it is a reason. Similarly, neither sympathy nor empathy are reasons to live – unless she likes/loves to feel sympathy or empathy. Again the reason hinges on liking/loving.

Consider duty: "I live because it is my duty." Here we need to ask, why the person wants to do her duty. If she likes to do her duty then we are back to the reason of liking and loving. Should she like life or her duty? Both provide reasons. For duty to be a reason to live, the actor must not only like to do her duty, but also like to live.

Finally consider beauty: "I live because there is so much beauty in the world." This reason works only if she likes beauty. If, for instance, she finds the beauty distracting or dangerous and not likeable, the reason crumbles.

Happiness is the most cherished candidate for an overarching reason from antiquity through modern utilitarianism: "I live because I am happy." This statement may fit some people, but it does not sound convincing. First, one may wonder whether happiness can be a reason to live if people mostly like to be happy. We can imagine a person, who does not like to be in a state of happiness at all time because then she cannot concentrate. Thus liking, again, may be the true reason.

However, it is inherently problematic to make happiness the goal of life as, for example, in a utilitarian calculus. Pursuing happiness may prevent one from achieving it. The playwright Bertolt Brecht says that human beings run after happiness, but that they should not run too fast, because happiness runs behind.[11] Happiness is not a real goal, but akin to the cheer that might come after a real goal has been achieved or during the attempt to reach a real goal. The thesis here is: Happiness is a reward our psyche gives us for acting out of love, i.e. doing the things it wants us to do. Happiness is an escort to acting out of love; it is a companion to love.[12] Accompanying or escort phenomena are achieved not by pursuing them but by pursuing the phenomena, they escort. Therefore one cannot successfully have happiness as a goal. Our psyche will punish us as ego-

---

11   Brecht, B. 1928. „Das Lied von der Unzulänglichkeit des Menschlichen Strebens," in: *Die Dreigroschen Oper. (The Threepenny Opera)*.

12   This definition of happiness overcomes some of its elusiveness. Such comprehension is necessary. For instance one may identify happiness with brain substances or brain states. But the definition of the brain substance is clearly not happiness. Thus there must be a way to identify happiness independently of the brain substance in order for the identification to make empirical sense. Also, many popular Likert scale studies need a better understanding of the concept of happiness. To measure expressions of being satisfied is, for instance, by far not the same as being happy.

ists. But all this emphasizes that endeavors other than acting out of love are a waste. As happiness is a companion to love, so is unhappiness. The emotional pain of losing in the battle of love can be devastating.

Pleasure is very different from happiness. Pleasure and pain are opposites; happiness and pain are not. A person may work hard for something she loves. She may suffer, be in pain and have reached her limit. Despite that she feels happy. A person may claim that her reason to live is the pleasure it gives. And pleasure is important. But to consider it as the reason to live leads to despair. Pleasure and pain are like happiness passive mental states although they consume a lot of energy. However, happiness is based on the activities of love and thus related to the unfolding of life.

The search for a meaning of life sometimes substitutes for the classical search for happiness. A meaning is a source of reasons and reasoning that can structure life. Although the search for meaning may seem to be a more modest approach than the search for happiness, it has a sinister side. For the most part, the meaning of a person's life is positive, constructive, and ethical. However, sometimes the meaning is something terrible, which suppresses ethics and destroys the life of many people, even nations and cultures. All the horrible deeds in history have been loaded with vigorous meaning. Thus meanings can be good or bad and they must be assessed by reason.

There is good as well as bad meaning and there are good and bad reasons. The question: "is it good?" can be asked about anything, including any meaning and reason. For a reason to be a good reason it must be true and at least not lead to the destruction of loving conditions for good people. A belief system, a social ideology, which is a source of reasons, must itself be good. It must not conflict with knowledge, be superstitious, or lead to destruction of life, love and happiness for good people.

The overarching reason is an expression of a basic attitude or value that drives the person. It is not to be confused with the feelings that are reactions to the situation the person observes. The person interprets observations from the perspective of basic values and this interpretation initiates the feelings. Thus love as an overarching reason is not a feeling but the basis for the emotional reactions to the observed world. For example, if a person observes that something she loves is in danger, then she gets upset, feels anger or fear, and gets ready to react: to protect, hide, fight, or flee. If she hadn't loved, her emotional reactions would have been different.

Likewise, if a person sees that what she loves thrives in the world, then she feels well and happy. Thus, if a person does not know what she loves, she might pay attention to her emotional reactions.

The basic tone of feelings is colored by the overarching reason whether it is love, fear, anger or something spiritual. If love is the overarching reason, then the feelings of anger or fear disappear when the threat is gone. If however, a person is controlled by anger or hatred, then anger does not disappear when the threat is gone.

People may be controlled by negative overarching values or attitudes such as fear, anger, or hatred. Although a loving and liking attitude is a strong drive, the person may learn that this motive is out of touch with the social realities in her life. Such experience is caused by the unbearable painful defeats of her love. In order to survive she feels forced to change and replace this hopeless approach to life with a more negative and sinister approach, such as indifference, anger or hatred. It's obvious that ethical actors have the duty to be aware of this danger and help people to avoid it. Children in particular get hurt because they do not have power over their lives; there is often little protection of their loving relations. People, friend and foe, need social support to achieve a loving and loveable life, to prevent people from suffering, committing suicide, or being captivated by dangerous aggressions. If negative overarching attitudes take hold, then happiness appears no longer possible. The accompanying reward may turn into scorn, contempt, *Schadenfreude* and similar emotions. As reasons to live they are poor. Some may live to get revenge, but the reason is paltry.

Finally, an important reason to live is fear, especially fear of death. In a loving context fear is a reaction to situations where something we love – whether something in life or life itself – is threatened. When the threat is gone, the fear disappears. Threats to something we do not love or that has no consequence for things we love, should not cause fear. However, fear may become a permanent state and replace love as the overarching reason. One may recognize dangers everywhere and all reasoning may concern dangers. When fear is the overarching reason, then paradoxically there is nothing to be afraid of anymore, because love has been replaced by fear as the basic 'value'. Such overarching fear prevents people not from living but from structuring and unfolding their lives. Fear of death as the reason to live is only a reason to stay alive. It produces no content to life, in contrast to the loving motive.

Courage is an answer to fear. It does not eliminate fear but prevents us from becoming victims of fear. Courage presupposes something to defend against threats.

In conclusion

Love is a reason to live: "I love, therefore I am." This dictum installs love as the foundation of reason. Its use of the word "therefore" expresses a reason, the reason to be. In Descartes' dictum, "I think, therefore I am", the word "therefore" does not express a reason to be. Logically it claims that "I am" is a conclusion that follows from the premise "I think." That does not make thinking a reason to be. I would like to focus on Plato and Socrates who are concerned with the love-based drive in our approach to the world and to philosophy. It is the love for knowledge that creates the ability to focus, learn and develop. Love creates the enduring identity in which things can unfold. Love gives us all the reasons we need. Cold reason does not. Pure emotionality does not. The formidable drive that created science and technology originated not in knowledge, which has no reward, but in the loving search for knowledge, which is full of reward.

With loving and liking life as overarching reasons, the ethics of goodness has an ontological basis that makes it applicable in practice. This is not only an is-ought bridge but a theory-practice bridge. With it we can question practice. For example: Are the decisions under consideration concerned with profit or do they create a loveable world? Am I in my life really concerned with things that I love and like? Do we communicate and develop practices that supports people's struggle to realize a loving reason? It is our ethical duty to create conditions for a loving approach to life, i.e. to create organizations, workplaces, homes, and an environment that people can trust, like and love. A great deal of social pathology arises when people cannot find a way to realize a loving approach and thus end up in destructive and self-destructive behavior. People need a story of their life in this form: "And then I did this, which I love; and then I did that, which I love; then I did this, which I love." An opposite story is "Then I did this which is boring; then I did that, which is a waste of time; then I did this, which I hate.". If this is the case, they lose self-respect, and unless they change course, pathological issues appear on the horizon.

The difference between what one loves and does not love is an important dimension of the person's self-identity. Society identifies the person with her body and history. She was born there/then, she looks so and so, she did so and so there/then etc. There is little distinction between what happened to the person, what she did voluntarily and what she was forced to. But in her own story-telling there is a great difference between the things she did because she loved them and things she did because they were forced upon her. The first things tell her who she really is. The other things tell her what conditions the world gives her. For instance, a person may like to work with customers but not to do the accounting. To the question: "Who are you?" she would like to answer by pointing out all the things she loves: "I am married to this good man, I work with customers. I live over there." She likes to mention the things she loves the most. If she did not like her husband or her work, she might not want to mention them. Thus this lady does not say that she does the accounting. She does not identify with things she does not like to do although needs to do them. The border between what she loves and likes and that which she does not love and like tells us who she is as a person and what she would want to give to the world. Her identity as well as the things that limit and hurt her become visible in that distinction.

The joy of being in the world, which is with us from the beginning, drives our development and creates loving relations. People need the chance to live their likings and to develop their loving. So they need freedom because neither liking nor loving can be commanded.

A number of issues deserve exploration. People do not only need to love; they also need to be loved. Without love, we cannot develop. Thus one might claim also that "I live because I am/was loved." However, there is little help in formulating demands for love if there is no love available. Love cannot be commanded. In order for people to get love, we need to enable their possibility to love, so that there is a love to get. Since to love is a basic drive and the source of happiness, one must wonder and ask, why it can be missing. Why has it been replaced by other overarching approaches?

The focus on love and liking calls for a reevaluation of our values. We need to find out, what – if anything – characterizes the loveable and the likeable. Are all the decisions driven by economics an adequate reflection of that which is loveable? Does it make the world more loveable?

Finally there are different forms of love and their interplay should be analyzed. The subjective and personal forms of love, which drive our relations and activities, must for many reasons be complemented by a general form of love, a universal love, which is open not only to those that belong to us (our family, our friends, our nation) but also has a place for other human beings and nature in general. Most important is the overarching love of life, the existential love. We all need the joy of living. It spreads out where it comes and colors all things beautifully. And if we don't love life we cannot make the best things shine and feel good. It is the basis for all other values. If that is missing, then also subjective personal love loses its blessing.

Brenda Almond

Finding a way in tomorrow's world
The challenge for applied ethics[1]

Citizens of the developed countries of the modern world are constantly reminded by the media of a host of social ills that threaten their personal and the public's wellbeing: crime, domestic and street violence, terrorist threats, family breakdown, environmental deterioration and educational decline. The boundaries between these areas are not solid. Concern about the environment, for example, raises questions about the uses of science and technology, and this in turn can connect with issues of trust and transparency in commercial transactions. Similarly, in another area of scientific progress, developments in genetics and in the new reproductive technologies have implications for family and human relationships, opening up broader questions about such ethically sensitive matters as gender, ethnicity, population numbers, and demographic trends.

And yet it sometimes seems that philosophy has its gaze fixed firmly away from specific practical matters like these, or at least that practical or 'applied' ethics is a very new arrival on the philosophical scene, gaining in significance only in the late twentieth century. But that is a hasty judgement. One of the most important of today's international journals, *Ethics*, first appeared well over 100 years ago, bearing the subtitle: 'a quarterly devoted to the advancement of ethical knowledge and practice,' which it retained for nearly half a century, only abandoning it, ironically

---

1   This article is based in part on the author's article 'Applied Ethics,' which was published in *Routledge Encyclopedia of Philosophy*, ed. E. Craig (London: Routledge 1998, 2011). Parts of that article are reprinted here with permission from the *Routledge Encyclopedia of Philosophy.*

as it turned out, as the world stood on the brink of the Second World War. Surprisingly, given today's assumptions about the novelty and uniqueness of applied philosophy, topics in the first issue of *Ethics*, published in Britain in October 1890, included war, fanaticism, industrial and class relations, land-rights, and legal punishment. It was the heyday of Victorian social and ethical concern, and a number of ethical and philosophical societies were formed at the time, some of which have survived to this day. These societies, which were not always tied to academic institutions, organised public lectures and seminars, but they were also committed to positive and practical humanitarianism, founding schools, orphanages and hospitals, and working to relieve poverty.

The kind of reflective philosophical thinking that spills out into the realm of practice is something that many thoughtful people take as natural. Many philosophical thinkers and social theorists in many diverse cultural contexts have engaged with public life and its social and political concerns. Nevertheless, it is true that philosophical involvement of this kind has developed in new and distinctive ways over the last few decades under the name of 'applied philosophy' or 'applied ethics'. The two terms are sometimes used as synonyms, but the scope of applied philosophy is broader and can be used to tackle philosophical problems that are not exclusively ethical in fields such as law, education, art, or artificial intelligence. In contrast, 'applied ethics' usually focuses on questions in a narrower range of areas that are more strictly ethical.

The mainstream of professional philosophy in the English-speaking countries at first tended to keep a not wholly sympathetic distance from applied ethics the more prominent form of applied philosophy. Possibly this is because some practitioners of the subject attributed less weight to ethics itself as a branch of philosophy than they did to the metaphysical speculations of philosophers of earlier centuries. But philosophy is a richer, less narrow, concept than this would suggest, and few of the great philosophers of the past have ignored the ethical, social and political issues of their day. Interest in these matters is not, of course, confined to philosophers, but there is a common thread that marks an approach to practical issues as distinctively philosophical. First, while it accepts that a concern for the relevant facts is a prior condition for sound moral reasoning, it also recognises a deeper requirement: an underlying interest in questions about human nature and human needs that expresses itself in reflection about what makes a good life, and what kind of society is most likely to make that good life possible. This means that the response of the philosophical inquirer to any particular practical question will not be merely a quantitative calculation based exclusively on factual assumptions, but rather a response in which ethical considerations play a central role, and may well trump the immediate interests of groups or individuals. This is a large claim to make on behalf of those ethical enquirers who have strayed into the world of public policy, and it is likely to be contested. To set it on a firmer foundation, and to place it in a broader historical context, a brief retrospective glance may be useful.

Philosophical roots

The Western philosophical tradition found its focus in ancient Greece from the sixth century BCE. There were thinkers in other traditions too, who reflected on these matters and understood that the deeper questions about the lives of human beings cannot be answered purely by observation, but require ethical reflection and at least some kind of speculative reasoning. Sources are limited, but as far as Western philosophy is concerned, fragmentary records make it possible to trace the ideas of some of its early precursors.

Of most interest from the point of view of applied philosophy, the very first thinker in that tradition, the Milesian philosopher Thales (624-546 BCE), is known to have used his philosophical and scientific speculations to ground his practical and social concerns. Indeed, while only a few enigmatic sayings of his remain, scattered records show that through his business judgment, his expertise in economic and legal theory, and his interest in government and politics he played a conspicuous role in the public life of his time. But while little is known of the lives and ideas of early pre-Socratic philosophers like Thales, the writings of their immediate successors, especially Plato and Aristotle, have survived and confirm that Western philosophy, from its origins, made a connection between reflection on questions about the good life and the good society and practical conclusions about personal behaviour and good government.

Following these ancient beginnings, it is possible to trace a more recent history of philosophical concern with questions that are both specific and practical. Examples include the *Summa theologiae* (Gilby 1963) of St. Thomas Aquinas (1225-74) which contains a discussion of marriage and the family and the *De jure belli et pacis* (Kelsey 1925) in which Hugo

Grotius (1583-1645) formulated the rules for a just war. Other thinkers and philosophers included Milton (1608-74) and Locke (1632-1704) who, living in a period of political upheaval and religious persecution, launched an ongoing debate about toleration (Milton 1644; Locke 1968). Later, the empiricist philosopher David Hume (1711-76) left an essay on the ethics of suicide to be published after his death, and the utilitarian philosopher Jeremy Bentham (1748-1832) put forward comprehensive theories of law and punishment. Bentham even drew up detailed plans for a new type of prison, to be called the Panopticon and, in his programme for legal and political reform, devised a complex system, called the 'felicific calculus' for applying utilitarian theory to particular cases (Bentham 1789). The forerunner of today's cost-benefit analysis, Bentham's theory was intended as a scientific approach to the measurement of pleasures and pains against each other, and the weighing of long-term considerations against immediate short-term desires.

Elsewhere, in a different European tradition, the ethical theory of the rationalist philosopher Immanuel Kant (1724-1804) provided a philosophical basis for ethical practice in such matters as truthfulness, promise-keeping and charitable giving, and also gave lasting substance to the principle of human dignity – a notion currently influential in national and international law, and sometimes expressed in the language of human rights (Kant 1785). But if Kant's conception of human dignity has helped to shape the modern world, the philosophy of his near contemporary Hegel (1770-1831) can also be said to have done so, for good or ill, in a very different direction. Hegel's philosophy of history (Hegel, 1821) had a dramatic impact on the course of subsequent world events, not so much directly as through its influence on the work of another political theorist, Karl Marx (1818-83) – a paradoxical outcome, since Marx himself had doubts about the ability of philosophy to influence practical events.

Marx lived in London as a political refugee from 1849 and wrote his major and most influential works on capital and communism there. The British philosopher John Stuart Mill (1806-73) also lived and worked in London at that time, writing extensively on social, economic and political affairs, and giving shape to a political code that would later become, for liberal thinkers, the ideological opposite of Marxism and communism. Mill was an advocate of women's rights and, at a time when universal education was being promoted across Europe, a supporter of free education for all who nevertheless warned against the dangers of a state monopoly of education. But it was particularly his essay on toleration that earned him the title of father of classical liberalism, and the arguments he advanced for freedom and toleration influenced some of the major social and legislative changes of the twentieth century, especially in Britain (Mill 1859). They continue to be part of any debate about the role of the state vis-à-vis the individual.

By the beginning of the twentieth century, then, philosophical reasoning to determine practical ends was far from unknown and had already begun to display its potential for wider application in public affairs. Many other names could have been added to this thumb-nail sketch, which is intended simply to counter the idea that philosophy is, and always has been, essentially an abstract pursuit of matters of academic interest only, which is a dismissive approach that leads to an undervaluing of ethics itself, whether theoretical or applied. But it provides the background against which a broader and more generous conception of ethics opened up, ready to take seriously the moral issues raised by the environmental challenges and scientific advances of the latter half of the twentieth century and the opening decades of the twenty-first. Applied philosophy began to be seen as an important contributor to the task of monitoring, criticizing, and influencing the path of social progress.

A new ethics

Not everyone saw it in this way, however, and some philosophers in the English-speaking world, preoccupied with empiricism, conceptual analysis, and other philosophical priorities, were at first reluctant to seize this opportunity. This was particularly so in the immediate post-second world war period. For whatever reason, they were slow to address either the new anxieties or older perennial issues of war, poverty and social injustice. However, the ground was already well-prepared for the concept of a *philosophie engagée* to emerge in various European countries over the next decades. The notion of *praxis*, for example, is familiar from various continental traditions, including Marxism, the Frankfurt School, and the philosophy of Habermas (Habermas 1985), while the idea of the philosopher as *engagé* – as concerned with playing a part in the world – is an important part of French existentialist thought, made familiar in the works of Sartre (Sartre 1943). The involvement of philosophers in practical decision-making also grew in importance in the USA, as medicine moved from being a practice with little power to influence the natural course of disease to becoming a powerful interventionist tool. At the same time, developments in science and technology opened up a related area of philosophical engagement which became known as bioethics.

Other reasons for the turn towards practical affairs on the part of professional and academic philosophers can be found in the global upheavals of the twentieth century caused by wars, internal conflicts, persecution, and the migrations and movements of peoples. Modern conflicts stirred philosophical debate (Walzer 1977) and increasingly, in universities and elsewhere, lectures, books and articles tackled such subjects as civil disobedience and the role of conscience, equality and diversity, race, gender, nationality and multiculturalism. Human mismanagement of the environment, too, moved from being a concern of specialists addressing specific problems such as the misuse of pesticides in farming, river pollution, or the destruction of rain-forests, to the wider forum of the general public. Environmental philosophers began to consider, too, the moral dimensions of human treatment of non-human animals (Regan 2004). Global developments such as these, often involving a risky conjunction of nature, technology and commerce, contributed to the growth world-wide of both professional and public interest in ethics and public policy, poverty and affluence (Pogge 2008). From the mid-twentieth century on, and as humanity's new and enormously expanded power to dominate its world became apparent, philosophers such as Peter Singer (Singer, 2004) were increasingly ready to address some of the problems those powers created and to treat the role of ethics with greater seriousness.

A Danish perspective

Amongst these, the Danish theologian and social philosopher Knud E. Løgstrup (1905-81) was a pioneer of the kind of rich understanding of moral philosophy that would be responsive to the new concerns. His own early philosophical development had been influenced by existentialism and phenomenology, and in *The Ethical Demand* (Løgstrup 1956) he makes constant reference to human needs and human experience. With a distinctive focus on the necessary engagement of philosophy with personal and community life, he describes the ethical demand as something that is based on recognition of the interdependency of human beings. It touches on human love and relationships, and has implications for policy in many areas of human interaction: war, politics, economics, and matters that concern the wellbeing of others. For Løgstrup, phenomena such as mercy, trust, fidelity, sincerity, and the kind of love that in the New Testament is called *agape*, are part of what he calls 'the sovereign expression of life' and they have an intrinsic claim on human beings as Niekerk (2007 p. xix) and Fink (2007 pp. 15-19) argue. Against this background, Løgstrup's philosophy emerges more clearly as a forerunner of the new approach to ethics that developed in the course of the latter half of the twentieth century. In particular, his rejection of routine and unreflective responses to moral problems places him alongside those more recent commentators who see direct personal engagement with a particular issue as the best way to confront the novel challenges of today's world. Løgstrup expresses his own view in terms of the notion of spontaneity: the Good Samaritan sees a need and responds to it. He writes:

> There is no point in asking whether a merciful act is good in itself without regard to its result. Such separation is impossible: a term like 'merciful' is at once a characterization both of the attitude of mind and of the intention behind the act (Løgstrup 2007 p. 77).

It is this kind of spontaneous response that Løgstrup sees as appropriate in face of another person's needs. Even so, he acknowledges that there are times when a simple response of this kind may be inadequate, and when it may be necessary to turn for guidance to established moral rules. The ambiguity in Løgstrup's position here can perhaps be reconciled, as some commentators (Pahuus 2007) have suggested, by drawing a distinction between the political and the ethical, i.e., between ethical situations affecting only or mainly a person's private life where existential choice may have a place, and where ethical situations at a larger social level where law and government are involved, and moral principles and legal rules may be needed to provide guidelines for action. Løgstrup sees a role for public deliberation in the search for compromise solutions in contentious cases such as, to use his own examples, nuclear arms or, at the personal or micro-level, contraception.

Løgstrup may have hoped to provide an appropriate approach to difficult cases like these. But applied ethics is necessarily a place of controversy and those who favour reasoning based on rules that have a solid basis in universal moral norms are unlikely to change their position. So while Løgstrup's distinctive perspective finds a place amongst contemporary approaches to applied ethics, it is not the primary contender. Instead, the debate that currently dominates the field is one between, on the one hand, a form of utilitarianism that increasingly looks to quantitative methods to make judgements and, on the other, a more Kantian approach based on respect for well-established principles and the concept of human dignity. If Løgstrup's theory cannot be said to fit easily into either of these categories, he can nevertheless be seen as a pioneer of the kind of applied ethics that finds its most important zone of activity in unresolved issues in the contemporary world.

Today's concerns

As mentioned earlier, one of the main reasons frequently offered for the gradual return of a more practically engaged view of ethics has been the increasing importance of biomedical ethics, and this is an area where ethical dilemmas often demand resolution in circumstances where decisions are urgent and cannot be postponed (Glover 1990, 2000). The most controversial of these tend to be found in areas where scientific discovery and technological advance have dramatically re-shaped people's expectations. Developments in genetics and reproductive medicine, for example, have begun to play a new and unanticipated role in the lives of ordinary people, affecting them in the most intimate and personal aspects of their lives, including illness and end-of-life care (Battin 1994), birth and death (Dworkin 1995), and family and identity (Almond 2008). In engaging with such issues, applied ethics is both more holistic in its approach and, paradoxically, more willing than traditional ethics to give attention to detail in the conclusions it reaches. It is also more ready to take advantage of the contribution that other disciplines such as psychology and sociology may be able to offer, or to learn from the insights of great literature. It is necessarily cautious in the use it makes of empirical findings, and reluctant to accept the goal of achieving human happiness as a reliable short-cut to settling difficult or controversial issues, for concepts of happiness, too, are matters for debate. There is a wide spectrum of alternative 'happiness' goals starting from such basics as food and shelter and continuing with a range of alternative goals from power, honour, and fame to wealth, security, and health. In light of this weakening of utilitarian assumptions, then, there will be no inconsistency in recognizing that justice and rights, morality and obligation, also have a role to play.

Moral dilemmas, 'free riders' and other challenges

The line between theory and practice, then, is not as sharp as it is sometimes thought to be. What is more important where applied philosophy is concerned is to be able to demonstrate the clarity of its methods and the validity of its arguments. But how is it to do this? Ethics often features as part of professional training and preparation for careers in, for example, medicine or social work and the use of individual case-studies is popular in these courses. But according to critics, this can have unintended consequences. The claim is that, in stressing that there are at least two sides to many ethical problems, and in presenting ethical theories as necessarily leading to conflicting conclusions, it risks generating a facile relativism the view that there are only opinions, not answers.

For similar reasons, this objection can be extended to the use of moral dilemmas, although it has to be recognised that moral dilemmas have been a part of philosophy for as long as philosophy itself. Today, though, they differ in a significant way from traditional dilemmas. They are not usually to be understood in the hard logical sense in which a person faces a situation in which each of two opposite courses of action is judged to be ethically mandatory or, alternatively, each is judged to be wrong, making it impossible to take the morally correct path. The dilemmas encountered in applied ethics are usually to be understood in a looser sense, as cases in which a choice between courses of action may be extremely difficult, and the arguments on both sides are compelling. In such situations, the person who must decide on a course of action is strongly influenced in opposing directions. It should be said, though, that choosing between options which are not morally equal is, strictly speaking, not a dilemma although, admittedly, it is likely to be emotionally traumatizing. Choosing between moral obligations that are indisputably of equal weight, on the other hand, is not itself a moral problem. The challenge for applied ethics in such cases may well be to determine not which option is the better choice (a utilitarian calculation), but rather whether or not the available options are indeed morally equal.

These are practical challenges, and as such, it may be that they can be dealt with by good practice. But there remain some challenges to the theoretical basis of applied ethics that are more difficult to meet. One of these is the universalisation problem. Better known as the 'free rider' problem, this looks for an answer to the question: "What if everyone did that?" Many things are judged to be wrong as a result of asking this question, even though, in a particular case, it might seem harmless and more convenient for an individual to ignore a general rule intended to apply to everyone while benefiting from the fact that everyone else is following it. The applied ethicist, like the theoretical philosopher must find a way to deal with this problem, but for the applied ethicist the problem is bound up with the need to employ what is sometimes called moral casuistry. However, while it is true that the term 'casuist' can be used in a derogatory way to mean 'sophist' or 'quibbler', this ancient science is not necessarily to be despised. It was not originally a term of abuse, and simply described an attempt to work out the 'right answer' to a difficult issue of conscience in a particular set of circumstances by working through the implications and arguments systematically. In contemporary terms, it has much in common with situation ethics and may indeed be the only way to deal with some intractable issues of conscience.

Because it is fundamentally a philosophical enterprise, applied ethics cannot avoid the need to respond to certain historic philosophical objections. Of these, the one most frequently heard, and most often advanced in criticism, is Hume's objection to attempts to derive an 'ought' from an 'is', sometimes called the fact-value distinction (Hume 1739-40). A second objection, which leads to a conclusion very similar to that of Hume, is G.E. Moore's argument that to identify moral characteristics with 'natural' or empirical ones is to commit a 'naturalistic fallacy' (Moore 2003). Although neither Hume nor Moore appear to have drawn the conclusion that there can be no philosophical solutions to practical problems, these arguments are commonly seen by contemporary writers as having erected a barrier between the facts that the applied ethicist must begin from, and the moral conclusions which it is the aim of the exercise to draw. Closing the gap, then, between factual descriptions of situations and related moral judgment is an essential task for applied ethics. However, the arguments for and against both Hume and Moore have been extensively debated in the literature, and it would be superfluous to rehearse them again here. Both, however, may be at least partially answered by pointing out that moral philosophers holding positions as opposed to each other as emotivism and intuitionism can find common ground in conceding that there is much scope for factual argument and causal reasoning right up to the point of an ultimate ethical judgement. And both of these concur in the view that at that point, reasoning gives out. It is a short step from that to recognise that some facts – torture, child-murder, genocide – 'speak for themselves'.

From a different direction, there are critics who challenge on a broader front the notion of applied ethics as an impartial and essentially reason-based approach to society's problems. Objections to the idea of universal moral norms and to foundationalist procedures in reasoning (the 'postmodernist' challenge) are associated with recent developments in Marxist theory, certain feminist approaches in ethics and epistemology, and the deconstructionist movement – schools of thought which may also adopt an analysis of power-structures in society incompatible with belief in individual freedom of action (Almond 1992). Supporters of these theoretical positions often make strong claims for the recognition of rights, but this may be no more than a tactic designed to take advantage of their opponents' preconceptions rather than an explicit recognition of universal ethical concepts.

Other critiques of traditional ethics may, however, be more sympathetic to applied ethics. On the basis of research revealing the contextual nature of many women's responses to ethical dilemmas, some feminist writers, most prominently Carol Gilligan, have argued that women in general are likely to adopt an ethic of care and responsibility to particular others rather than an abstract morality of principles, rights or justice (Gilligan 1982). Such an approach may well seem better adapted to the resolution of 'hard cases' in, for example, health care or social work. Similarly, although proponents of 'virtue ethics' may regard applied ethics as a rival theory, its emphasis on seeking the good in particular situations means that it, too, can be seen as complementary to applied ethics, rather than an alternative to it.

Finding a way in tomorrow's world

Method in applied ethics

This suggests a need to approach the question of method more directly. How should one proceed in seeking clarification in matters of morals or conscience? A suggestion which combines some of the best features of the examples discussed here can be compared to the method used by a designer or sculptor who starts with a blueprint, but has to adapt it to the materials to hand and to the situations in which it is required. This way of proceeding bears some resemblance to the Hegelian method of dialectical reasoning, or to the method of reflective equilibrium favoured by John Rawls (1971). In this approach, intuitions in response to particular cases are measured against moral principles that the person concerned is inclined to accept; this initial response is then revised and its implications for other particular cases are considered again in the light of that revision. According to this view of the subject, the method of applied ethics is neither purely deductive nor purely inductive. For others, however, the deductive model is more powerful, and the question to be answered in any particular case is simply under which (inviolable) principle it falls. Others again would favour the inductive model, according to which, by clearly seeing what is right in particular cases, it becomes possible to formulate a general principle to cover both these and other particular judgments. In general, then, if it is to justify its claim to be a philosophical rather than an empirical science, applied ethics must aim to address the question of what is the right moral response to a situation by seeking the highest possible degree of generality and abstraction.

This takes us back to the question of what kind of study applied ethics is. Is it simply a scholarly study, or is it committed to the promotion of change in the world? Is it conservative or radical, reactionary or revolutionary? The answer to this last question is that it can be either. Reflection sometimes encourages people to seek change for what they believe will be better; others, however, may want to resist change in order to preserve what is best from the past. It is probably true to say that until recently, despite differences of religious or ideological background, a common moral approach could in general be assumed, and accepted norms of moral behaviour could be taken as a starting-point for ethical reasoning. But it is no longer possible to assume a moral consensus of this kind, and in practice the defence of an absolutist conception of morality is often left to those with a religious perspective. But this divergence of opinion is not necessarily a disadvantage, and the controversial nature of most of the issues involved is itself a spur to their philosophical study.

Applied ethics, then, is part of a whole view of the human condition and takes a broad view of ethical decision-making. It is compatible with a range of political opinion, and it would be wrong to link it to a stereotypical set of views, for it is of the essence of applied ethics that it approaches individual issues in their own right and not as part of an ethical or political package-deal. Nevertheless, in relation to practical policy, it recognizes and respects the constraints imposed by moral norms that are capable of commanding universal respect. Its object can be summed up simply: it is to gain clearer perceptions of right and wrong, with a view to embodying those insights in manners and institutions.

References

Almond, B. 2006/2008. *The Fragmenting Family*. Oxford: Oxford University Press.

Almond, B. 1992. Philosophy and the cult of irrationalism. In: *The Impulse to Philosophise*, ed. A. P. Phillips-Griffiths, 201-17. Cambridge: Cambridge University Press.

Aquinas, T. 1266–73/1963. *Summa theologiae*, ed. T. Gilby. London: Eyre & Spottiswoode.

Battin, M. B. 1994. *The Least Worst Death: Essays in Bioethics on the End of Life*. Oxford: Oxford University Press.

Bentham, J. 1789/1996. *An Introduction to the Principles of Morals and Legislation*, ed. J.H. Burns and H.L.A. Hart. Oxford: Clarendon Press.

Andersen S. and van Kooten Niekerk, K. eds. 2007. *Concern for the Other: Perspectives on the Ethics of K. E. Løgstrup...* South Bend, IN: Notre Dame Press.

Fink, H. 2007. The conception of ethics and the ethical. In: *Concern for the Other: Perspectives on the Ethics of K. E. Løgstrup*. Ed. S. Andersen and K. van Kooten Niekerk, 9-28. Indiana: Notre Dame Press.

Fletcher, J. 1966. *Situation Ethics: The New Morality*. Louisville, KY: Westminster John Knox Press.

Gilligan, C. 1993. *In a Different Voice: Psychological Theory and Women's Development*, 2nd ed. Cambridge, MA: Harvard University Press.

Glover, J. 1990. *Causing Death and Saving Lives: the Moral Problems of Abortion, Infanticide, Suicide, Euthanasia, Capital Punishment, War, and Other Life-or-Death Choices*. London: Penguin.

Glover, J. 2000. *Humanity: a Moral History of the Twentieth Century*. New Haven, CT.

Habermas, J. 1985. *Theory of Communicative Action*, trans. Thomas McCarthy. Cambridge: Polity Press.

Hegel, G.W.F. 1821/1991. *Elements of the Philosophy of Right*, Cambridge: Cambridge University Press.

Hume, D. 1739/1978. *A Treatise of Human Nature*, ed. L.A. Selby-Bigge.

Phillips-Griffiths A.P., ed. 1992. *The Impulse to Philosophise*. Cambridge: Cambridge University Press.

Kant, I. 1785/1964. *Grundlegung zur Metaphysik der Sitten*, trans. H.J. Paton. (Originally: *The Moral Law.*) London: Hutchinson, 1948. Reprinted. New York: Harper & Row.

Kant, I. 1797. On a supposed right to lie from altruistic motives. In: *The Philosophy of Immanuel Kant*, trans. L.W. Beck, 346-9. Chicago, IL: University of Chicago Press.

Grotius, H. 1925. *De jure belli ac pacis,* vol 2, trans. F. W. Kelsey. In: *The Classics of International Law*, ed. J. B. Scott. Oxford: Oxford University Press).

Locke, J. 1689/1968. *A Letter concerning Toleration*, ed. J.W. Gough and R. Kilbansky. Oxford: Oxford University Press.

Løgstrup, K. E. 1956/1977. *Den etiske Fordring.* Copenhagen: Gyldendal. Trans. H. Fink and A. MacIntyre as *The Ethical Demand.* South Bend, IN: University of Notre Dame Press.

Løgstrup, K. E. 2007. *Beyond the Ethical Demand*, ed. K. van Kooten Niekerk. South Bend, IN: University of Notre Dame Press.

Mill, J. S. 1859/1982. *On Liberty,* Harmondsworth: Penguin Books.

Milton, J. 1644. *Areopagitica,* London.

Niekerk, K. van Kooten 2007. ‚Introduction', In: *Beyond the Ethical Demand* p. ix- xxxii.

Pahuus, A.M. 2007. The use of principles in ethical situations. In: *Concern for the Other: Perspectives on the Ethics of K. E. Løgstrup*, ed. S. Andersen and K. van Kooten Niekerk, 103-11. South Bend, IN: Notre Dame Press.

Pogge, T. 2008. *World Poverty and Human Rights.* Cambridge: Polity Press.

Rawls, J. 1971. *A Theory of Justice.* Oxford: Oxford University Press.

Regan, T. 2004. *The Case for Animal Rights.* Berkeley: University of California Press.

Sartre, J.-P. 1943/1957. *Being and Nothingness*, trans. H. Barnes. London: Methuen.

Singer, P. 2004. *One World: the Ethics of Globalisation.* New Haven Ct: Yale University Press.

Walzer, M. 1977. *Just and Unjust Wars.* New York: Basic Books.

Terje Mesel

Adverse events as moral challenges in health care

Abstract

Adverse events, such as patient suicide, unfortunately happen. For the health care worker such tragic events can activate emotional responses and inadequate coping mechanisms through which the moral implications of the situation are not fully met. The thesis of this article is that a contextual clarification of the concepts of guilt, shame, and responsibility can help to facilitate better coping. First, it is necessary to make a clear distinction between responsibility and guilt. Being responsible implies moral lucidity and a willingness to make clear one's reflection and action in the given situation. However, it does not imply guilt. Second, the question of guilt is complex, especially in health care where so many factors are outside our control. This fact, however, does not diminish our responsibility for what is outside our control. Third, other-oriented feelings of guilt provide a much better ethical bridging than self-oriented feelings of shame. Thus, it is important both to recognize and facilitate for feelings of guilt rather than feelings of shame. However, excessive feelings of guilt can be crippling, and it ought to be a responsibility for the professional community to contribute to emotional calibration in order to facilitate individual coping mechanisms that meet the moral implications of the events.

A narrative

John has just finished an internship and started his first year of residency in psychiatry. The ward on which he works is badly understaffed, and all beds are occupied, a combination that makes his days both hectic and challenging. John experiences a growing dissatisfaction, as he does not have enough time for his patients; he is unable to offer them the therapy he thinks would give the best effect. There simply isn't enough time!

On this particular Friday, his schedule is full, and his first session is with a young man whom we will call Fred. John has been his therapist for some time and is optimistic for Fred's future, as the young man seems to be recovering well from his depression and anxiety. Today they will focus on Fred's moving back into his own apartment, and this will be their final talk before his parents pick him up around noon. The ward desperately needs vacant beds, as several new patients are on the waiting list for admission. But Fred has been feeling anxious and insecure. Moreover, he has said that he is afraid to be alone with his thoughts.

Just as John arrives at his office, he hears people screaming and running down the corridor. Fred's body has just been found in his room hanging from the ceiling. John's world shatters in an instant: "It is my fault. I am a dangerous doctor. I pushed too hard to get Fred's discharge through and didn't see his anxiety. I am to blame for Fred's suicide!"

Although several years have passed since this Friday in his first year of residency, John can still describe every detail; time, place, smells, the faces of colleagues, patients, Fred's parents. At times, feelings of guilt still overwhelm him. (based on interviews with Norwegian psychiatrists fall 2010)

Introduction

Adverse events in health care happen for a variety of causes. For example, medical procedures sometimes produce negative effects. Communication breaks down, and vital information is lost. Patients get hurt, and patients die. Sometimes the health care worker is to blame; he or she may have performed inadequately (Berlinger 2005; Rosenthal 1995). Sometimes adverse events happen due to the inherent fallibility of medical knowledge (Gorovitz & MacIntyre 1975; Rørtveit & Strand, 2001; Strand, Rørtveit, Hannestad, & Schei 2010), and sometimes they just happen out of sheer bad luck (Dickenson 2003; Fredriksen 2005). Not surprisingly mental strain and fatigue are linked to healthcare personnel making diagnostic errors (Hilfiker 1997). Even though the healthcare worker is not necessarily to blame, the emotional strain they experience can at times incapacitate them. Empirical studies also document that the stress caused by feelings of distress and guilt are key factors in understanding burnout among health professionals (Glasberg 2007; Sporrong 2007).

It is well documented that patient suicide is an important stressor in psychiatric practice (Collins 2003; Fothergill, Edwards, and Burnard 2004). Since the etiology of such deaths in general is more difficult to establish than that of deaths in somatic medicine, these deaths can end up in a moral grey zone where they are suspected to be the consequence of some sort of therapeutic failure because of the practitioner's lack of insight. In terms of the health worker, this can activate strong emotions of feeling responsible, guilty and shameful, and opens up the possibility of evasive coping mechanisms where the moral implications of the situation are not adequately addressed.

My preliminary thesis is that a clarification of the concepts of responsibility, guilt, and shame as they relate to a specific event can contribute to and facilitate better coping mechanisms in relation to oneself, colleagues – and in the long run – the bereaved. There is clearly no opportunity for an elaborate discussion in the context of this paper[1]. Rather, I will outline a possible clarification in light of the narrative above.

First, I will try to give a contextual clarification of the concepts of responsibility, risk, and guilt. Second, I will try to clarify self-conscious emotions (such as shame and guilt) as potential responses to responsibility, risk, and guilt. Third, I will attempt to suggest certain strategic points in order to facilitate health care workers' improved management of and coping with these events.

Moral responsibility

Empirical studies show that moral responsibility is a key philosophical term in order to understand both clinical practice in general and dealing with adverse events in particular.[2] But how can moral responsibility be

---

1   This article is based on depth-interviews with 25 Norwegian health care workers (doctors, nurses, and psychologists) who have been in situations where for various reasons clinical treatment has gone terribly wrong. (I will publish this extensive material in a forthcoming book.)

2   In his doctoral thesis, Holm (1997, p. 125 ff.) uses the concept of protective responsibility as a core category in order to explain the ethical reasoning of health care professionals. On the basis of a fairly extensive body of empirical material, he further qualifies the concept as, e.g., the responsibility to protect from harm. In my own doctoral work (2009, p. 151, 198) involving in-depth interviews with 23

understood in this context? The concept of responsibility touches upon central discussions within philosophy, psychology, and jurisprudence.[3] Vincent (2011) argues for the need for a whole taxonomy of responsibility perspectives if we want to address the complexity of the concept. Poel (Poel 2011), who identifies nine different perspectives on responsibility, places them on a time-axis as backward and forward looking responsibility. This notion of forward- and backward looking responsibility, has also been used as an analytical tool in empirical studies (J. Fahlquist 2006; Fahlquist 2009; J. N. Fahlquist 2006). To further complicate the picture, in a professional setting such as health care, one can also distinguish between levels of responsibility connected to role, function, system, and so forth.

In this context, however, the focus will be on the professional responsibility the clinician has for his/her patient. Even though the moral complexity of such a relationship calls for a whole array of philosophical perspectives in order to give a thorough analysis, I will limit myself to weave together a forward looking perspective on responsibility, defined as our status as moral subjects in the world, with a backward looking perspective as our willingness to answer as moral subjects when things go wrong.

The word responsible comes from the Latin word *respondeo*, which means to answer (Lucas 1993, p. 5). Thus, acknowledging oneself as being morally responsible can be understood as a readiness and willingness to account for the actions and attitudes that define us as moral subjects in the world. Schoeman captures this point very clearly:

> It matters to us whether we are responsible because being responsible suggests our potential – that we are engaged as active and self-aware beings with perspectives on what we do and with a contributing and creative role to play in what we become. To see ourselves as not responsible is to confront our limits – to regard our lives as passively reflecting personality factors beyond

---

    hospital doctors, I tried to show how loyalty to their patient overrode nearly all other professional loyalties they might have had, including loyalty to colleagues. This loyalty seemed to be grounded in a strong sense of professional responsibility toward the patient, which in turn left many of them extremely vulnerable when adverse events happened.

3   For an introduction, see e.g. J.R. Lucas 1993, P. Cane 2002 as well as Widerker and McKenna 2006, Schoeman 1987b, Smiley 1992a, Sabini and Silver 1998 and Walker 2003, p. 27; 2006.

our capacity to effectively restructure, however good our reasons for doing so may be, and with at most an attenuated sense of self – leaving us in a diminished position in the great chain of being (Schoeman, 1987a).

Moral responsibility therefore defines us prior to any possible action that can be judged as blameworthy or not. In other words, being morally responsible for causing harm to others is a consequence of the fact that we are considered as persons capable of being morally responsible for causing harm. Lucas (Lucas 1993, p. 5.) defines responsibility as an answer to the question: "Why did you act/not act as you did?" Stated differently, being responsible is when you acknowledge your contributing role by giving reasons for your actions. This understanding needs to be further specified: First, it seems to imply a recognition of the fact that anyone has – in a given situation – the right to make such a demand.[4] Second, it implies a recognition of the fact that you are the correct recipient of that demand. Third, it implies a willingness to respond to the demand made on you.

In the narrative above, John can recognize that Fred's parents make a moral demand for an explanation of what has happened. As Fred's psychiatrist, John can also recognize that he is the correct recipient of such a demand; however, this does not necessarily mean that he is willing to answer, to give an open and thorough account of what has happened prior to the tragic event. Feelings such as shame, a sense of failure, fear of litigation, and so on, can make him withdraw and not accept the full responsibility for what has happened. When not answering to the demand of the bereaved, John not only violates their moral demand for an explanation but also undermines himself and the fact that he is a morally responsible person. Conversely, he can acknowledge that he is the correct recipient, meet with Fred's parents and respond to their questions. What he is most likely to experience is that the need of the bereaved is largely concerned with trying to understand what happened to their son and why, and to share their grief with John. Indeed, the "blame game" is more likely to start if he evades his responsibility.

---

4 In a Levinasian tradition the Other will always have a demand on me. Proximity is only possible as responsibility in the sense that being-with is inseparable from being-for. For further positioning of this fundamental moral point of view, see e.g., Vetlesen 1997.

Moral guilt

At the same time, accepting responsibility does not imply that you are blameworthy.[5] Establishing blameworthiness or responsibility for guilt seems in the philosophical discussion to imply meeting certain criteria such as freedom of will, intentionality, sufficient information, and absence of coercion. A classic example is found in Feinberg's definition: "Guilt consists in the intentional transgression of a prohibition, a violation of a specific taboo, boundary, or legal code, by a definite voluntary act" (Feinberg 1970, p. 231).

The discussions of definitions and applications of these criteria are extensive within moral philosophy and cannot be taken up at the present time. I will therefore only point to a few relevant factors in this context. M. Smiley (1992b) shows how these discussions of formal criteria are ill-fitted to meet the challenges of complicated practice. In real life, such as in the narrative above, it is nearly impossible to establish guilt or blame because the formal criteria are seldom fully met; on the contrary, they are only met to a certain degree. Let me give an example. Was there any element of coercion when John decided it was time for Fred to move back to his apartment? If so, should we postpone the question of who is to blame? On the one hand, there was undoubtedly an element of coercion. It was Friday, and John desperately needed a couple of vacant beds that the ward staff could make ready for weekend admissions. On the other hand, it was up to John's clinical judgment as a psychiatrist to decide what action should be taken, and he could have let Fred stay if he thought that would be best. Smiley's argument is that formal theoretical discussions of different criteria fall short when applied to the complexity of empirical practice; instead, she proposes the pragmatic principle of fairness, which tries to take into account as many relevant contextual factors as possible. In John's case, there was an element of coercion due to the fact that they needed vacant beds for weekend admissions. But there is also the structural setting within which he has to use his good clinical judgement and exercise professional responsibility. It is also the nature of clinical judgement that it operates within an area where access to information very often is insufficient and the etiology unclear. However, this

---

5   In a more thorough analysis, there are important distinctions to be made between the moral concepts of guilt and similar concepts, e.g., blame, regret regarding the matter of intentionality. (These will be omitted in this short article). For a recent contribution to the discussion, see Katchadourian 2010.

lack of information cannot postpone John's professional responsibility, as he has to make clinical decisions within the framework of the actual context. This uncertainty or lack of control introduces the concept of moral luck.[6] In other words, establishing blame or guilt requires careful contextual analysis of the relevant factors known at the time. For instance, a retrospective evaluation of John's clinical judgement cannot be based on the fact that Fred later chose to commit suicide, because this tragic ending of Fred's life was unknown to John when Fred's decision was made. Such an evaluation also has to take into account the fact that the connection between John's planned discharge of Fred and the latter's subsequent suicide can be merely coincidental and due to factors beyond John's control (Fredriksen 2005). It seems obvious that any retrospective evaluation should keep these distinctions clearly in mind. However, in my experience as empirical researcher in this field, it is not always so. Evaluations both from colleagues and health authorities sometimes lack sufficient conceptual clarity, thus muddling distinctions between responsibility and guilt, and making emotional coping more difficult.

Being at risk

However, the question of whether or not John is blameworthy does not alter his responsibility – nor do factors that are outside of John's control. The framework of his professional practice is fraught with uncertainty, structural pressure and insufficient knowledge. This is the nature of the game for a psychiatric resident in an understaffed ward, and it is within these boundaries he is responsible for responding to the moral demand of Fred's parents. Walker describes the moral position of John very clearly:

> The fact is our perfectly predictable entanglement in a causally complex world, with imperfectly predictable results. Part of the normal and required self-understanding of human agents is a grasp of that fact, of the loose and chancy fit between undertakings and impacts, and between where we'd choose to find ourselves and where we actually do. This fact requires us to understand and respond to our actual situation of being at moral risk,

---

6   For further reading, see e.g., Athanassoulis 2010; Dickenson 2003; Nagel 1991; Williams 1981.

> i.e., of being subject to assessment both for results of what we have (uncontroversially) done and for our actions under circumstances morally fraught, where these results and circumstances are determined in important part by luck. The truth of moral luck, which the rational, responsive moral agent is expected to grasp, is that responsibilities outrun control, although not in one single or simple way (Walker 1993, p. 26).

To sum up, the attribution of blame in the narrative of John is contextually complex and hinges on many factors. However, the idea of responsibility concerns more than the questions of blame and control. Being responsible in a complex and unpredictable world is what Walker calls "impure agency," meaning to be able to keep a coherent and responsible moral posture even when our actions seem to have negative and unforeseen consequences. The alternative to such moral lucidity and steadfastness is often avoidance and denial (Walker 2003, p. 27).

Emotions of shame

Shame can make John evade his responsibility; it is a difficult emotion to handle because it involves a negative devaluation not of our action but of ourselves (i.e., who I am) (Katchadourian 2010, p. 24; Tangney & Dearing 2002, p. 24)[7]. For example, facing Fred's parents in a responsible way is difficult for John because it feels like a display of his failure as a person. The choice of pursuing an evasive strategy is often the result of feelings of shame because devaluation of the global self is too heavy a load (Tangney & Dearing 2002, p. 105). John can withdraw and hide as best as he can from facing both the parents and his colleagues, thus contributing negatively not only to the pain of the bereaved by not taking on responsibility but also by making his own coping difficult. Another evasive manoeuvre is displaying anger as a defensive retaliating reaction where scapegoating is used to shift the burden of blame (Doug-

---

7   The discussion of the concept of shame is extensive within several disciplines. For further discussions, see e.g., Pattison (2000, p. 21), Nussbaum (2004, p. 172), and Deonna et al. 2011. In this paper I stress shame as a self-conscious emotion underscoring the possible ethical consequences of its predominant evasive character in comparison to guilt-feeling, even though there are obvious and important distinctions to be made between e.g., pathological (chronic) shame and shame as a more acute and reactive emotional response to a given situation.

las 1995). In order to manage his shame, John can point to the psychiatric nurse or other colleagues who have not informed him properly of the anxiety Fred has displayed during the previous nights: "It is impossible for me to make good clinical judgments when others do not do their work properly!" Thus, he makes himself morally responsible for a situation where he definitively is to blame by subverting to scapegoating mechanisms and vertical violence. The paradox is that evading responsibility because you feel a sense of shame often strengthens the shameful emotion you are trying to evade: "I am not only a terrible psychiatrist, I cannot even take responsibility for my own actions."

Thus the moral problem of shame is that it seems to be evasive in nature to the extent that when adverse events happen and patients or those bereaved experience loss (or even at times feel violated by the health care professional), shame contributes negatively to all parties involved. The emotion of shame seems to be a poor tool for bridging the gap between the health care worker and the patients or the bereaved.

Emotions of guilt

Contrary to the above-mentioned feelings of shame, emotions of guilt can make John take on responsibility more easily. As a self-conscious emotion, guilt involves a more articulated condemnation of a specific behaviour or action (i.e., what I did) (Katchadourian 2010, p. 24 pp.; Tangney & Dearing 2002, p. 24). In other words, guilt can be understood as an other-oriented emotion that focuses on our harmful action or behaviour and thus brings the violated into focus. Therefore, in this respect the emotion of guilt is a better tool for bridging the gap between ourselves and the one towards whom we feel guilt. Thus, it is, ethically speaking, a more productive feeling than shame. In John's case, the emotion of guilt connects him to the moral fact that he might be to blame for the actions that led to the death of his patient, and might also lead him to take responsibility for it by acknowledging the need for reconciliatory action in relation to the bereaved.

However, if the emotion of guilt is to play a bridging role in ethics, it needs calibration. The emotion of guilt needs to be connected to the specific time and place in history where the event took place, and it needs to be calibrated to the event itself. John's guilt can be so all-encompassing and all-consuming that it renders him unable to respond in a responsible manner. Such an excessive feeling of guilt is not only incapacitating for John, it also leaves the bereaved parents in a situation where, e.g., rightful attribution of blame, anger, and subsequent reconciliation are made difficult. Walker's (2003, p. 27) call for moral lucidity (that is, keeping a coherent and responsible moral posture) seems to hinge on the calibration of guilt. In this respect both excessive guilt – or lack thereof – can be pathological and thus lose its function as ethical bridging (Katchadourian 2010, p. 112 ff).

Professional community

It is my experience that, for some health care professionals, excessive feelings of guilt are predominant and require careful and nuanced analysis with regard to the question of calibration. However, in this context I will focus on three aspects related to the professional community:

First, calibration of guilt is seldom trustworthy as an individual exercise. It is not something John should do alone. Instead, he needs a good colleague who can sit down with him and go through a patient's medical journal and evaluate the clinical decisions that John made. Thus, calibration entails connecting the emotion of guilt to the facts and clinical evaluation of these in the professional community. John's clinical judgment has become clouded, and he needs to get his clear vision back. This recovery matters not only to himself but also to the bereaved and John's future patients, who need him to be brave, sound, and responsible. The professional community possesses the resources to help John with a critical evaluation of his actions. Questions of appropriate sanctions decided between colleagues (or by health authorities or in a court of law) need to be clinically as well as ethically informed. The question, however, is whether the professional community has sufficient focus on the necessity of making clear distinctions between concepts such as responsibility, guilt, and emotions of guilt and shame in situations such as these.

Second, the burden of maintaining a coherent and moral posture seems to be correlated to several factors. Let me focus on two of them. It is well documented that personality factors are important in deciding whether we respond with either shame or guilt (Tangney & Dearing 2002; Jessica L. Tracy, Robins, & Tangney 2007). In other words, these emotions are not entirely context-specific, but are different emotional responses in a given situation (Tangney & Dearing 2002: 20 ff.). Thus, there seems to be little empirical evidence for categorizing events in themselves as either shame-inducing or guilt-inducing, even though, ethically speaking, they imply blameworthy action or behaviour (Keltner 1996; Tangney & Dearing 2002, p. 17; J. L. Tracy & Robins 2006). Thus, if calibrated emotions of guilt are more ethically valuable than those of shame, and personality factors seem to be important in deciding how we respond emotionally, it is crucial that the professional community facilitates guilt-inducing responses and not shame-inducing ones. If John's colleagues remain silent and avoid talking about what has happened, the chance of John responding with shame is increased.

Third, the gravity of the situation seems to be correlated to the burden of maintaining a coherent and moral posture (Gerrity, Earp, DeVellis, and Light 1992). Even though the normative judgment in itself would not necessarily take into consideration the burden of taking on responsibility for blame, clinical practice should. When we assert ethically normative claims about what ought to be done in a specific situation, we should allow this normative judgement to be informed by a sociological analysis of whether it is actually possible. As far as I can see, this is the underlying premise of Smiley's (1992b) principle of fairness. With regard to John, the burden of responsibility, moral lucidity, and steadfastness (Walker 2003, p. 27) can be too heavy to carry alone. For instance, the bereaved parents may go to the media, or John's colleagues might turn their backs on him, fearing their own involvement and discredit. John might be made a scapegoat for both the grieving parents and the administration of an understaffed ward. What John needs is a supportive professional community. Thus, it makes good sense to ground a forward-looking moral responsibility within the professional community to facilitate sound ethical responses and coping mechanisms when things go wrong.

Concluding remarks

I have attempted to demonstrate that factors of uncertainty inherent in clinical practice create unclear demarcations between concepts such as responsibility and guilt. A clarification of these concepts seems necessary in order to both distinguish between them in a clinical context and correlate possible guilt to the clinical facts in a given situation. Coping with the events of a possible clinical error is difficult for health care personnel. Calibration of emotional responses seems to be important in order to maintain moral responsibility and steadfastness in such situations. The professional community plays a key role in this calibration, and it seems appropriate to make both the handling and coping with these events a forward-looking responsibility for the professional community.

References

Athanassoulis, N. 2010. *Morality, Moral Luck and Responsibility: Fortune's Web*. Palgrave: Macmillan.

Berlinger, N. 2005. *After Harm Medical Error and the Ethics of Forgiveness*. Baltimore: Johns Hopkins University Press.

Cane, P. 2002. *Responsibility in Law and Morality*. Oxford: Hart.

Collins, J. M. 2003. Impact of patient suicide on clinicians. *Journal of the American Psychiatric Nurses Association* 9:159-62. doi: 10.1016/s1078-3903(03)00221-0

Deonna, J. A., R. Rodogno, and F. Teroni. 2011. *In Defense of Shame: The Faces of an Emotion*. Oxford & New York: Oxford University Press.

Dickenson, D. 2003. *Risk and Luck in Medical Ethics*. Cambridge: Polity.

Douglas, T. 1995. *Scapegoats : Transferring Blame*. London: Routledge.

Fahlquist, J. 2006. Responsibility ascriptions and public health problems. In *Journal of Public Health* 14: 15-19. [?doi: 10.1007/s10389-005-0004-6.?]

_____. 2009. Moral responsibility for environmental problems: Individual or institutional? *Journal of Agricultural and Environmental Ethics* 22:109-24. [?doi: 10.1007/s10806-008-9134-5.?]

_____. 2006. Responsibility ascriptions and Vision Zero. *Accident Analysis & Prevention* 38: 1113-18. [?doi: 10.1016/j.aap.2006.04.020.?]

Feinberg, J. 1970. *Doing & Deserving : Essays in the Theory of Responsibility*. Princeton: Princeton University Press.

Fothergill, A., D. Edwards, and P. Burnard. 2004. Stress, burnout, coping and stress management in psychiatrists: Findings from a systematic review. *International Journal of Social Psychiatry* 50: 54-65. [?doi: 10.1177/0020764004040953.]

Fredriksen, S. 2005. *Bad luck and the tragedy of modern medicine*. Oslo: Faculty of Medicine Unipub.

Gerrity, M.S., J. A. L. Earp, R. F. DeVellis, and D.W. Light. 1992. Uncertainty and professional work: Perceptions of physicians in clinical practice. *American Journal of Sociology* 97: 1022-51.

Glasberg, A-L. 2007. *Stress of Conscience and Burnout in Health Care: The Danger of Deadening One's Conscience*. Ume: Ume Universitet.

Gorovitz, S., and A. MacIntyre. 1975. Toward a theory of medical fallibility. *The Hastings Center Report* 5: 13-23.

Hilfiker, D. 1997. *Healing the Wounds*. 2nd ed. New York: Pantheon Books.

Holm, S. 1997, *Ethical Problems in Clinical Practice : The Ethical Reasoning of Health Care Professionals*. Manchester: University Press.

Katchadourian, H. A. 2010. *Guilt : The Bite of Conscience*. Stanford, CA: Stanford General Books.

Keltner, D. 1996. Evidence for the distinctness of embarrassment, shame, and guilt: A study of recalled antecedents and facial expressions of emotion. *Cognition & Emotion* 10: 155-72.

Lucas, J. R. 1993. *Responsibility*. Oxford: Clarendon Press.

Mesel, T. 2009. *Legers profesjonsetikk : refleksjon og mestring i en sykehuskultur*. Kristiansand: Hyskoleforlaget.

Nagel, T. 1991. *Mortal questions*. Cambridge: Cambridge University Press.

Nussbaum, M. C. 2004. *Hiding from Humanity*. Princeton: Princeton University Press.

Pattison, S. 2000. *Shame. Theory, Therapy, Theology.* Oxford: Oxford University Press.

Poel, Ibo van de. 2011. "The Relation Between Forward-Looking and Backward-Looking Responsibility". In Vincent, N. A., van de Poel, I & Hoven, J. (eds.), *Moral Responsibility. Beyond free will and determinism* (Vol. 27, pp. 37-52): Springer Netherlands.

Rosenthal, M. M. 1995. *The Incompetent Doctor: Behind Closed Doors*. Buckingham: Open University Press.

Rørtveit, G., and R. Strand. 2001. "Risk , uncertainty and ignorance in medicine" . *Tidsskrift for den norske legeforening,* 121: 1382.

Sabini, J., & Silver, M., eds. 1998, *Emotion, character and responsibliity*. Oxford: Oxford University Press.

Schoeman, F. 1987a. Introduction. *Responsibility, Character and the Emotions,* Cambridge: Cambridge University Press.

_____. 1987b. *Responsibility, Character, and the Emotions: New Essays in Moral Psychology*. Cambridge: Cambridge University Press.

Smiley, M. 1992a. *Moral Responsibilities and the Boundaries of Community*. Chicago: The University of Chicago Press.

_____. 1992b. *Moral Responsibility and the Boundaries of Community: Power and Accountability from a Pragmatic Point of View*. Chicago: University of Chicago Press.

Sporrong, S. K. 2007. *Ethical Competence and Moral Distress in the Health Care Sector*. Uppsala: Uppsala Universitet.

Strand, R., G. Rørtveit, Y. S. Hannestad, and E. Schei. 2010. Risk, uncertainty and indeterminacy in clinical decisions. *Primary Care: Clinics in Office Practice,* 12: 232-33.

Tangney, J. P., and R.L. Dearing. 2002. *Shame and Guilt.* New York: Guildford.

Tracy, J. L., and R.W. Robins. 2006. Appraisal antecedents of shame and guilt: support for a theoretical model. *Pers. Soc. Psychol Bull.,* 32: 1339-51. doi: 32/10/1339 [pii]10.1177/0146167206290212.

Tracy, J. L., R.W.Robins, and J.P. Tangney. 2007. *The Self-conscious Emotions: Theory and Research.* New York: Guilford Press.

Vetlesen, A.J. 1997. Introducing an ethics of proximity. In *Closeness. An ethics,* ed. H. Jodalen and A.J. Vetlesen, 1-19. Oslo: Universitetsforlaget.

Vincent, N. A. 2011. A structured taxonomy of responsibility concepts. In *Library of Ethics and Applied Philosophy* 27: 15-36.

Walker, M.U. 1993. The virtues of impure agency. In *Moral Luck,* ed. D. Satman [pages?]. New York: New York University Press.

_____. 2003. *Moral Contexts.* Lanham, MD: Rowman & Littlefield.

_____. 2006. *Moral Repair: Reconstructing Moral Relations after Wrongdoing.* Cambridge: Cambridge University Press.

Widerker, D. 2006. *Moral Responsibility and Alternative Possibilites.* Burlington: Ashgate.

Williams, B. 1981. *Moral Luck: Philosophical Papers 1973-1980.* Cambridge: Cambridge University Press.

Hannes Nykänen

Morals
An instance of political correctness?

My aim in this paper is to show some aspects of the way I think moral difficulties and violations are repressions. More specifically, they are repressions of what I take to be the fundamental moral relationship, the I-you relationship. Our difficulties with the I-you relationship urge us to create a kind of secondary morality that I call collective morality or, depending on the context, collective pressure, collective norms, or simply collectivity. The I-you relationship is founded in conscience, which is a fundamental engagement between human beings. But instead of engagement one should perhaps speak about sympathy or, better yet, love.

I do not have space enough to discuss the concept – if it is a concept – of conscience to make it clear. I have done so elsewhere; see Nykänen 2002, 2005 and forthcoming work. Instead, I will discuss some of the ways conscience is repressed or, in other words, collectivised. What is repressed and unconscious is, on Freudian terms, taken to be an elusive psychic material that reveals its existence only on particular occasions (dreams, slips of the tongue, free association) and only to experts in the field. What I say is an implicit critique of this conception (even if I also agree with much that Freud says). Actually, one of the awkward aspects of the unconscious is that it is fully "visible." Of course, it is not visible in the same way as that which is not unconscious. Therefore, we need to talk about the different ways in which things show themselves and the different connections that they have to what we call the inner. We might also remind ourselves of the fact that psychic disorders involve that one sees the world in a twisted sense. What is fully visible becomes distorted because the way it actually is, is intolerable.

If the unconscious is fully visible, then this means that repression is not a process where something is hidden, but a process where a transformation takes place. A disturbing meaning is avoided by transforming it to one that appears to be more tolerable; this is similar to the way in which throwing oneself into a psychic disorder appears to be more tolerable than dealing with the meaning that disturbs. This mechanism can function as long as its avoiding function is not acknowledged. Obviously we have to take a look at how this transformation takes place. This, then, is the subject of this article.

Since the distorting point of view is, as I will show, collective, it is achieved by a form of agreement. This agreement itself must also have an essential repressed aspect to it, an aspect that cannot be discussed. This unspeakable something determines the common and sayable meanings. Still, what represses must have some connection to what is repressed. The common meaning must be connected to the repressed meaning, replace it, and by this, secretly reject it.

I am speaking about an implicit and at once repressed and repressing agreement. Such an agreement involves that the bonds between the persons agreeing are unconscious and repressed/repressing. This repressed unity encompasses everyone who shares the agreement. I call this kind of unity "collective." In other words, "collectivity" does not refer simply to "togetherness of people" but to a fatally pervasive mode of it, where the togetherness is constituted by individual self-understandings that are collective in the sense I discuss here. For a collective to have the power of transforming understanding, the collective and unconscious agreement must have authority in and of itself. Can we find evidence of this?

Consider the fact that a completely crazy activity may acquire a certain degree of plausibility simply if many persons are involved in it. Conversely, something that is perfectly sensible may appear completely crazy because only one person stands for it; this is so even if it would obviously be the morally right thing to do (defending the strange guy whom everyone accuses of being a pedophile simply because of his strangeness). If a group of persons have agreed to do something, then it is taken to be sensible in the collective understanding. However, "collectivity" is not a collection of ideas and activities taken to be sensible on the grounds of some general criteria. Rather, it is a tacit acknowledgement that some kind of criteriality determines what is taken to be intelligible. Terrorists are condemned but at the same time, in a way, acknowledged in and through this condemnation while the single person talking about, say, the end of the world on the corner is not "even" condemned but simply ignored as being insane. I do not mean to imply that a single person could not be completely enthralled by collectivity. Indeed, the problem of collectivity is precisely a concern for the individual. My aim was to introduce the topic by pointing to one aspect of collectivity, namely the authority of sheer numbers and the implicit agreement it creates.

The important thing about agreement is not its explicit aspect but the repressed one. The repressed agreement gives opinions the weight of being good, questionable, or reprehensible, and gives their adherents the dignity of being allies or enemies. These determinations involve a kind of reasoning that is essential in that it represses the I-you perspective.

I will begin my elucidation of collectivity by trying to show how it represses the I-you relationship. After that I will broaden the topic and discuss some of the different forms of collectivisation.

Moral reasoning

Suppose I have let down my friend in the most terrible way. Suppose, further, that I do not want to acknowledge this. How do I deal with the problem? I cannot simply ignore it. (I cannot discuss this point any further, but it is not possible to simply rid oneself of one's conscience without causing further consequences.) I will try to show how my difficulty with the other – the "you" – appears as different ways of diminishing my sense of being an I and of the other being a you. Instead, I depersonalise myself and the other. Doing this involves numerous collectivising tendencies. "Depersonalisation" in my sense is not a psychological term or a diagnosis, but a moral concept that is an aspect of the way the primary moral relationship between "I" and "you" is transformed into collective morality, the latter being a repression of the former.

In my difficulties with you, isn't it important that I try to find good or acceptable reasons for my acting? ("I mean, no one can expect me to…") The important thing to notice is the kind of work moral reasoning performs here (though there is no room to go more deeply into this concept). When I reason along these lines, I am presupposing that the problem I am facing can be clarified and perhaps solved by intellectually analysing and comparing different moral concepts that belong to "our" moral language.

In making these moves I affirm the idea that morality consists of shared values and norms that we affirm in different ways and to different degrees. This does not mean that collective moral language would be a collection of norms and values. Rather, the essence of this language has its source in that repressed and repressing spirit where the nature of moral understanding is, without question, assumed to consist of norms, values, judgements, blame, praise, moral reasoning, etc. Whatever agreements and disagreements we have about moral behaviour, there is the secret agreement that what is moral shows itself in terms of norms, values, judgements, etc. The important thing is not what is or should be the outcome of moral reasoning, but the idea that moral issues are assessed by way of moral reasoning and the concepts that go with it. Collective understanding is a repression not because it would safeguard the subject against moral accusation, but because it transforms our conscientious difficulties with each other into moral accusations or, to put it differently, it transforms bad conscience into guilt. Guilt and moral reasoning concerning when and to what degree anyone is guilty of something appears to be more manageable than hearkening to one's conscience. It appears to the same extent as when one in the collective understanding appears less as an I and the other appears less as a you.

If one wants to measure the possibilities of moral reasoning, then moral philosophy and political action are good places to start. When one explores these fields, one gets more than depressed about what has been taken to be "morally sensible" to say and do. The only "politically realistic" thing to do, according to the moral values of the West, seems to be to continue abusing developing countries. Philosophers on their part, besides claiming that there might be good reasons for killing innocent people, seem to think that the question of whether other persons have a mind at all must be seen as a serious philosophical question. This being the case, entering the realm of classical moral reasoning does not seem to be very challenging for anyone. The problem is, of course, not that philosophers have been intellectually incompetent. The problem is that if you stay within the discourse of collectivity, moral problems will inevitably appear in the way I've described above.

Hannes Nykänen

Moral truth and splitting the mind

Moral reasoning in its classical sense is, like any kind of reasoning, a public affair. The validity and relevance of arguments and counterarguments must be assessed according to commonly accepted norms and procedures. Within this kind of reasoning, the particular person whom one has wronged vanishes together with one's sense of being an I. The issue is, rather, expressed in general, and so impersonal, terms: "If someone does such and such a thing to someone else, is that morally acceptable?" Here the other, the you, has become anyone, your relationship to her has become a "type of action"; your conscience grinds at you about a matter of common moral assessment and judgement. Once the question has been framed in this generalising mode one can, "quite legitimately," refer to all so-called uncertainties in moral reasoning, including relativism (and, implicitly, even subjectivism: "No one can know how I feel about this."). At issue is the validity of a moral statement; not what I have done to a particular person, a you. This move involves both transformation and avoidance, i.e., repression.

The idea that moral reasoning is the only way "we" can assess moral conflicts is part of the repression. It is within this same discourse that the existence of other minds has been seriously questioned and the rightfulness of occasionally killing innocent people seriously suggested. How many philosophers would be prepared to say these things in a real situation to an innocent person who has, by reference to some "good reason," been chosen to be killed? And what would you think of philosophers who – referring to their arguments – would maintain that she must be killed? In case you think it would revolt you, you see how much is repressed in the discourse of moral reasoning. On its own terms, moral reasoning is taken to be quite legitimate; one might even argue for the option of killing innocent people. (When atrocities are actually carried out, the meanness of the cruel thoughts – "mean" by the way originates from the Old English *gemæne* which means common and public – has a considerably higher pitch than in the seminar room. This is, "of course," quite normal. I will return to the concept of normalcy later.)

We have, on the one hand, a tendency to make it appear as if moral issues were about knowing what is right and wrong. This is the objectifying tendency of collectivisation. In "knowing," that which is known can be assessed in general terms. On the other hand, there is a tendency

Morals

to make it seem as if the "deepest" moral responses are unknowable and emotional. This is the subjectifying tendency of collectivisation.

Philosophers, being more obsessed with rationality than the general population, tend to choose between these two tendencies (sometimes, as with Kant, after many complications), but in ordinary life they are often found in combination. The tendencies are internally connected and they both repress moral understanding, not by positing moral truth as nonexistent or hard to find, but by representing moral understanding in terms of a truth to be found. Both the claim "there are no moral truths" and the claim "there are moral truths" are articulated in terms of knowledge, and it is this fact that is central to the repressive tendency of collectivity. (The objectifying and subjectifying tendencies are obviously connected to the "problem of other minds," but I cannot elaborate on it here.)

Addressing the other

Truths are established and questioned in public discourse. Whatever else we want to say about truth, we assess it within common and shared standards of reasoning. We may disagree about much, but this disagreement must itself be expressed within common standards of reasoning. This means that if an issue is couched in terms of common standards, then it is by the same token thought of in terms of those standards. Is not saying this stupid? Perhaps, but then consider the fact that when the very being of the other is couched in these common terms, the question arises of whether the other has a mind at all. In other words, when we think in terms of common standards, it is both reasonable and respectable to question whether there are other minds. And if this is a serious question, how could morals even be considered?

I am speaking as if there were an alternative to collective language. There is. For we do address each other in the sense of an I to a you. It is not even possible to do this in terms of collective discourse for it is a repression of the I-you relationship. When you greet a friend and say, for instance, "Hello Sigmund! How are you?" etc., you are using language in common ways, but the way you address Sigmund cannot be accounted for by analysing the meaning of the words. It is, rather, your addressing Sigmund that gives sense to the words. One could say that the relationship between you and Sigmund is unmediated. No turn of words, no logic and no convention can capture the openness between you. To the extent that you really would wonder whether he has a mind or whether he can feel pain, you would not be addressing him; you would not stand in this openness. Instead, you would ask whether certain kinds of claims about him are valid or not.

(It is in this kind of discussions that Wittgenstein encourages the philosopher to ask herself whether she really responds to a particular person – to a you – in the way assumed by the philosophical notions she uses (Wittgenstein 1988, §420, and 1993, pp. 381, 383.)

I am not making psychological observations about attending to others but about a fundamental feature of the way we understand each other. The openness between I and you precedes concepts such as wondering, knowing, establishing, doubting, claiming, etc. When it comes to being open with the other, these words have no epistemological role to play. You can doubt, claim, and know things about the other only within this openness. In a sense then also the difficulty with the other, with openness, occurs within openness. When the openness with the other becomes difficult, you can reject the other by reference to some doubts, but now "doubting" has a moral meaning. At stake is not to doubt whether the other has a mind or whether there are moral truths, but your rejection of the other. But to withdraw from the openness with the other (which of course can never be fully achieved) means that you begin to use those collectivising strategies that I discuss here. Taking those strategies at face value means that you ignore, in the sense of repressing, the fact that they announce themselves as ways of withdrawing from the openness with the other. (Someone might wonder whether listening to one's conscience means that one is open to all sorts of violent intrusion from others. But turning down such intrusions is not about rejecting openness but rather about rejecting closedness in the form of manipulation and psychic violence. In fact it is a matter of conscience not to yield to such things.)

You could talk for hours with Sigmund without ever using collective discourse. During the whole discussion you would just be listening to what he says and he would just be listening to what you say. If collective discourse enters into the discussion, it could be, for instance, a statement that he was intruding on your privacy. In that case, you might say with moral indignation, "Please show some respect!" You want him to keep his distance and you do this by referring to common ideas about respect. At this point something happens. You say something that makes it impossible for Sigmund to merely listen to you. This is

Morals

because in an important sense it is no longer you talking. You place before him a perspective where he is invited to view himself and his acting against the backdrop of the general idea of conduct. This action falls just the other side of your pushing him further away from yourself, of your being closed to him.

If your conflict deepens, new aspects of collectivity enter the picture. Let us assume that what started as a friendly, open discussion ends up in bitter hatred. What is it that takes place in this process of depersonalisation? I will now list and shortly discuss some mechanisms of depersonalisation.

Forms of repression

1. First, one creates distance from the other by referring to common ideas about respect and integrity. Distance is an essential feature of collectivity and, as Kant noted, distance in the form of respect opposes love (Kant 2000, p. 215).
2. Objectifying the other: this happens not by treating the other as a thing (that is not even possible), but as an object of gaze. In collective terms "moral perspective" means deliberating, assessing, judging, blaming, acquitting, etc. Human beings are viewed, and view themselves, from a perspective where they are standing before a gaze. Depending on how they are judged (and judge themselves), human beings appear one way or another. Moral understanding is seen here as analogous to a court of law (Kant 2000, p. 189). The you has become appearance in the face of collectivity. This is the transformation of the you. Even if the I and the you are inseparable and even if all forms of repression involve a transformation of this inseparable I-you relationship, there are still particularly striking analogies between the collective perspective and the I-you perspective. One could in this connection point to the way Kant associates "moral friendship" with the claim that the "human being is a being meant for society" and also point to Kant's observation that the human being "feels strongly the need to *reveal* himself to others" (2000, pp. 215-16.) In my view, Kant has here, in a very compact and yet confused way, brought together the fact that collective morality is a repression of the I-you relationship. Moral friendship (which involves love) is associated with the al-

legedly social nature of man while the urge to reveal oneself (in my account, the "standing before a gaze") is discussed as if it were the same as openness.

3. You transform yourself into an anonymous, epistemological entity: "*One* cannot know…". The I is transformed into an anonymous "one" of a collective. This is the transformation of the I. (cf. Heidegger's "they" or *das Man*, 1992, § 27.). In rational terms this "one," in the sense of "no one in particular," is understood as the pronoun of logical validity. But how could "no one in particular" have a conscience?

4. A certain aspect of conscience is transformed into a discourse of knowledge, e.g., when it is said that no one knows what is right and wrong; that there are some self-evident valid moral truths; that there are no moral truths, etc. Moral awareness, conscience, is transformed into claims about moral knowledge. (You might say that "original sin" consists in making morals appear to be a discourse of knowledge.)

5. Another aspect of conscience is transformed into guilt. Placed into the limelight of collectivity, everyone appears guilty, for this is discourse where one can question whether the other even has a mind. Nothing about you is as such beyond questioning. The power of collective pressure to question everything means that, insofar as you partake in collectivity, you will feel guilt. Being placed into the limelight of collectivity is part of the grammar of the collective perspective. Stated differently: the "court of law" nature of collective morals implies guilt, as it were, grammatically. This is why the apparently tautological formula "innocent until proven guilty" has a point. It is like a collective, repressed reminder that we should not confuse the sense in which we all are, collectively speaking, guilty in the sense in which a person can be guilty of a particular violation. Collectivity can acquit a person of particular charges of guilt but not of the general feeling of guilt. (Heidegger and Freud saw some aspects of this general guilt but were, in the main, confused about it.)

6. Emphasising specificity of content and formality. This point is difficult to articulate.
   a Collectivity is implicitly and explicitly constituted by specific norms, values, traditions, etc. However, the first step to collectivity is specification as such. Specification represses openness sim-

ply by way of being specifying. Any borderline that can be drawn between me and the threatening other can function as a repressive defence. We notice repressive content when it appals us, but often we are much less appalled than we would like to think. For more on this, see Žižek's discussion on ideology (2008).

    b Formality in human relationships regulates intimacy so that people can maintain a "proper distance" from each other. Recall Kant's elaboration on love and respect. One could also point to the many formalising practices in all cultures, e.g., the forms of addressing the other depending on the other's rank, age, degree of familiarity, etc.

7. Normalising discourse. "Normalcy" is the fundamental mood of collectivity. This is why most psychic disorders, "abnormalities," involve an uneasiness with collectivity and why it is so difficult to detect psychopathy, which is the tendency to repress conscience (i.e., the personal moral awareness), by substituting collective norms to a strikingly high degree. Hence the "callous" tendency of psychopathy.

Arendt mistook normalising for banality, while E. S. Herman's notion of "normalising the unthinkable" is too narrow (Herman 1995, pp. 97 ff.). Collectivity is inherently dissonant with itself (not only, as Herman would say, "cognitively"). Collective responses can be wildly self-contradictory yet without necessarily giving rise to any conscious sense of contradiction or corruptness. This is because collective understanding and normalcy define each other. For instance, a person who trusts collectivity firmly (call her conservative) can accuse a person who criticises certain aspects of it (call her radical) of being paranoid and sick: "You see conspiracy and corruption everywhere. How sick you must be!" Then, if evidence proves the critic right, she changes her accusation, stating that the radical person is naive and innocent: "Did you really imagine that torture could be avoided? Did you really believe that the terrorists were politely asked whether they knew some other terrorists and that, if they said 'no', they were simply left alone? How gullible can one be!"

First it appeared normal that no responsible state would tolerate torture. When this proved to be wrong, the most "natural" explanation available was sought. And should not one always look for the most natural explanation? And when it is found, as it always is, it really makes everything seem quite normal, even the claim just made.

Here is another example of this normalising tendency. A person I know works as a civilian in a military base. He does not wear a uniform. After some time he was stopped because he looked like a civilian, and his case was brought before his superiors. It was then stated that a person working permanently in a military base absolutely cannot wear civilian clothes. So he was given a uniform and he wore it until it was learned that he had no military education. His case was considered again. It was now stated that a person who has no military education absolutely cannot wear a uniform. And so he switched to civilian clothes again.

In these cases, there is no sense of contradiction between points of view. This is because collectivity is seen as that which simply "is" normal. The problem is to assess what it is or should be. In the first case the, as it were, conservative collectivist thought that it is sick and abnormal to suspect that, say, the government of the United States of America would allow torture. Then, when the evidence became overwhelming, she began to think that torture was normal because the government and other people that matter thought it was necessary. Moral ideas themselves do not decide what is normal. That is decided by the normalising mood of collectivity. The emperor can be without clothes or people can be killed by thousands in a nearby camp; it can all be normal. And then, what is seen as normal can change to something abnormal almost overnight.

It is perfectly possible that the radical person in our above example also is moving within the discourse of collectivity. In this case she sees only that the collective trespasses some of its own norms. She then criticises the conservative for being inconsistent or dishonest, i.e., for not staying in line with collective norms. But what if the radical person thinks that torture is morally wrong? Does that make a difference? What would that mean? Certainly, the conservative person thought initially that torture was morally wrong. Probably she did not even change her view. She only thought that there are situations where evil is unavoidable. This and similar thoughts are results of normalisation and express themselves as moral reasoning. Due to normalisation, ideas about what should count as moral change (it is appropriate/inappropriate to be topless) are overruled by "more important matters." That moral ideas change is taken to be quite natural. This kind of change has even been thematised as an essential historicity. In my view, what changes is only the discursive devices that repress conscience. In different times and cultures, different groups of people set the tone of what is used as repression.

Here is yet another aspect of normalising. Think of the "convincing" character of a voice with an ordinary and everyday tone. In a public debate, the person who can make herself appear more ordinary will win, from the collective point of view. (Think also of the ordinariness, not to say boredom, in the tone of voice of the flight-captain addressing passengers.) On the other hand, it is also normal to appreciate, within limits, exaggeration and drama. Given this, more "extreme" expressions are, of course, disarmed in advance, for they are not judged by content but by their degree of deviance from normality. ("They are going too far...") If collectivity is by definition, and not by content, normal, then nothing is extreme. It is only the degree of deviation that can be extreme and hence unacceptable. As it was said in a French movie, "A moderate excess is only good for you".

8. Within the grammar of collectivity, certain conceptual relations are taken as a matter of course. One concept is taken to lead "naturally" to another. For example, "One cannot help becoming hurt if someone picks on you." Thus, being wronged "leads" to revenge, being unfaithful "leads" to divorce, speaking nicely to a person "makes" her feel good, etc. Consider how in a revenge culture such as traditional Sardinia, violating individual honour is taken to be a completely collective issue (Newman and Lynch, 1987). The violated person has no say: he must exact revenge whatever his own understanding of the situation. Many of the above-mentioned mechanisms enter into the discussion here (the importance of formality, specificity of meaning, "standing before a gaze"), but I will focus on the issue of matter of course relation between concepts.

In the Sardinian culture it is as if the whole culture wants to make sure that violation of honour leads to revenge. The idea that it would not is intolerable. In my view revenge cultures show something important about collectivity, namely, that it creates conceptual relationships of the kind I am discussing by expecting "morally" that people act according to those relationships. This collective pressure is not the result of abstract theorising but of common anguish about the I-you relationship. In a revenge culture your killing another person becomes, collectively speaking, an impersonal deed demanded by tradition. You are not responding to another by whom you are addressed but you are carried away by collective meanings.

There are still other mechanisms that I cannot discuss here: scapegoating and bullying, ritualisation, hierarchisation, the craving for leadership. Let me instead elaborate on some of the points mentioned above. Since the transformations in question are responses to difficulties with the other, they are all, despite the inherent loss of sense for the other, also connected to experiences of comfort. Respect and distance are felt to be precious; appearance seems deeper than mere superficial traits (perhaps why excessively explicit attention to appearances might be disturbing to some persons); collective togetherness gives a sense of commonness simply because it arouses emotions; the pursuit of moral knowledge appears sincere because it seems both "heartfelt" and reasonable; guilt does not feel only bad. Since guilt is both a sign of and cement for collective belonging, it also offers masochistic enjoyment.

The discourse of collectivity predetermines you to certain reactions where you lose sight of the other even if you seem to be dealing precisely with her. You can escape into this predetermining discourse when the other threatens to come too close. Suppose the other asks you, without evil intention, a question that you find very disturbing. You now interpret the question as an offence and now you can "legitimately" reject it: "One cannot help being annoyed if someone becomes intrusive."

Also, this reaction is possible: "One cannot help being hurt if someone picks on you." And of course one pays back every offence, gets angry if provoked; of course one cannot help becoming depressed if one fails badly at something. And of course this is why any kind of offensive behaviour should be forbidden. But still, and of course, a young person with social problems is considered violent.

Within collectivity one has the feeling of being part of something bigger. (See Heidegger in *Being and Time* § 74, and *Logic as the Question Concerning the Essence of Language*. See also Haidt 2012.) This is because one has lost both one's own I and the other, the you. Instead, one has an engaged feeling of belonging together, a feeling that "gives meaning" in the sense that it predetermines you. You feel that you have a "mission." Heidegger, approvingly, calls this destiny, *Geschick*.

If, in your encounter with the other, you get hurt (embarrassed, annoyed, hateful,), feel a desire to hurt her (or are consciously trying to avoid hurting her), or try to affect her with what you say and do (being kind and taking it to be morally justified to expect kindness of her -- an expectation so automatic that it is hardly ever recognised except when, rarely, it is not fulfilled), then you are not open to her. Instead, you use language with the expectation of making her feel a certain way. When you try to hurt her, when you yourself become hurt, and when you try to affect her, you are counting on the effects that this is "bound" to have within collective discourse.

These effects are not, within collectivity, understood in any uniform way even if they are predetermined. Whether you feel hurt or have hurt someone else, some people will side with you while others will side with the other person.

It is all important to realise that language works differently in the I-you perspective than it does in collectivity. For instance, in collectivity, moral language is about evaluating and assessing criteria for judgment and about determining whether someone has violated moral norms or not. This perspective, which I have characterised as repressed/repressing, is mostly taken to be what morality is about. When Kant says that moral assessment takes place as if in the face of a judge in a court room, he affirms collective morality without realising it.

To cite a more modern example, Jonathan Lear says: "For the super-I is not merely the intrapsychic manifestation of values, ideals and prohibitions; it is the internalization of an *observer* of the self. It is one of the ironies and paradoxes of human existence that the self comes into being by the internalization of a self-observer" (1998, p. 208.) Here conscience is identified with collective pressure. Note also how the repressive force of "standing before a gaze" is understood as an internalisation of the observer.

Conclusion

How many times has it been claimed that morals are about our common values, ideals, and norms? The grammar of this "morals" consists of observation, judgement, blame, and punishment, and all this is characterised by the mode of being observed. The feeling and understanding that corresponds to being observed is guilt. When you are observed, the general sense of guilt cannot be removed even if you can be acquitted in particular cases. The collective sense of morals depends on a conscience-like feeling that both Kant and Lear confuse with conscience. Guilt responds to this collective pressure and thereby represses the you.

Conscience is different. It does not place you in front of a court of law where your moral acting is judged and where what you are morally is determined by how you appear before collectivity. Instead, conscience is the perspective through which you see the other. This perspective is always there even if it strikes us with particular force when we wrong the other: "How could I say that to her!" To follow one's conscience and acknowledge one's violation means that one wants to ask for forgiveness. This is what I would call having a "bad conscience." But if one represses conscience, the bad feeling will remain. This is because conscience cannot be simply erased. As a result of repression the badness remains and is transformed to guilt: a feeling where one avoids the other and where one appears as a bad person.

What is called "political correctness" occurs when it is commonly realised how a certain common way of speaking covers over a moral issue. What I have tried to show is that this is no special case, but that what are usually taken to be paradigmatic cases of moral understanding in moral philosophy and other areas, actually function in the same way. One could speak of "collective correctness." If the conscientious I-you relationship were taken into account, the perennial problems of moral philosophy would dissolve. I think, for instance, of the troubling split between seemingly objective and seemingly subjective sides of moral understanding; the problem concerning moral truth; the problems concerning conflicts of duty; the schism between deontology and consequentialism; the often ignored paradoxical problem between stating, on the one hand, that moral understanding is deeply personal and, on the other hand, that morals is about common values and norms; the seemingly perplexing fact that the most terrible atrocities in human history have been collectively committed. And I've named only a few of the problems.

In the I-you relationship one cannot speak about either subjectivity or objectivity, for it is about the way we address each other. Or better yet, it is about the fundamental openness between I and you. Despite our difficulties with it, this openness is always already there when an I addresses a you. For without I and you there is no such thing as addressing another human being.

References

Haidt, J. 2012. *The Righteous Mind. Why Good People Are Divided by Politics and Religion*. New York: Pantheon Books.

Heidegger, M. 1992. *Being and Time*. Oxford: Blackwell.

_____. 2009. *Logic as the Question Concerning the Essence of Language*. Albany: State University of New York Press.

Herman, E. S. 1995. *Triumph of the Market: Essays on Economics, Politics, and the Media*. Boston: South End Press.

Kant, I. 2000. *The Metaphysics of Morals*. Cambridge: Cambridge University Press.

Lear, J. 1998. *Love and Its Place in Nature*. New Haven: Yale University Press.

Newman, G. R., and M.J. Lynch. 1987. From feuding to terrorism: the ideology of vengeance. *Contemporary Crisis* 11: 223-42.

Nykänen, H. 2002. *The "I", the "You" and the Soul (An Ethics of Conscience)*. Åbo: Akademi University Press.

_____. 2005. Heidegger's Conscience, in: *sats* 6: 40-65.

_____. Conscience and Collective Pressure. *Philosophy, Psychiatry & Psychology* (forthcoming).

Wittgenstein, L. 1988. *Philosophical Investigations*. Oxford: Basil Blackwell.

_____. 1993. *Philosophical Occasion*, ed. J. Klagge and A. Nordmann. Indianapolis: Hackett.

Žižek, S. 2008. *The Sublime Object of Ideology*. London: Verso.

Patrik Kjærsdam Telléus

On teaching applied ethics
A controversy between theory and application

Abstract

This paper will address the relationship between ethics as a philosophical or theoretical discipline, on the one hand, and ethics as an applied or normative form of action and reasoning, on the other, in the context of teaching practices. Using the review of a debate between Robin Lawler and David Benatar published in the *Journal of Medical Ethics* over the course of several years, this paper discusses the role of ethical theories when teaching courses in applied ethics to, for example, medical students. The aim of these courses is to generate and improve moral reasoning among the students. In this case, the controversy between a theoretical approach and an applied approach can be summed up by the question of whether to teach ethical theories in applied ethics courses. This paper maintains that the conditional settings, with the actual lecturer as a key figure, constitute the balance between what I call "moral notions" and "moral phenomena" necessary to generate the intended moral reasoning. In this sense, whether to teach ethical theories or not is a question subordinate to the primary issue of one's role as a lecturer with regard to the participants in a given course.

> O' for a muse of fire that would ascend the brightest heaven of invention…
>
> – William Shakespeare

On teaching applied ethics

Last Christmas, I was baking cookies with three of my four children. They were, at the time, between the ages of 6 and 13. Having a Swedish father and a Danish mother, they have heard us sing a children's song about a baker in its Swedish and Danish versions. The two versions are almost identical, with one important exception: the Swedish version ends by singing, "If you are kind, you may have some [pastry], but if you are mean you have to go." The Danes sing, "If you have money, you may have some, but if you have none, you may not." I didn't interfere as I overheard my children talking about this difference. They had all noticed it, reflected on it, and now they were debating with themselves which version was the best. By the best they meant – without explicitly saying so – more morally just; and what they were comparing – without explicitly saying so – were the moral essences of the songs; and what they wanted to achieve – without explicitly saying so – was a normative, moral judgment on fairness applicable in this particular case.

Had I recorded this conversation, an analysis of the children's conversation would have illustrated several implied references and presumptions related to certain ethical theories and principles. We might, with some slight adjustment, also be able to detect which theory or principle they ended up supporting. The question I ask myself is: If my children had been explicitly aware of the vast field of ethical theoretical information that such an analysis could provide, would it have improved their discussion and conclusion? And more importantly, had it improved whatever reasonable awareness they gained by the end of that afternoon?

Since 2003, I have taught ethics to philosophy students, computer engineers, business and administration students, and of course, students in medicine and biotechnology. The courses have ranged from introductions of one session of 45 minutes to 10 sessions of 90 minutes each. I have also been involved in a few more advanced and detailed studies of particular ethical positions or ethical dilemmas as well as forms of applied ethics.

All this has made me aware of the difficulties related to these teaching practices, and especially those concerned with applied ethics courses. One such difficulty is the question of ethical theories. To what extent should ethical theories be included in courses aimed at students who are not students of moral philosophy, but students of applied ethics? The purpose of these courses is to engage students in particular practical moral problems and improve their ability to reflect ethically on these problems. Therefore, the question of ethical theories is linked to the question of understanding the moral reasoning of these students.

Here, I approach this difficulty by reviewing a typical debate on the issue. I conclude with a statement on the importance of addressing the conditional setting of these courses and the role of the lecturer.

Setting the scene

The discussion of courses in applied ethics, i.e., courses in ethics taught in academic fields other than philosophy, is not a uniform or well-defined topic, but I will try to sketch briefly some general features and conditions of these courses.

If we look at the development of university education and university programs, it is clear that different philosophical topics, methods, and perspectives have typically been intertwined with almost every other educational program. Ole Ravn 2004 has studied the history and content of so-called *filosofikum* within the Danish university system, and Sten Lindroth 1997 has carefully and extensively told the story of university and scientific development in Sweden. The traces of philosophy in the progression of scientific and academic areas are often linked to the initial phase of development, namely the formulation or definition of the particular subject matter. But philosophy also appears later, mainly in terms of epistemological and ontological concerns, involving topics such as the development of rational procedures and validations and the use and abuse of essential concepts (Kragh 1999, 2004, Kjærgaard and Kristensen 2003, Haaning 1998). The concept and practice of *filosofikum*, as one example of mandatory philosophy education for all university students, illustrates this application and design. When formally created during the nineteenth century, *filosofikum* focused on epistemology, logic, and psychology. Later, psychology was removed from the curriculum because it developed into its own field, leaving the *filosofikum* first and foremost to provide training in philosophical analytics, working with arguments and propositions and the principles and analysis of truth (Ravn 2004).

The philosophical aspects of modern academic programs could agreeably be associated with the role of philosophy in relation to science that Ayer constructed in his classic work *Language, Truth and Logic* (first published in 1936 and again with slight changes in 1946). Ayer states clearly that philosophy is the logical analysis of principles, facts (or sense-data), statements, and forms of empirical justification, and as such, is the rationality of reason, being both the architect and the custodian of rational judgment. Consequently Ayer removed all metaphysics from the work of philosophy, and with that also a lot of what we call practical philosophy (such as moral philosophy, aesthetics, and the philosophy of life). He did so not because these things did not matter or were irrelevant to people, but because he believed that philosophy was/is the business of rationality, and as such, the business of logical analysis and empirical validity. This position is also apparent in Ayers tribute-like description of John Locke:

> For he [Locke] is content, in his own words, "to be employed as an under-labourer in clearing the ground a little, and removing some of the rubbish that lies in the way of knowledge"; and so devotes himself to the purely analytical tasks of defining knowledge, and classifying propositions, and displaying the nature of material things. And the small portion of his work which is not philosophical, in our sense, is not given over to metaphysics, but to psychology (Ayer 1987, p. 70).

Philosophical contribution, as a supplementary element in university educational programs, is viewed mainly as a tool for developing general rational skills and for providing valid and basic conceptual framework. This framework also excludes the metaphysics of life from the realm of science and academic programs. The philosophical contributions are effectively realised through their inclusion in the supportive disciplines of methodology and philosophy of science. These disciplines can largely be viewed as applications of epistemological and ontological perspectives and are generally well-established parameters in most university educational programs, as well as (more or less) integrated parts of most student projects and reports.

This rational and "Ayer-like" perspective is obvious in the new Danish university regulations concerning the mandatory teaching of philosophy of science in all academic programs. The aim of the regulation is to provide the students with an understanding of the cogent development of their particular academic program and scientific subject matter. The purpose of this is to basically explain the scope and advancement of the discipline's theoretical account and validates the methodological procedures in the field. (See also Pedersen and Kragh, 2000).

However, what Ayer argued was left to the psychologists to explain or, in the worst cases, was lost in the speculations of metaphysicists has been given an opportunity to be reformulated as science. During the last 50-60 years, scientists have become increasingly aware of the moral, social, and environmental implications and consequences of their work. The field of applied ethics first emerged in the treatment of humans as research subjects, then in the treatment of and effects on nature, the risks and possibilities of technological developments, and finally in subject areas such as business administration and management, law and politics, information technology and communication. (Dige 2011, Cohen and Wellman 2005, Flyvbjerg 2001, Plough 2009). The main operative areas for applied ethics, however, continue to be the fields of medicine and biotechnology (Kuhse and Singer 2006, Landeweerd, Houdebine and ter Meulen 2006, Balling and Lippert-Rasmussen 2006).

The development of the field of applied ethics has allowed ethics to become a formally integrated part of many university educational programs (Telléus 2006). Ethics is a philosophical discipline with a long and well-established tradition as moral philosophy. So when moral philosophy is applied to the fields of science, it is only natural to expect that it will be applied in the same way as epistemology and ontology, i.e., as tools for rational improvement or rational scrutiny, providing a form of background or foundational conceptual framework. Due to such presumptions and expectations, courses in applied ethics have tended to focus on the following elements: a) procedures, regulations and guidelines; and b) ethical theories. This has been done to promote the development of analytic abilities and principal knowledge which, in turn, can ensure the capacity for rational ethical judgment within a particular discipline's range and involvement with society (Baune 2006, Landeweerd 2006, Fink 2003).

It is fascinating to witness the influence of an "Ayer-like" perspective on the realisation of applied ethics. It promotes a focus on the analytical assessment of factual value/values[1] as a way of "removing the rubbish," and

---

1   In his 1946 foreword, Ayer claims that values can be analyzed if the ethical statement that states the value adequately refers to or contains an empirical statement of fact. However, this is not a complete reassurance because normative expressions of value can always be contradicted due to the nonsensical nature of such statements. Ayer concludes, "For, since the expression of a value judgment is not a proposition, the question of truth or falsehood does not here arise" (Ayer 1987 p. 29).

validates and evaluates the costs and benefits of scientific endeavours (Forsberg, 2006). And it provides a form of moral rationality as the architect and custodian of norms and principles for science[2] (Merton 1946, Beauchamps and Childress 1977).

The players

In 2007, Robin Lawler wrote an article in the *Journal of Medical Ethics* that discusses the use of theory in teaching applied ethics. David Benatar wrote a critical response to Lawler and out of this exchange emerged a brief debate between the two (Lawler 2007 2008; Benatar 2007 2009). In 2010, Ben Saunders wrote a summary of the debate and introduced his own perspective on the matter. I shall present a brief outline of each author's position and arguments as an example of how the issue of applied ethics courses and ethical theories is deliberated. All three authors are philosophers, working with moral philosophy, and they are affiliated with philosophy departments at two British and one South African universities. In that sense, they fit the archetype of where and who are usually appointed the task of composing an introductory course in ethics for non-philosophy students.

Lawler (2007) advocates against the use of theory-based teaching. He objects to the conceptualisation of applied ethics as being the act of taking an ethical theory (i.e., a theory that claims unified or foundational principles of morality) and then applying it to a particular problem or actual setting. Lawler claims that it is impossible to teach anything but caricatures of the theories, either as oversimplified presentations that leave students unable to judge the theories properly or by providing such a large amount of theoretical information that it is impossible for students to comprehend the theories. Both scenarios induce students to regard moral philosophy as either a relativistic pick-and-choose, anything-goes defence strategy or an abstract bundle of words without any real impact on their very real problems and issues.

---

2   When talking about norms and principles, the main philosophical influence is Immanuel Kant (which is also pointed out in Landeweerd 2006). When I say "Ayer-like," I refer to the idea of grounding and framing the ethics of the scientific profession by analogy to Ayer's conception of philosophical analysis providing the grounding and framing for the justification of true empirical statements, i.e., the epistemology of the scientific profession.

As an alternative, Lawler presents a piecemeal concept of applied ethics. He suggests addressing the particular issues directly, confining the moral reasoning to a particular problem. The teacher of applied ethics must realise that he is not teaching future moral philosophers, but future doctors, engineers, business executives, etc., who do not need to know ethical theories in order to solve their moral problems. Lawler does introduce a concept of hierarchical thinking in terms of the amount of moral philosophy that students need (and can eloquently process?), but it remains unclear what he actually suggests, apart from something as simple as the idea that students can advance their argumentation by spending more time on reading, writing, and reflecting upon it.

Lawler's claim is also presented as an analogy to a physicist wanting to understand motion not through a unified theory of everything but simply by focusing on motion. The analogy may be that the moral philosopher is the physicist searching for the theory of everything, and the "applied ethicist" student is just interested in motion. Later, in his responses, Lawler is much clearer regarding how his approach is to be understood.

Benatar 2007 does not support the idea that ethical theories must be taught in applied ethics courses. However, he insists that there are some benefits to teaching ethical theories that should not to be overlooked in the debate. His position rests on two distinct claims. The first is that all of us, whenever faced with a practical moral problem, make use of theoretical frameworks by appealing to presumptions, emotions, and principles that are not always expressed but that are related to ethical theories of consequentialism, virtue ethics, contract theory, etc. Benatar suggests that making this theoretical framework explicit in teaching applied ethics enhances students' abilities to understand and argue for and against their initial positions; it gives them a vocabulary to articulate aspects that might have been otherwise difficult to address. Furthermore, it provides them with coherent ethical positions, thereby allowing them to become aware of paradoxes or deductions that strengthen their overall capacity for passing moral judgments.

Benatar's second claim is a practical pedagogical one. By debating moral issues from a theoretical standpoint, students are more apt to explore the issues because they can do so through objective abstractions. If they were to debate from their initial interest-oriented and emotional positions, they would be less likely to rationally articulate their position and, more importantly, would be more defensive and less open minded.

In his paper, Benatar fails to account for exactly how this theoretical expression may help to develop students' abilities to address practical issues, problems, and concerns. Why is it better to know that you are a consequentialist when you are solving a practical problem such as patient prioritisation? Also one might ask how the theoretical exploration and abstract articulation increase the students' abilities to make the actual and relevant moral judgment, and how that moral judgement qualitatively differs from their initial opinion, emotional response, or interest.

These objections were also raised by Lawler in his response to Benatar's critique (Lawler 2008). However, Lawler concludes that the benefits of which Benatar speaks, mainly the enhancement of the ability to pass moral judgment based on rational awareness and articulation, can be gained without the use of ethical theories and without abstracting from the initial opinion. Lawler's point is that if the student is passionately engaged in the issue, he is much more likely to also engage in finding support for his opinions or solving contradictions in his beliefs than if he is restricted to theoretical articulations and personally detached from the issue.

Lawler advocates a piecemeal approach, which either ignores ethical theories altogether or reduces them to brief or casual treatment. This becomes clear as he addresses Benatar's own example about the consequentialist. Lawler shows how to engage the students in a discussion by simply asking more questions, or making explicit confrontations within the style and vocabulary of the discourse, or by presenting the students with *reductio ad absurdum* arguments in relation to their opinions.

After publication of the second article by Lawler, Benatar replied that he believed it ought to be optional as to whether to use theory in teaching applied ethics (Benatar 2009). Although that is an insubstantial conclusion, he persists in claiming that there is an unresolved problem in Lawler's position: how to handle the vague difference between mentioning and teaching moral theories. Benatar links this point to his earlier claim about the benefits of using theory to expose already present but silent theoretical assumptions.

Concluding the debate, Ben Saunders 2010 wrote a piece in which he sums up the arguments and offers his own opinion. In Saunders' view, there is no real controversy between Lawler and Benatar because Lawler does not completely deny the use of ethical theory but simply promotes a more case-based and issue-oriented pedagogy (casuistry). Saunders reads this position into Benatar's articles as well, although Benatar emphasises the possible benefits of using theory within this teaching practice. For Saunders, the real issue is not whether theory should be taught, or even how much theory ought to be taught, but rather how to teach ethical theories.

Saunders criticises theory-based teaching practices for creating confusion and providing simplifications, which in turn can produce apathy and mechanical or relativistic approaches towards the application of ethical theories to real moral problems. Like Lawler he advocates for case-oriented teaching within applied ethics. In response to Benatar, Saunders suggests that case-based teaching benefits from introducing ethical theories early in a course. Contrary to Lawler, Saunders suggests that, rather than staying within the vocabulary and style of the discourse, the introduction of ethical theories is made by focusing the discussion on a theory-building schema. The schema is presented through eight steps or principle criteria (consistency, explanatory power, completeness, etc.), which lead to the recognition, use, or creation of a solid ethical theory.

Saunders seems to express the classical rational dream within moral philosophy, namely, that we become enlightened by turning our ordinary common sense or intuitive morality into abstract principles and comprehensive ethical theories, which we then use to make sound, valid, and clear moral judgments. To be fair, Saunders' intention is somewhat modified with regard to the students in applied ethical courses, who may not, he suggests, have to engage in moral philosophy. Here, the ambition is simply to create a "heightened awareness" through engaging in serious (i.e., philosophical) and critical reflections guided by the teacher's knowledge of ethical theories.

The plot thickens

At first glance, the debate seems rather dull and banal, perhaps even redundant and pointless; it is difficult to determine who the three writers are addressing and what the intention of the debate is. It is not a philosophical debate because it is not a philosophical problem. It is not a pedagogical debate because theories of learning processes or didactics are not presented or discussed.[3] The best way to characterize this debate is probably as one of opinions on or attitudes toward factual practices. However, we lack

---

3   Lawler's first article makes one reference to a work on didactics.

tangible examples (with one notable exception) and references to the genuine experience and the factual practices they are discussing. Therefore, one should perhaps regard the different sides in the debate as declarations of assumptions and recognise that these assumptions are not targeted at a clearly articulated audience.

However, the debate has something interesting to offer and teach us. When engaging in a debate on teaching ethical theories to students of applied ethics, it is necessary to specify whether one is representing and addressing practical or philosophical concerns and perspectives. A third purpose of the debates could be to bring forth different scientific concerns and problems, e.g., pedagogical, sociological, juridical, historical, organisational, economical etc. However, from the perspective of philosophers and practicing lecturers/teachers, the first two interpretations appear to be the most natural choices.

For practitioners, there are many issues to discuss, e.g., the differences between teaching a theory through concepts and literature or through examples and arguments, using value-oriented or comparative presentations, and so forth. The issue of time, which is related to questions of formally declared aims and intentions as well to as the very important issue of examination, is also important to address. And matters such as whether to use one teacher or several, perhaps with different scientific profiles; the combination of excursions, experiments, and theoretical interpretations; and the composition, attitudes, and motivations of the students as both a group and as individuals. I will not elaborate here, but the debate I have presented can be read as useful, yet lacking in the context of these issues. For instance, Lawler's practical example of a discussion can certainly be appreciated on a hypothetical level, but in practice, there are some restrictions, most notably the number of students in the classroom.

Instead, let us try to be philosophers. What philosophical issues are at stake in this debate? There are a number of interesting topics here, and Lawler indicates several of them in his first paper, e.g., the question of what we mean by applied ethics, the concept of the unified theory, conditions for verification, moral attitudes vs. ethical theory, etc. (Lawler 2007).

One of the questions I'd like to pose to the authors is what we actually mean by a practical moral problem. All the contributions seem to take for granted both the notion of ethical theory and the notion of practical moral problems, and although we might be able to gather the references and correspondence into a concept of ethical theory (e.g., a coherent and consistent explanatory system for the experience and use of values or the good), this is less easily performed for the term "practical moral problem." There are important differences between phenomena such as patient priority, confidentiality on the Internet, dismissing a coworker, consumer awareness, stem cell research, etc. The gap in question can be viewed through inquiries, such as who must deal with the problem, where the problem is located, and what creates the problem. The results of this type of analysis display a huge range of possibilities from individual, particular circumstances and social, practical communities to universal, theoretical concepts. This begs an essential question: Do such differences have (or should they have) any impact on whether the problem is moral or not?

What we actually mean by moral is an important philosophical issue. Related to that issue is the classic debate in moral philosophy on whether we conceptualise different things/phenomena with the notion of moral and with the notion of ethics. The lack of clarity regarding this issue is a huge part of the difficulty in teaching applied ethics because we consequently become unclear about what constitutes the actual subject we are supposed to teach. Are we teaching morality (e.g., appropriate awareness and normative behaviour); are we teaching ethics (e.g., virtuous principles and explanatory theories of goodness); or are we teaching something in between or a little of both?

Moral philosophy can help us as lecturers and help the students. Through working with the concept of ethics and the concept of moral, we are able to identify culture-bound norms, compulsory principles, righteous rules, and unconditional demands (Fink 2007). By focusing on basic philosophical notions such as ethics and morals, we are provided with a conceptual framework that enables us to distinguish between essential aspects of particular as well as abstract phenomena simply by looking at the way we apply or use the notions given to us. As Hans Fink 2007 has demonstrated, the significance is not that these notions are used in a universally correct way, but that they are used in a particular fashion, with a certain intent and having influential consequences. Fink illustrates a difference between intuitive sentiments and the norms and attitudes that are dependent on culture and that justify how we ought to value them and how we ought to act according to one or the other (Fink 2007).

The distinction between ethics and morals is not the only one that is useful as an analytical tool to clarify these issues. Ludwig Wittgenstein, in his lecture on ethics, makes another distinction. He recognises that we use the notion good, on the one hand, in terms of measurable achievements and actions, and on the other hand, in applications regarding the meaning of life, where the notion seems to echo a rudimentary feature of things and attitudes (Wittgenstein, 1965). This distinction is then recreated in several other similar distinctions, such as between trivial and ethical meaning, relative and absolute judgments of value, natural and supernatural beings, and so on. For Wittgenstein, this generates a conceptual framework that enables us to explore systematically what we can reasonably assess in terms of morality. He emphasises the difference between what we can adequately express through language and the corresponding states-of-affairs and what must be considered beyond language and the factual world (Wittgenstein 1965). Another example is one of many categorisations that Jürgen Habermas employs, namely between pragmatic, ethical and moral reasoning (Habermas 2005a). These three basic philosophical notions come to refer to different discourses and domains of action, which gives Habermas a conceptual framework for analysing, e.g., a democratic principal such as rights in divergent ways. This constitutes a hypothesis about what can be represented and misrepresented as well as what can be achieved by a society acknowledging this principle (Habermas 2005b).

I have attempted to demonstrate that both the execution and content of the debate between Lawler and Benatar would benefit from a clearer conceptual framework. I propose that this is a task where moral philosophy may be helpful, by providing different illustrations of some basic philosophical notions with which we can critically reflect on our own or other uses of presumptions about those notions. This is a form of deliberation that comprises the framework within which we comprehend practical moral problems as well as ethical theories. This evokes another interesting philosophical issue, i.e., the question of what is intended by moral reasoning. It is clear that Lawler, Benatar and Saunders all seem, to a different extent, to believe in the power of rationality in questions of morality. I also adopt this position; however, I will discuss this stance further with the help of two Finnish philosophers.

Matti Häyry 2005 has addressed the issue of rationality and morality within applied ethics in a short article in which he asks if arguments can address concerns. Häyry makes an important observation about applied ethics: there are logical and conceptual inferences as well as states-of-affairs that philosophers can address through ethical arguments and ethical theories. But this form of comprehension of the moral phenomena is not necessarily equivalent to the concerns that are expressed as anxieties, worries, and fears. These types of concerns are more successfully addressed through actions and reassurances. Here Häyry becomes a little vague because he does recognise that moral philosophy can help to clarify the presumptions and provide some arguments for and against the different choices with which a particular person is faced. However, he maintains the idea that the actual choice is a different matter and cannot be handled through ethical conceptualisation and argumentation. He has two main arguments: one is that the ethical demand on universally accepted solutions is not possible because the concerns are local and specific, and the second is that even if we rationally and ethically reach a conclusion (choice), this does not automatically remove the concerns.

Häyry rightly notes that when we are talking about moral problems and concerns, those concerns cannot be reduced or translated into purely logical, rational arguments based on ethical assumptions or into structured, empirical settings or conditions. These types of problem also indicate emotional commitments, contradictory but sustained values, projections into the unknown, and speculative change, and more importantly, they are always locally contextualised and particular in nature, carrying all the contingency of such an occurrence. Häyry does not conclude anything in his article but simply wants to raise a concern about the idea of reason making sense of moral judgment or moral choices through explicit conceptualisations and critical philosophy and to some extent, through ethical principles and ethical theories. Perhaps, Häyry seems to argue, this is not a complete answer to the challenges expressed within applied ethics.

Häyry has a point. Working out a coherent and appropriate conceptual framework is essential to moral reasoning and to problems and issues addressed in applied ethics, but it is not sufficient. There is always a wide range of emotions involved with these issues and problems. The question is whether these emotions can be addressed in the teachings of applied philosophy, which, as we have seen, is related to the development or improvement of moral reasoning. It has been suggested in this paper that the emotional side to these issues cannot be properly addressed through theory, i.e., language or propositions, or through factual cases, i.e., the explanatory states-of-affairs of practical problems. However, I have also indicated another answer by accentuating the use of basic moral or philosophical notions. Using a conceptual framework that contains the problems and theories is not simply a question of logical coherence and identification of the subject matter; there is also a performative aspect involved, in the sense of dressing ourselves, our actions and attitudes, in the moral cloth that such notions generates.

To elaborate further on this issue within the framework of moral reasoning, I now turn to another Finnish philosopher, Lars Hertzberg, and the work he presented in a conference paper entitled "On knowing right from wrong" (2009). Hertzberg presents us with the case of P. G. Wodehouse, who while imprisoned in Germany during World War II, made some radio broadcasts for German Radio aimed at the American market. Wodehouse was later accused of treason for these acts, but defended himself by claiming that he didn't understand that his actions could be interpreted in this way. Using this case, Hertzberg discusses the concept of moral ignorance.

Hertzberg identifies moral ignorance with a) the failure to understand the moral scope of one's actions and b) the failure to understand notions with a moral content. He makes a brief reference to the word "idiot," which is derived from the Greek word for private person, to indicate that moral ignorance can also be viewed as not relating to others, not realising consequences that go beyond oneself, not being sensitive to the needs and wishes of others, and not being aware of others' interpretations and judgments of oneself and one's actions. By discussing the notion of betrayal, with the focus on how we typically use the word, Hertzberg claims that knowing moral notions is by definition knowing their domain (or meaning) to be right or wrong in an ethical sense. One cannot claim that a particular act is an act of betrayal while denying that the particular act is also a wrongful act. Instead, he says that if one does not believe that the particular act is wrong, one would try to show that it is anything but an act of betrayal.

His point is that awareness of ethical principles and moral beliefs includes knowing what is indicated as right and wrong in relation to the principle and belief regardless of agreement or disagreement with the principle or belief. This is also indicated by the responses and evaluations we receive from and together with others. To know moral notions without knowing the relevant moral judgment of right and wrong is, as Hertzberg calls it, a philosophical fantasy. In this sense, both signs of moral ignorance are based on sensitivity to the world around oneself and to different forms of social assessment more than on the cognitive ability to make logical definitions or causal calculations.

Hertzberg recognises that morality is about how we act as people, and a morally ignorant person is one who acts inappropriately in various ways. The morality of people is tied to an emotional and rational awareness, in the sense of realising the significance of one's actions and choices beyond one's personal situation. Consequently, moral ignorance is not realising this significance, significance being the practical consequences as well as the approval or disapproval of others.

Hertzberg also relates the relevance of this discussion to courses in applied ethics. He claims that such courses are not ways of raising the moral quality of the students (to become ethical experts) or removing moral deficiencies in an epistemological sense (learning to make ethical judgments through arguments and deduction). Rather, they are ways of deepening students' sensitivity to their role as professionals and encouraging them to reflect on the scope of their profession, in terms of the possibilities for actions, consequences, and the aspects of integration that the profession establishes and in which it takes part. "What one is acquiring should not be thought of as a specialized skill; rather one's attention is drawn to things that tend to get overlooked in more conventional forms of professional training" (Hertzberg 2009).

The alertness, awareness, or sensitivity that Hertzberg considers a necessary requirement for, or integrated part of, the comprehension of basic moral notions may be conceived as the performative aspect of these notions. They are not merely theoretical hypotheses or even deductions; neither are they simply practical presumptions or intuitional reactions; instead, they constitute the conceptual framework in which I am engaged as a moral, reasonable actor, and in that sense my performances become equivalent to what I consider valuable.

... gently to hear, kindly to judge, our play

William Shakespeare

In this paper I have addressed different aspects of teaching applied ethics. The first perspective I examined attempts to explain the academic development of applied ethics as an analogue or continuation of other forms of applied philosophy or philosophical application. The point here was to stress the importance of reflecting on what philosophy and the philosopher have to offer with regard to courses in applied ethics. I suggested that this should be understood as providing a conceptual framework and promoting the practice of reasoning. However, I also indicated that there are some pitfalls inherent in this perspective. If we unreflectively or hastily translate conceptual frameworks into theory and reasoning into method, we run the risk of not applying philosophy, in terms of actually philosophising, but reduce this opportunity to a guarantee or a sanction of repeating theoretical explanations and executing given procedures.

Then, I turned to the debate between Lawler and Benatar in the *Journal of Medical Ethics*. The purpose of this section was to illustrate the first perspective and also to make the potential misconception even more clear. The debate was to a large extent a debate on how to teach applied ethics to ensure or evoke the method of moral reasoning and judgment by initiating the validation of the conceptual framework through theoretical or practical means. I attempted to show that, if this idea were reduced to debating a step-by-step procedure of going from theory to case or going from case to theory, the debate became trivial and insignificant. However, if the debate were elaborated upon in terms of philosophy, it would reveal the importance of the philosophical contribution to the teaching of applied ethics.

In the final part of this paper, I attempted to express the idea of moral philosophy as a way of conceptually deliberating on the use and meaning of basic moral notions. This is the process of constituting the conceptual framework as such and thereby providing us with a philosophical, analytical saturation through the use of the notions in question. By looking at the emotional side of moral notions or the phenomena presumably addressed by those notions, I imply that the relevance of moral reasoning is situated in a personal as well as a social environment. The same point was punctuated by Hertzberg's epistemological analysis of the mutual intersection of understanding and using moral notions.

I am now back where I started, promoting what I believe to be the ethical (as in moral philosophy) contribution to applied ethics. The claim, naïve as it may appear, is that teaching can never be purely theoretical or simply practical because it will not allow the students to exceed their presumptions or habits. Instead, it must be envisioned and enacted, that is, performed as a conceptualisation that challenges the given framework by recreating a reasonable framework. This framework is expressed through the simultaneous use of moral notions and engagement with moral phenomena.

We can stage the issues demonstrated through the example in my introduction. Here I illustrated a moral reason that was equally devoted to its phenomenon and to its notions. Who is to say whether it was the difference in moral notions or the moral actions in the song or the actual activity of baking that initiated my children's speculation? Their discussion was committed to the contextuality of the circumstances but at the same time able to transcend the given framework. They critically evaluated the notions in use and reconfigured the comprehension of the moral significance of the notion. This was done in terms that were reasonable to both their personal experience and the social realms of the concurrence, semantically both in a linguistic sense and as an acted situation. This example also indicates the importance of who participates, where the reasoning occurs, and on what grounds it is developed.

Considering these ideas within the teaching context, it is essential that the lecturer first knows him/herself and knows the students before addressing issues of theoretical or case-based approaches. From this point, it becomes possible to explicitly address the conceptual framework that discloses itself in the students' (and the lecturer's) articulations and enactments of relevant moral phenomena and dilemmas. Only in this way does the lecturer know what must be addressed in order to evoke moral reasoning within the students so that they can embark on the ethical journey from the given and trivial framework to a reasonable and significant framework in which to comprehend the issues at hand. In this sense, the issue of theory based or case-based teaching becomes a subordinated question. First it is necessary to articulate the contextual dependent, conceptual comprehensions in play.

References

Ayer, A.J. [1936/1946] 1987. *Language, Truth and Logic*. Middlesex: Penguin Books.
Balling, Gert and Lippert-Rasmussen, Kasper, eds. 2006. *Det menneskelige eksperiment*, København: Museum Tusculanums Forlag.
Baune, Ø. 2006. Conceptual ethical tools and common morality. In *BioTechnology: Ethics an Introduction*, ed. L. Landeweerd, L-M. Houdebine, and R. ter Meulen. Firenze and Baltimore: Angelo Pontecorboli Editore – International Association for Arts and Sciences.
Beauchamps, T.L., and J.F. Childress. 1977. *The Principles of Biomedical Ethics*. New York: Oxford University Press.
Benatar, D. 2007. Moral theories may have some role in teaching applied ethics. *Journal of Medical Ethics* 33: 671-72.
_____. 2009. Teaching moral theories is an option: Reply to Rob Lawler. *Journal of Medical Ethics* 35: 395-96.
Cohen, Andrew I. and Wellman, Christopher Heath, eds. 2006. *Contemporary debates in Applied Ethics*, Oxford, UK: Blackwell Publishing.
Dige, M. 2011. Praktisk etik – en oversigt. In *Filosofisk etik – normativ etik, praktisk etik og metaetik*, ed. A-M S. Christensen, Aarhus: Aarhus Universitetsforlag.
Fink, H. 2003. Universitetsfagenes etik. In *Universitet og videnskab*, eds. H. Fink, P.C. Kjærgaard, H. Kragh, and J.E. Kristensen, København: Hans Reitzels Forlag.
_____. 2007. The conception of ethics and the ethical in K.E. Løgstrup's *The Ethical Demand*. In *Concern for the Other: Perspectives on the Ethics of K.E. Løgstrup*, ed. S. Andersen, and K. van Kooten Niekerk, South Bend, IN, IN: University of Notre Dame Press.
Flyvbjerg, B. 2001. *Making Social Science Matter*. Cambridge: Cambridge University Press..
Forsberg, E-M. 2006. The ethical matrix – a tool for ethical assessments of biotechnology. In: Landeweerd, L. Houdebine, L-M. and ter Meulen, R. eds. 2006. *BioTechnology: Ethics an* Introduction, Firenze and Baltimore: Angelo Pontecorboli Editore – International Association for Arts and Sciences.
Habermas, J. [1991] 2005a. Om det pragmatiske, etiske og moralske brug af den parktiske fornuft [Von pragmatischen, etischen und moralischen Gebrauch der praktischen Vernuft]. In *Demokrati og retsstat*København: Hans Reitzels Forlag.

_____. [2001] 2005b. Den demokratiske retsstat – en paradoksal sammenknytning af modstridende principper? ["Der demokratische Rechtsstaat – eine Paradoxe Verbindung widersprüchlicher Prinzipen?"]. In *Demokrati og retsstat* København: Hans Reitzels Forlag.
Hertzberg, L. 2010. *On Knowing Right from Wrong*. Conference paper presented at "Wittgensteinian Approaches to *Ethics and the Philosophy of Culture*" organized by the Nordic Wittgenstein Society, Åbo, Finland.
Haaning, A. 1998. *Naturens lys – vestens naturfilosofi i højmiddlealder og renæssance 1250-1650*. København: C.A. Reitzels Forlag.
Häyry, M. 2005. Can arguments address concerns? *Journal of Medical Ethics* 31: 598-600.
Kjærgaard, P.C., and Kristensen, J.E. 2003. Universitetets idéhistorie. In: H. Fink,
Kjærgaard, P.C., Kragh, H. and Kristensen, J.E. ed. 2003. *Universitet og videnskab*, København: Hans Reitzels Forlag.
Kragh, H. 1999. *Videnskabens væsen – en søgen efter sand erkendelse*. København: Forlaget Fremad.
_____. 2004. *Naturerkendelse og videnskabsteori – de uorganiske videnskabers filosofi og historie*. Århus: Århus Universitetsforlag,
Kuhse, Helga and Singer, Peter eds. 2006. *Bioethics – an anthology. Second edition*, Oxford UK: Blackwell Publishing.
Landeweerd, L. 2006. Moral theory and bioethics. In: Landeweerd, L. Houdebine, L-M. and ter Meulen, R. eds. 2006. *BioTechnology: Ethics an Introduction*, Firenze and Baltimore: Angelo Pontecorboli Editore – International Association for Arts and Sciences.
Landeweerd, Laurens, Houdebine, Louis-Marie and ter Meulen, Ruud, eds. 2006, *BioTechnology-Ethics an introduction* Firenze, Italy/Baltimore, USA: Angelo Pontecorboli Editore – International Association for Arts and Sciences.
Lawler, R. 2007. Moral theories in teaching applied ethics. *Journal of Medical Ethics* 33: 370-72.
_____. 2009. Against moral theories: Reply to Benatar. *Journal of Medical Ethics* 34: 826-28.
Lindroth, S. 1997. *Svensk lärdomshistoria band I-IV*. Stockholm, Sverige: Nordsteds Förlag.

Merton, R. K. [1942] 1973. The normative structure of science. In *The Sociology of Science – Theoretical and Empirical Investigations*, 267-78. Chicago: The University of Chicago Press.

Pedersen, O., and Kragh, H. 2000. *Fra kaos til kosmos – verdensbilledets historie gennem 3000 år*. København: Gyldendal.

Plough, T. 2009. *Ethics in Cyberspace – How Cyberspace May Influence Interpersonal Interaction*. Heidelberg: Springer.

Ravn, O. 2004. *Exploring the Borderline – A Study on Reflections in University Science Education*. Ph.D. thesis. Aalborg: Department of Learning and Philosophy Aalborg University.

Saunders, B. 2010. How to teach moral theories in applied ethics. *Journal of Medical Ethics* 36: p. 635-38.

Telléus, P. 2006. Is there one set of ethical principles? *Philosophy and Science Studies – Working Papers*. Vol. 1. Aalborg: Aalborg Universitet.

Wittgenstein, L. 1965. A lecture on ethics. *The Philosophical Review* 74: p. 3-12.

Thessa Jensen

Designing for relationship
Fan fiction sites on the Internet

How can design reinforce a culture of acknowledgment and support? This article looks into the world of fan fiction as it is found on two different web sites. Using the ethics of Løgstrup as its fulcrum, this article tries to show how fan fiction sites through their design nurse the writers and readers, creating a culture that can be described only as special with regard to the ethical conduct of site participants.

Further narrowing the topic, this article uses the British television series "Sherlock" as its case in point.

In summer 2010, the BBC broadcast the first episode of the new television series "Sherlock." The series is a modern retelling of the original stories, bringing Sherlock Holmes into the age of mobile phones, websites, blogging, and texting. It revolves mainly around the relationship between Sherlock Holmes and Doctor John Watson, which, in addition to the modernisation, is a new approach. To date, "Sherlock" has run for two seasons, each with three, 90-minute episodes. The second season was broadcast in January 2012 on the BBC. A third season was in production during Spring 2013.

Despite having relatively few episodes when compared to the ongoing American series [e.g. "Elementary", "The Mentalist"], which also focuses on criminal cases solved by an eccentric sleuth, "Sherlock" has had a remarkable impact on social media. It is the sixth highest-ranking fan fiction fandom on fanfiction.net, which in turn is the largest media platform in the field of fan fiction. "Sherlock" gains between 25 and 50 new stories daily. By comparison, the American series "CSI" gains fewer than 10 stories each day.

Fan fiction as a genre is special in more than one way: it is written by women for women. Another characteristic is that it is typically "in progress," being developed as it is read and commented on by the readers. Fan fiction stories evolve around establishing a relationship, including sex, between two or more characters of the original show/movie/book/comic/game. The readers and writers are highly supportive of each other; flaming, hating, or trolling are extremely rare and frowned upon.

With the above in mind, the hypothesis examined here is that the culture of fan fiction entails an ethical behaviour, which helps nurturing the so-called spontaneous life manifestations as described by Løgstrup. The question here is: How does the design of a fan fiction platform motivate or restrict such behaviour? To answer that question, I explore examples from the two largest fan fiction sites on the Internet, i.e., fanfiction.net (ffnet) and archiveofourown.org (AO3).

This article contributes to the field of social media, creative writing, and Løgstrup's ethics of the "Other".

The ethical demand

> No one is more thoughtless than he who makes a point of applying and realising once-delivered directives. His claiming that the directives are radical really makes no difference. Thinking and imagination become equally superfluous. Everything can be carried out quite mechanically; all that is needed is a purely technical calculation. There is no trace of the thinking and imagination which are triggered only by uncertainty and doubt (Løgstrup 1997, p. 114).

For Løgstrup the starting point of ethics is not universality or laws on morals and ethical behaviour. His starting point is the specific meeting of two people. This meeting places demands on the two people involved. The Other places an unspoken demand of trust, openness of speech, mercy, and a wordless appeal for nonviolence on the "I." These demands are the sovereign expressions of life and they will, according to Løgstrup, always be present when two people meet each other. The sovereign expressions of life can be seen as an undercurrent of the meeting. Even though the life expressions are present, they will never be met fully. As Løgstrup says in *The Ethical Demand* (English translation):

> The radical demand says that we are to care for the other person in a way that best serves his interest. It says that but nothing more. What this means in a given situation is that a person must discover for himself in terms of his own unselfishness and in the light of his own understanding of life. This is why in the very nature of things it is impossible to obey the radical demand on the basis of motives which are foreign to the demand (1971, p. 58).

So the radical demand is based on the actual situation, the actual people involved in it, and how the person determines what is in the best interest of the Other. While the radical demand underlies the interaction between the two persons, the actual outcome is by no means a given. Løgstrup does not apply rules, norms, or laws. Yet he explains why people in general are likely to demand laws, rules, and norms:

> The social norms, on the other hand, give comparatively precise directives about what we shall do and what we shall refrain from doing. We are usually able to conform to these directives without even having to consider the other person, much less take care of his life (Ibid.).

Socially accepted rules make living and interacting with people easier. People do not have to think about what would be in the best interest of the Other since all they must do is follow the rules. But applying the rules in the relationship turns the Other into a means instead of an end. Thus the "I" does not have to recognise the needs of the Other, does not need to actually "see" the Other as a person, as long as the rules are obeyed.

The sovereign expressions of life: Life manifestations

But what are the expressions of life and when do they become visible? Løgstrup talks about different expressions and is not always clear about what is actually seen as an expression in and of itself and what is merely acting on behalf of the expression. This can be explained by the very nature of his ethics, which are not rule or norm-based, and thus are heavily dependent on actual situations.

The following expressions of life are mentioned in *The Ethical Demand*:

- mercy;
- openness of speech (honesty);
- trust; and
- wordless appeal of nonviolence.

Other works by Løgstrup 1996, 1983 give additional examples.

At this point it might be appropriate to emphasise that Løgstrup is trying to explain his ethics independently of any kind of religious foundation. His aim is, in fact, to show how deeply rooted these expressions are in the social life of human beings, rooted prior to any kind of religion, universal laws, and the like.

The four expressions of life are also described as life manifestations, which can be explained by the following characteristics. Life manifestations are usually latent, underlying every kind of interaction between people but not normally visible. Life manifestations will become visible typically in the event of a crisis or conflict since the manifestations will be noted by their absence rather than their presence. On becoming visible they may be turned into ethical norms and rules in order to prevent a new crisis or conflict.

Life manifestations are unconditional, but if they are turned into a goal, an end, they disappear. Thus, the visibility of a missing life expression often renders it superfluous because people will try to develop rules for the situation in which it became visible.

Life manifestations depend on acting and deliberately choosing an action. In the introductory passage in this chapter, Løgstrup explains how rules tend to become ends in themselves, turning interaction with other people into the means for meeting the rules.

Løgstrup explains the difference between "need" and "life expression" as needs being something that people can satisfy. People can develop new needs, and needs can be created by others. On the other hand, people either have or don't have life expressions (Pahuus, 1991). Life expressions are spontaneous, sovereign, and individual. This can be surprising, but individuality arises through the context and upbringing of a given person. One cannot create life expressions, but they can be nurtured during the upbringing and through the behaviour of people toward each other.

Life expressions can be suppressed easily, but they will then turn into something else. According to Løgstrup, suppressed life expressions can turn into needs. Hence, the ever-growing needs of people can be explained by a society that suppresses life expressions.

In other words, life expressions cannot be created, but they can be nurtured. Life expressions underlie every kind of human interaction, but are visible only when they are violated, negated, or suppressed.

The following will try to show how Løgstrup's ethical approach can give an understanding of the dynamics of fan fiction communities as social media, and how their design influences the behaviour of their participants.

Social media and relationships

Social media is a term that denotes different media platforms, all contributing to a framework for social interaction in one way or another. Boyd and Ellison (2007) provide the following definition:

Web-based services that allow individuals to:

- construct a public or semi-public profile within a bounded system;
- articulate a list of other users with whom they share a connection; and
- view and traverse their list of connections and those made by others within the system

Social media are only a framework for communication and, more importantly, for creating and maintaining relationships with other people on a given platform. The "bounded system" is no more bounded today than many social media platforms going cross-media, making it possible for people to communicate across perceived media boundaries, collecting material from one medium for use on another without needing to login or logout.

At the same time, the list of users, list of relationships to any given person, can also be used across boundaries. In this way it is possible to maintain relationships with the same people in different environments, which make possible different types of relationships.

Chayko notes that people, in fact, perceive their relationships with others on the social media platform as important):

> People can feel so close to one another, so strongly bonded, in portable communities because proximity and presence are perceived by us in ways that transcend the physical. When we connect with others, we experience real feelings of nearness to them: we may feel intimacy, love, happiness, anger (2008, p. 37).

Social media can be seen as a digital way of maintaining and achieving relationships with people, in cases where people know each other in the physical world, and, in other instances, where people never meet each except in the digital world.

Social media can be divided roughly into two categories determined by the motivation to participate (Gudiksen 2013):

1. The community exists because of the social connections, with Facebook as the main example; or
2. The community exists because of a shared interest.

The starting point for this article is my interest in exploring the ethics of a relationship if said relationship is conducted and developed via a social media because of a shared interest. However, this article also narrows the field by analysing the relationships made possible via the framework of two fan fiction sites.

The two sites maintain two different ways of supporting relationships. Thus the participants can interact with each other in different ways, leading to different kinds of support between the writer and the reader.

When working with relationships on the Internet, typical mentions of trolls, haters, and shit-storms are part of the way people interact (Shitstorm, 2011). Trolls and haters can become really vicious (i.e., Guardian 2013) in their verbal attacks. Interestingly, these kinds of attacks are very rare in the fan fiction communities. Since January 2012, I have been a reader, commenter, and writer on the two largest fan fiction sites on the Internet since. During that time less than a handful of instances of trolling or hating were observed and were typically rebuked by other readers and commenters. In a few cases, the writer abandoned the story.

The shared interest in fan fiction is reading and writing stories about the favourite One True Pairings (OTPs) of favourite characters in a specific fandom. In the following passages, the specifics of social media and thus fan fiction and its ethical demands are explained further, showing how the design of the sites and the writing process nurses the development of Løgstrup's life manifestations.

In the world of social media, fan fiction platforms like fanfiction.net (ffnet) and archiveofourown.org (AO3) in principle deliver the same framework as Facebook or Twitter, a platform that would be empty if the users didn't generate its content. But, as said above, the interactions on the fan fiction platforms differ greatly from Facebook or Twitter in the way content is generated and in the interaction between the users. Hence, the interaction relies heavily on shared interests.

Women's folly: Writing fan fiction

Fan fiction as a genre started in the 1970s when specialty magazines were publishing stories written by fans of a particular movie, television series, and the like. Since the stories more often than not involved sex, at times even pornography, these stories were not openly published or distributed. With the Internet developing new ways of communication, fan fiction moved from print to online places, so-called social media.

A fan fiction writer is usually a woman – 80-90 percent of all writers are women – who writes about the possible relationship between the characters in a given film. For the television show "Sherlock," this would typically be Sherlock Holmes and John Watson, but other pairings of the characters in the series are possible. The typical fan fiction story would revolve around the relationship of the two characters, trying to make it probable that this relationship is taken further than in the actual film or television show.

Since the stories focus on the feelings and closeness between two characters, Woledge 2006 coins the term "intimatopia" to describe the development of the relationship. Sex is only part of developing this closeness between the characters; the other part is to explain how the two characters come to understand, trust, and respect each other.

Writing fan fiction in a social media context is not a solitary process. The community of fans will comment on each short story, often giving advice or ideas for further work. A writer typically has a so-called beta, who reads the story and reviews it before it is published. When a story is developed over several entries, every entry gets comments, which can lead the writer into new paths or develop the storyline into a new direction.

This process is described as community-centred creation of content (Busse and Hellekson 2006). The community of a given fandom can partake in the creation process. Often one story can develop into artwork, YouTube films, and other stories, which take one or more characters from the "original" fan fiction into their universe.

The people in fan fiction communities typically give credit to each other's work, by stating who had the idea(s), who did the artwork, who translated the story, and so on. The process is open and there are no restrictions as to who is entitled to work on a new idea although plagiarism is frowned upon.

There seems to be some differences between fandom groups. Several of the "Sherlock" fans state that the people in this particular fandom are more supportive than in other groups in the fan fiction universe. This could partly be because of the story itself, having the relationship between two men at its core, thus touching the very foundation of fan fiction. On the other hand, many of the "Sherlock" participants are led to writing fan fiction for the very first time by this series. And these people seem to be women with families, and for that reason may be being more supportive than younger women.

Fan fiction as it is developed and created in the "Sherlock" fandom shows again how important the initial trust and openness of speech is when people meet. The interaction, communication, and community-centred creation of a story can only be accomplished if the fans involved trust each other, even though they do not know each other in the physical world.

Considering some fan fiction works, it is amazing to think that it is all done for free, including translations, beta-reading, writing, artwork, videos, and the like. Some of the stories are the length of novels, running more than 200 pages. Other stories have gone viral, with people developing new fan material from them. And the only credit these people get is from their peers; the producers of the "Sherlock" series have stated that they do not read fan fiction to avoid being sued for stealing ideas.

So, how are fan fiction sites designed for a relationship between readers and writers?

Designing for support and acknowledgement

In the following pages, two sites, ffnet (figs. 1 and 2) and AO3 (figs. 3 and 4), will be examined with regard to the different possibilities for interaction between reader and writer.

A writer sets out to create her story, starting by uploading the first chapter; she has a work in progress. Depending on the writer, stories can be finished when the first chapter is published, or can still be in progress. Further development will depend on the input the writer gets from her readers.

The easiest way of reacting to a story is to read it. This will be registered as a "hit" in AO3, and as a "view" in ffnet. Interestingly, ffnet does not show the number of views to potential readers, while AO3 makes it optional for the writer to display the number of hits.

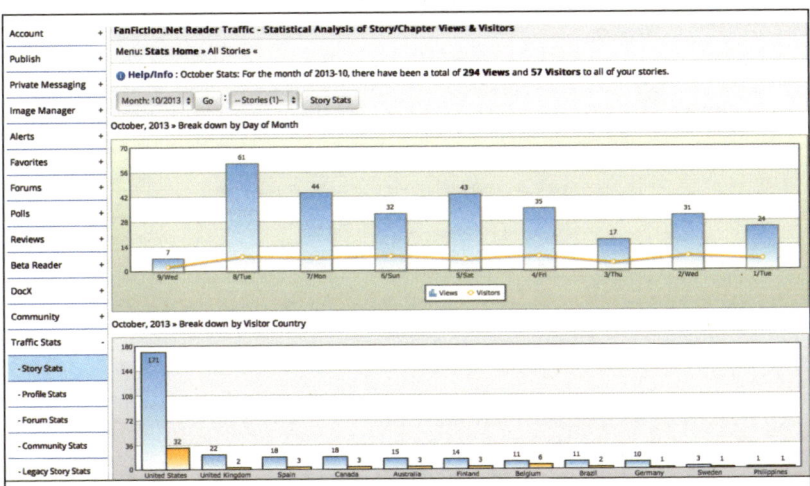

Fig. 1. ffnet – the writer's perspective

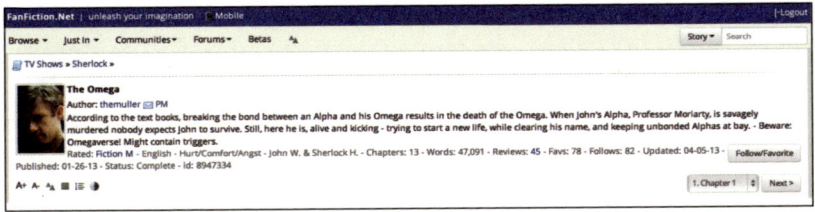

Fig. 2. ffnet – the reader's perspective

Designing for relationship

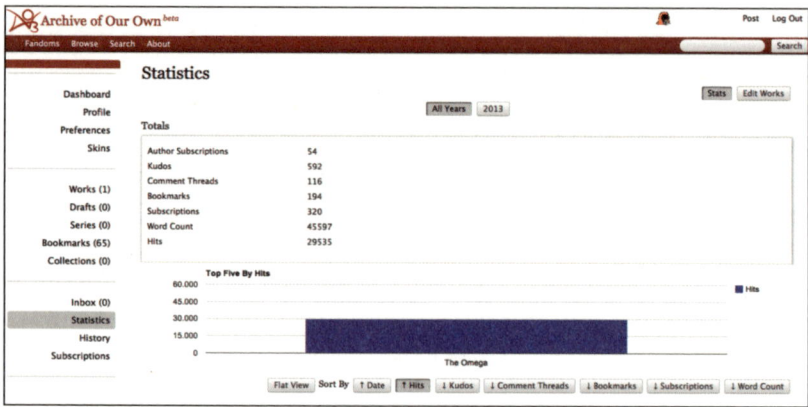

Fig. 3. AO3 – the writer's perspective

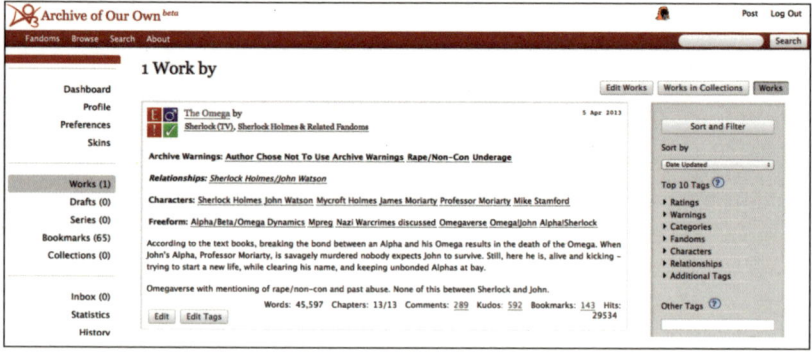

Fig. 4. AO3 – the reader's perspective

In ffnet the reader can "favs" (favourite) the story or its writer. In AO3 the reader can give "kudos" to the story. Kudos and favs (though only story favs) will be shown to potential readers. "Bookmarking" (visible either to other readers or only to the writer) is another way of reacting to a story on AO3.

"Subscription" to either story or writer on AO3 and "alerts" (as seen by the writer) or "follows" (as seen by the potential reader) on ffnet informs the subscriber or follower about updates.

Finally, the reader can "comment" on (AO3) or "review" (ffnet) the story. While the writer can answer a comment in public on AO3, a review can only be answered with a private message to the reviewer.

Thus the two media frame the writing in different ways, giving the development of a relationship between writer and reader different constraints and possibilities. Through different kinds of feedback, the writer gets instant gratification when uploading a new chapter. Normally the comments provide encouragement and positive input.

Negative criticism is often displayed by anonymous commenters, and can mostly be explained as trolling. As said above, it is extremely rare and most often admonished by other readers, who try to convince the writer to continue the story despite the trolls.

Another speciality quality of the fan fiction writing process is the beta, another reader or writer who helps a given writer with her story. A beta can help with the plotline, the characterisation, grammatical issues, or other problems. The writer sends the beta a new chapter before publishing, and the beta gives feedback on different parts of the manuscript. In this way the writer can improve her story, especially when she is a newcomer or is not a native English speaker. Furthermore, in the "Sherlock" fandom, writers can ask for a Britpicker, ensuring the story is written in British English and that the situations are authentically British. Several British writers write so-called Metas on different subjects concerning the conduct and traditions in Great Britain, i.e., how to visit a pub, how to become an army doctor.

The above examples show how supportive the community is around a given writer. Instant feedback gives the writer the needed support to continue the writing and the will to improve the story.

Writers create fan fiction for different reasons. Some write to improve their writing, hoping to become professional. Others write just to express their love for a given character, while still others use fan fiction to express a part of their talent, which might not yet be publication worthy.

The interaction differs slightly between participation on AO3 and ffnet. The threshold is low for both sides, yet AO3 gives the easiest access to supporting a writer by a reader through giving kudos. Both sites give the reader the possibility to comment. While the AO3 site makes other comments visible with one click, keeping the reader on the page of the story, ffnet gives the reader the possibility of reviewing without being able to see other reviews at the same time. Either the reviewer is on the page of the story, reviewing or reading the reviews without being able to read the story at the same time.

A writer, on the other hand, can reply to a review on ffnet solely by sending a private message (PM) to the reviewer. If she wants to reply in public, e.g., for other readers to see her reply, she has to do so in the next part of her story.

A writer on AO3 can reply in the same comments section as the reader, thus doing so in public, reinforcing the support from the reader to the writer as well as from the writer to the reader the writer acknowledges the reader by replying to the comment.

This interaction is quite interesting since the public acknowledgement of the reader through the writer enhances support from other readers. Some writers choose not to answer comments, often because they simply receive so many comments that it would take more time to answer them than to write the next part of the story.

Often this choice of not communicating is put into words by the writer, thus showing their concern for the reader and typically acknowledging the readers in a note at the end of the story. A writer might say thank you to everybody who commented, sent kudos, and the like.

Looking back at Løgstrup's life manifestations, two others stand out: mercy and the wordless appeal of nonviolence.

When a writer uploads and publishes her story, she is at the mercy of the readers. In this respect even successful writers are intimidated every single time they upload a new chapter. Here the immediate feedback through the number of hits, comments, favs, and kudos shows the writer if she has succeeded in keeping the audience interested in her story.

Every published chapter makes the writer vulnerable. The higher the stakes, the farther the fall. To explain this part of life manifestations, one can look at the term "ethos." The writer is given ethos by her audience, who tells her how interesting, riveting, or in character her story is. With a new update, this ethos is challenged. More demands more, and the wordless appeal of nonviolence, as it is described by Løgstrup, can be found in the excuses and the appeal for feedback made by the notes in the beginning or end of a chapter. The writer tries to keep her ethos, but is the vulnerable Other, who has to rely on the "I" for not hurting her through a spiteful comment.

Rules or freedom?

Ffnet is the oldest and largest fan fiction site, established in 1998 with 2.2 million users. Because of its size the site has implemented several rules and restrictions for publishing a story. Thus, it is not allowed to publish material that requires a rating of R or above. The highest permissible rating is M for "mature." The rule has been enforced several times by deleting offending material. This in turn has led to a migration of writers from ffnet to AO3, most recently in May 2012, when a large number of writers decided to use AO3 instead because the site didn't have censorship.

One of the problems with deleting stories is that the comments a writer has received also vanish.

AO3 has been open for publication of fan fiction since 2009, though in beta. AO3 is part of the Organization for Transformative Works (OTW), which not only tries to enhance possibilities for writers but for other producers of fanworks as well. OTW has several publishing sites as well as an online magazine, with among others Henry Jenkins on its board (http://transformativeworks.org).

While ffnet has strict rules about ratings and language -- even private messages are censored -- AO3 has no censorship at all. The readers chose what to read. This means that anything can be published on AO3 as long as the writer is meticulous in tagging her work. Wrong or insufficient tagging is one of the few situations that can set off flaming, simply because the reader might have some trauma that is triggered by the description of a rape or a non-con (nonconsensual sex) situation in the story. Other potentially traumatising depictions might also set off flaming.

Conversely, ffnet has a very restrictive policy on links in the stories, comments, or private messages. They are simply not allowed and ffnet will automatically remove links. The only place links can be used is in the profile description of the user.

While ffnet claims that the policy on links is used to avoid spam, the users perceive the restrictions as a way to keep the user on ffnet, not allowing any promotion from third parties. This also means that the writer is unable to link to artwork, translations, and other works in her story, even if this fan work takes its starting point from her story. This puts a severe restriction on the interaction between writer and reader when the reader becomes a producer and would like to be acknowledged for her work.

On AO3 there are no such restrictions, enabling the users to publish fan art inside a given story, to link to other stories or translations, thus acknowledging the work of their peers and nurturing the relationship between reader and writer.

Designing for relationship

As I hope I have shown above, design has an effect on how a relationship can be enhanced or restricted, depending on how the design enables interaction among the users of a given site.

Fan fiction sites may be a small part of the vast possibilities for interaction and content production on the Internet, but it is becoming interesting as a place where design directly influences the ethical behaviour of the users.

Taking into account how vulnerable a writer is when she publishes her story, every reader and designer of a fan fiction site has an obligation to assure and support her. This can be done in many ways; acknowledgement and immediate feedback are only a few of the numerous possibilities found on the above- mentioned sites.

It would be interesting to take a look at how the design and the conduct of readers and writers in fan fiction communities could be implemented in other contexts, perhaps to even enhance the composition of research articles.

References

Boyd, D., and N.B. Ellison. 2007. Social network sites: Definition, history, and scholarship. *Journal of Computer-Mediated Communication* 13 [use page numbers (1), Article 11].

Busse, K., and K. Hellekson. 2006. *Fan Fiction and Fan Communities in the Age of the Internet.* Jefferson N C: McFarland

Chayko, M. 2008. *Portable Communities: The Social Dynamics of Online and Mobile Connectedness.* Albany: State University of New York.

Guardian. 2013. http://www.guardian.co.uk/media/2013/jan/21/mary-beard-suffers-twitter-abuse?INTCMP=SRCH (Accessed 29/03/13.)

Gudiksen, S. 2013. Volunteering and user creation in communities. In *Handbook of Experience Economy*, ed. J. Sundbo and F. Sørensen, Cheltenham: Edward Elgar Publishing.

Løgstrup, K. E. 1997. *The Ethical Demand.* South Bend, IN: University of Notre Dame Press.

Pahuus, M. 1991. Holdning, spontaneitet – pædagogik, menneskesyn og værdier, Kvan.

Shitstorm. 2011. http://www.anglizismusdesjahres.de/anglizismen-des-jahres/adj-2011. (Accessed March 29, 2013.)

Wikipedia. 2013. http://en.wikipedia.org/wiki/Organization_for_Transformative_Works (Accessed March 31, 2013.)

Woledge, E. 2006. Intimatopia: Genre intersections between slash and the mainstream. In *Fan Fiction and Fan Communities in the Age of the Internet*, ed. K. Hellekson and K. Busse, Jefferson N C: McFarland.

Veselin Mitrović

The human enhancement
Toward the creation of patterns of injustice?[1]

Abstract

Transhumanism justifies the use of the new enhancement technologies, not only for the sake of treatment and disease control, but, more importantly, for the sake of enhancing and improving human capacities and traits in the transition from humanist to posthumanist society. Conversely, bioconservatives express their opposition regarding these ways of changing human beings. Representatives of the "middle approach," on the other hand, think that the constant growth of technology renders the bioconservative position untenable: once research is initiated in countries of market economy, and once its effects, such as better quality of life quality and longer life expectancy, are manifested, technology can no longer be easily obstructed.

With these ideas in mind, the language of sociological imagination poses the following question: Are developed countries ready to change their socio-economic and political structures, or is it, in fact, easier to gradually and progressively approve individual modification along with cultural complicity? Advocates of the "middle approach" point out that the challenge involves simultaneous observation of individual suffering as well as criticism and opposition to the system that creates such suffering.

---

1   I am indebted to Jörg Zeller and Marjan Ivković, a fellow sociologist and Ph.D. student at the University of Cambridge, for the commenting on a previous version of this paper. The responsibility for the content remains with the author.

Keywords: enhancement, bioconservatives, transhumanist, in-the-middle approach (the middle stream), the genetic elite, human enhancement technologies (HET)

Enhancement: social context and origin of the idea

One of the *well-known* and most contradictory definitions of enhancement is a directed use of new biotechnical power through direct intervention in order to alter the "normal" functions of the human body and psyche – not the disease processes – and to increase or improve the innate capacities and performances of the body (The President's Council on Bioethics, 2003,).

After World War II, unprecedented advances in biomedicine enabled its commercial use and application to healthy individuals. The beneficial effect of biomedicine on health protection and its use in medical treatment is considered to be one of its most valuable contributions to society.

But what happens if these scientific inventions and technology are applied to healthy people? Could we call that human enhancement?

Answers to these questions involve not only the analysis of the medical implications of the enhancement interventions, but also a debate on whether better is always good.

Thus, it is necessary to know to what extent biomedical enhancement supports or clashes with the socially accepted activities such as training, study courses, language or music lessons, talent building, immunizations, etc. Quality of life enhancement raises a number of ethical and social issues. With respect to them, enhancement could not be assumed as the opposite of therapy. The dichotomy "enhancement-therapy" is valuable in cases such as cloning and genetic engineering in general, but in other cases, such as vaccinations, it could be very seductive.

For that reason we will indicate several possible research approaches to the enhancement of healthy people: the different ideological and theoretical approaches; analysis of human enhancement technology (HET); research into the socio-epistemological implications that arise not only from scientific and laboratory work, but more often as the result of monopolization of the personal moral compass in bioethical regulatory institutions. The dominant ideological stream determines the usage and type of the biotechnology whose implications could be projected beyond objective results. Such projection could be used for perpetual justification of more hazardous procedures.

Different approaches to enhancement: Ideological and theoretical trends[2]

Transhumanists are strong advocates of human enhancement. According to Savulescu, "Not only can we enhance, we should enhance" (2007, pp. 516-517). They do not share the view that enhancement and therapy differ significantly (Bostrom and Roach 2008, p. 3). According to Savulescu, for instance, "enhancement" means helping healthy people to live a longer and/or better life than normally expected. By enhancing, the author refers to biological enhancement exclusively, with special focus on the genetic (Savulescu, pp. 516-517).

Bioconservatives accept the use of biotechnology for therapeutic purposes and find it worthy of support and public funding. However, they do not have the same view of enhancement (Bostrom and Roach 2008, p. 3). These authors share ethical concerns arising from threats to human nature and dignity (Fukuyama 2002, pp. 168-172; Kass 2000, 1996, 2007; McKibben 2003, pp. 5-6).

---

2   In addition to the three above-mentioned ideological stands of the present-day enhancement debate, we can observe a relatively new trend: so-called "moral enhancement." In the paper "The Myth of the Moral Enhancement: Back to the Future?" *Filozofija i društvo* 23 (2012): 111-123 (in Serbian) [DOI: 10.2298/FID1202111M]. I try to shed some light on the origin of the idea of moral enhancement, its epistemic and moral foundations. This requires a comparative analysis of similar ideas present in various areas of bioethics today: the analysis of the very roots of Poter's global bioethics; the idea of moral enhancement; the break between advocates of moral enhancement and John Harris, their transhumanist colleague, with whom they used to share the same perspective. In this article we identify some basic starting points, similarities, and differences between global bioethics and moral enhancement, and draw lines of demarcation between transhumanism and moral enhancement. One of the most prominent advocates of moral enhancement today is the ex-transhumanist Julian Savulescu, whose ideological path of conversion I marked as the transition "from the moral obligation to enhance (by using biotech power) ourselves and our children" (Savulescu 2007, p. 517) up to the obligation of moral enhancement (with the usage of pharmacological means: Oxicontin, Ritalin, etc.) of the dangerous people (i.e., the people who could misuse biotech power) (Persson; Savulescu 2011). This insight, which has contributed to the transformation of Savulescu's theoretical position, and which could even be considered an instance of "personal moral enhancement," could be of great significance for a deeper understanding of the concept of moral enhancement in general.

The in-the-middle approach argues that the danger lies in the dialectical relationship between "capitalism and medicine." The authors of this trend perceive access to and the application of biotechnology as instruments for securing a better social position in a given society. Advocates of this trend argue that constant technological development renders the bioconservative position untenable.

According to them, once research is initiated in countries with market economy, and once its effects, such as better quality of life and longer life expectancy are manifested, this process can no longer be obstructed easily (Bogdanović 2010, pp. 73-74; Elliott 1998; Parens 1998).

Human enhancement technologies (HET)

HET involves the use of medicine, surgery, and other kinds of medical technology, not only to cure or control illness, but also to enhance or improve, human capacities and characteristics (Elliott 1998). Interventions involving therapy and enhancement are not different activities. The difference lies in the health of the individuals under treatment. However, there might be differences between these interventions since their use may either alter certain functions or change the characteristics of human physiology, which changes (improves) the being as a whole.

Consequently, this leads to the establishment of new medical as well as cultural norms that are typical for the kind (Mitrović 2010). Therefore, it is necessary that research within enhancement studies and the analyses of complex issues arising from the use of HET are based on an interdisciplinary approach that includes medicine, law, philosophy, theology, and sociology, to name just a few. Four major branches of HET, referred to as "convergent technologies," include the nano-bio-info-cogno disciplines (NBIC):

a nanoscience and nanotechnology;
b biotechnology and biomedicine, including genetic engineering;
c information technology, including advanced computing and communications; and
d cognitive science, including cognitive neuroscience (Roco and Bainbridge 2002: pp. vii-ix).

Besides the NBIC typology, HET can be recognized as natural or traditional (training, music lessons, etc). There is also a typology based on the location and timing of usage. In that sense, we can differentiate between technologies that are used inside or outside the human body, technologies of periodical or eternal use (Spohrer 2002, pp. 101-117). All of these aspects intersect or overlap with each other.

Transhumanists claim that "human nature" possesses an inherited tendency towards enhancement. In that sense, they create a continuum between natural and genetic interventions. Its purpose is to justify the usage of new biotechnologies as evolutionarily more functional and leading to longer lasting changes (Bostrom and Roache 2008; Savulescu 2007, pp. 521-522; Harris 2007; Agar 2004).

On the other hand, at first glance the group of bioconservative authors makes a sharp distinction between (1) natural or traditional enhancement and (2) changes caused by biotechnological means. However, some authors (e.g., Fukuyama 2002, pp. 75-79) who take this view do not distinguish, for the most part, between the use of temporary means of enhancement (pharmacological means) and the use of genetic modifications (eternal). This kind of equalizing results in the mitigation of negative effects that could result from genetic engineering. Bioconservatives emphasize the need of saving "actual human nature" and warn us about possible nonfunctionality, which serves for them as a kind of moral discontinuation between natural and new or genetic enhancement.

The third-stream (in-the-middle) approach treats as unacceptable the use of HET, which jeopardizes the biological heterogeneity of humankind and creates insuperable social gaps. Third-streamers are convinced of the wrongness of the claim that biotechnologies use the same means as older ones. It is true that we were always striving for enhancement, but it is not true that new biotechnology means serve as the realization of old ends. Regarding that, the ethics of every particular aspect or type of HET must become a special case (Parens 1998, pp. S13-S14). It is a kind of moral distinction. Keeping in mind all the possible technological combinations, the realization of enhancement and the prolonging of human life become real and possible through small but certain steps. Such a potential situation has several social and moral implications, which we will analyze from the perspective of the in-the-middle approach.

The in-the-middle approach and HET

The issue of human enhancement as a social goal, i.e., "to be better, smarter, healthier," combined with the biomedical approach to healing, can easily blur the boundaries between the value of social and health care on the one hand, and the goal of enhancing healthy people on the other. It is important to remember that many health conditions, which are nowadays considered illnesses, used to be simply aspects of human life before biotechnological development. The in-the-middle-approach supports ideas such as gene therapy for cystic fibrosis. However, it discourages people from experimenting with genetics in order to intervene in personality, intelligence, or physical appearance. The advocates of this stream argue that genetic engineering may lead eventually to the destruction of the biological and cultural heterogeneity of humankind, society, and the biosphere. It is not uncommon that certain disagreeable personality traits are referred to as illnesses, even those that are not very negative. For instance, ethical and psychiatric literature increasingly discusses shyness as if it were a kind of mental disability (Elliot 1998).

Keeping in mind the above-mentioned technological divisions, it is clear that the ethics of enhancement depend to a great extent on the type of technologies used (their functionality, range of effect, etc.) and divisions between the natural and artificial types of HET. Sociologically speaking, the importance of the scientific and technological roles in the enhancement debate lies in the scientific (as well as in everyday) language or explanations of scientific improvements. Let us consider one of Deegan's comments on that topic: "The explanatory choice between genetic determinism and environmental determinism is a false dichotomy. There are times when a powerful genetic prediction is possible; carrying the gene for Huntington's disease, for example, strongly predicts that the disease will ultimately appear. Even here, however there are large variations in severity and age of onset. Most diseases lie far from this polar extreme and general characteristic such as intelligence and athleticism farther still. The point is not that genes don't matter for such characteristics, or that science will never find "genes for" them, but rather that the relative power of the genetic explanation should not be projected from the case of Huntington's, where it is high, to the case of alcoholism or schizophrenia or, worse still, to criminal proclivity or intelligence" (Deegan 1995, p. 253).

This example is a motive for the research of "ideological" usage of the scientific facts: the creation of patterns of injustice. In the following pages we will try to explore such usage through a kind of epistemological clinch. Using this clinch situation, we will try to describe the landscape of the contemporary enhancement debate as well as the necessity of an alternative approach to it.

Epistemological reductionism

Despite the ideological and the theoretical differences, all three streams clinched with regard to one of the most important social aspects of enhancement: social division.

According to the bioconservative position (as well as some of in-the-middle-approach authors), these biomedical interventions and unequal access to biotechnologies lead to a genetically divided society (two classes: Natural and GenRich.)[3] Within these social divisions, transhumanist ideas follow two directions.

The first direction supports the idea that such class dichotomy is not a special or new ethical case: "We must remember that nature allots advantage and disadvantage with no gesture to fairness. Some are born horribly disadvantaged, destined to die after short and miserable lives. Some suffer great genetic disadvantage while others are born gifted, physically, musically, or intellectually. There is no secret that there are 'gifted' children naturally. Allowing choice to change our biology will, if anything, be more egalitarian, allowing the ungifted to approach the gifted. There is nothing fair about the natural lottery: allowing enhancement may be fairer" (Savulescu 2007, p. 530).

The second direction within the transhumanist position is Nicholas Agar's techno-optimistic idea of innovation and diffusion. The innovation of enhancement technologies tends towards greater polarization of

---

3 See in: Lee Silver 1998. *It's not the meek who will inherit*, http://www.timeshighereducation.co.uk/story.asp?storycode=105415 Accessed October 10, 2012.
One scenario that has been envisaged is the idea of human society divided between the "gene enriched" and the "naturals". Some people have the resources to exploit all aspects of technology to improve their lives, while others are left to live and breed naturally. Lee Silver believes that although such a dystopia is not imminent, it is plausible and could eventually lead to two species of humans. "If the accumulation of genetic knowledge and advances in genetic enhancement technology continue at the present rate," Silver says, "then by the end of the third millennium, the GenRich class and the natural class will become the GenRich humans and the Natural humans – entirely separate species with no ability to cross breed and with as much romantic interest in each other as a current human would have for a chimpanzee".

society, but the process of diffusion of these technologies points in the opposite direction, promoting their spread (Agar 2004, p. 140).

The middle stream focuses on the fact that we are faced with the actual problem of an unequal allocation of social power, which is even more problematic if one has in mind the availability of biotechnologies to powerful social groups, that is, their substantially greater purchasing power of "genetic material." Those who have economic resources already will readily gain access to new technologies, and these new technologies, in turn, make them stronger competitors for more resources. Those who had access to technology would, as a result of their newfound productivity, win more resources. Those without resources to purchase new technology would be that much farther behind. "Parenthetically, we should note that it is logically possible that all members of our society might gain access to the same technology, thereby providing no competitive or positional advantage to anyone" (Parens 1998).

I argued that the problems related to this idea (which is common to all three streams) are rooted in bio (class) reductionism. In the following debate I will explain this problem from the perspective of the most correctly comprehending possibilities (the above described middle stream or Parens' case) of social power acquirement. Considering Potter's classification of surviving types,[4] as well as Murray's note on the distinction between enhanced persons and people who make profit from developing, possessing, and selling enhancement products or interventions, it seems that Parens overlooks the contingency of this process. As a result, I try to make fine sociological distinctions between GenRich and Naturals.

Following Parens' idea (a similar argument can be found in Fukuyama 2002), in the context of the competitive character of developed socie-

---

4   See Van Rensselaer Potter, Lisa Potter "Global Bioethics: Converting Sustainable Development to Global Survival," in *Medicine and Global Survival*, www.asmalldoseof.org/people/Potter.global.bioethics, *1995:* "Millions of people in various parts of the world and within each country are presently surviving in categories described as "mere," "miserable," "idealistic," "irresponsible," and "acceptable." The term "acceptable survival" is proposed as a bioethical goal of global survival, looking beyond the twenty-first century to the year 3000 and beyond. The frequently used alternative term is "sustainable development," but in most contexts this is an economic concept and does not imply any moral or ethical constraints, except where these are spelled out. Acceptable survival, broadly defined, means acceptable to a universal sense of what is morally right and good and what will continue in the long term. The expanding dominant, but irresponsible, world culture is not an acceptable type of development because it cannot survive in the long term."

ties, a sociological analysis of social mobility could suppose that the socio-economically stronger groups should be directly classified as a potentially genetically superior class. Those who do not have enough socio-economic power will lose their standing within the social hierarchy by staying in a "natural" condition (Parens, 1998). But this claim is not completely true. The existence of two bioclasses is not the cause behind the creation of future society, but its logical consequence. So the analysis of this type of society depends on the grade and manner of the use of biotechnology. With respect to this, such an analysis could be done on the basis of social status as well as using the power elite approach.

The variables that are important for such an analysis are: the level of the economic and technological development of society; social layers or classes involved in socio-technological reproduction; the particular technology that is used (reversible or irreversible effect, outside or inside the body), etc. Therefore, this claim is perhaps most effectively presented through an intersection between Wright Mills' *The Power Elite*[5] and M. Foucault's concept of "contractor" or user [6] in *The Birth of the Clinic*.

Following this perspective, a group with a better structural position has the power to impose new social and medical norms. We suppose, also, that the very same group has the power to finance and create new techniques and technology, which provides them with certain biotechnological power. But biotechnological power does not yet mean the genetic superiority of the class that creates such power. In order to capitalize biotech power, groups of people who are educated for the usage of biotechnology are needed. That group is a class of specialists who will try to secure a greater share of power. In the process, they not only publicize the procedure but also experiment with more powerful and riskier

---

5 W.C. Mills 1956, *The Power Elite* (New York: Oxford University Press, p. 3-4). "The power elite is composed of men whose positions enable them to transcend the ordinary environments of ordinary men and women; they are in positions to make decisions having major consequences. Whether they do or do not make such decisions is less important than the fact that they do occupy such pivotal positions: their failure to act, their failure to make decisions, is itself an act that is often of greater consequence than the decisions they do make. They are in command of the major hierarchies and organizations of modern society. They rule the big corporations. They run the machinery of the state and claim its prerogatives. They direct the military establishment. They occupy the strategic command posts of the social structure, in which are now centered the effective means of the power and the wealth and the celebrity which they enjoy."
6 I prefer the term 'user' in place of Foucault's concept of "contractor."

The human enhancement

techniques. There are also groups of socio-economically lower classes who represent a potential experimental group whose safety is compromised although they (the patients) may be the last ones to know this (Murray 2007, p. 500). And last but not least, there is the group that should justify such interventions – a class of bioethicists (Elliot 2007, pp. 45-46). We must have in mind that the middle group (the proletarians from Marx's earlier class dichotomy), is, in this case, the one that does not possess biotechnology. Foucault's idea in *The Birth of the Clinic* gives a certain dynamic to such a class constellation. In a free-market society, the clinic discovers the possibility of stimulating, in a group of rich men, investment in medical research. The clinic establishes a gradual payoff for the other contractor – a payoff which, from the perspective of the pauper, is actually interest paid for the clinical capitalization that the rich man had in fact approved; this interest has to be understood in all its complexity, as we are actually referring here to a compensation that is part of an objective interest in science and of an existential interest of the rich man (Foucault 1994, p. 87).

This implies that it is possible to identify several strata in the "enhanced society." Today there already exist big biomedical magnates (e.g., Geron, PPL-Therapeutics) who possess biotech resources. Therefore, in the context of new biotech research, we can recognize a stratum of specialists who, because of their professional skills, have a particular social position. After all, there are ambivalent, structurally intermediate classes, who are neither GenRich nor Naturals. Today we already know of such strata: "transgenetic organisms created for xenotransplantation" (Cohen 2002,); "babies with DNA from two mothers" where cytoplasm is transplanted from a healthy woman to a second woman whose ovum has sick cytoplasm (Frankel 2003); children with surgically created anatomical traits (Ouellete 2009). On the other hand, genetically engineered organisms would represent a transition from an ambivalent to an unambiguous class of genetically enhanced men. Only through a dialectical relation of the mentioned socio-technological process with all the transitional strata is it possible to realize a transition from the economic to the "genompital," genome- based capital.

This dynamic might remind us of Agar's idea of the diffusion of technology to the lower social layers, but at the same time it raises the question about the nature and range of such diffusion. From a sociological perspective, it is the question of the structure and function of such processes. As we already described, the structure of "diffusion" represents an expansion of the prior biomedical effects toward an experimentation phase. The real advantage stays in the higher circles, gradually moving from an economic compensation for the specialists, through the objective interest ("knowledge") for science, to the final and accident-free genetic enhancement for its sponsors.

This process is provided with the help of cultural complicity, including the special role of the class of bioethicists, in which their community spots the partial interests that are determined with the possession of social power. It is obvious that so-called "Agar's diffusion" cannot be assumed as a type of cultural diffusion, but rather as cultural-technological hegemony.

How then do we operate with enhancement?[7]

1 Enhancement as moral boundary
   Enhancement is often used to delineate moral boundaries within the realm of biomedicine: enhancement is contrasted with "medically indicated" treatment. Health professionals might find enhancement to be a useful boundary marker that sets off the actions which health professionals are not ethically obligated to do – namely, enhancements – from those that they are required to do out of professional and moral obligations to patients, i.e., therapeutic interventions.

   The public and private institutions that pay for health care may use enhancement as a boundary. Enhancement helps set boundaries on biomedical research. What risks to humans subject to research are acceptable if there are no health benefits in the offing?

   Thus enhancement leads us out of the field of medicine and towards the wide range of goals, values, and social institutions.

2 Enhancement as moral signpost
   Recognizing enhancement as a signpost does not settle moral questions. On the contrary, it warns us that important values might be at stake. Parents regularly seek nonbiomedical means of enhancement for their children such as language or music lessons. However, what if

---

7   I borrow the subtitles Enhancement as Moral Boundary and Enhancement as Moral Signpost, from Thomas Murray 2007, p. 491-516.

the means are biomedical and the goals not related to health? Certain "enhancements," such as education, development of moral virtues, or immunization against infectious diseases, are not only good but might become an important moral obligation of the adults towards children.

Naming something an enhancement tells us little about our moral attitude towards the intervention and what it should involve. The task is more difficult and therefore more interesting: to base our moral judgments on the understanding of the goods sought and the values prized in the sphere of human practices at issue (Murray 2007, p. 493-495).

3 Enhancement as valued human practice?
The goodness of any particular enhancement depends first of all on the goodness of the goal to which it is directed. As we think about biomedical interventions as enhancements, we must bear in mind that similar ends may be reached by quite different means. For that purpose we differentiate the end, means, and intermediary state.

Social and Ethical Implications

1 The principle of beneficence and social values: Relativization of a child's talents and their variety
If we argue that "enhancement as a social goal" is a problematic issue, we have to show that certain interventions violate important social goals or values. For example, the increasing use of human growth hormone (HGH) sends the message that height is a very important personal trait. The same resources might be used to promote and develop a child's talents – and to ensure that the child does not "come up short" – in music, intellectual achievement, inventions, creativity, art, and any other human activity.

2 Technological perfection and the principle of autonomy
Is the increasing technological efficiency in selecting a child's characteristics one result of free choice or an open door to tyranny? This issue is related to the neutrality of technologies. The technique that was originally created to help people screen out certain characteristics has developed in a different direction: it enables people to import, to screen in, desirable characteristics.

But where does one draw the line? Should we screen out for short stature or screen in for eye color? (Frankel 2003, p. 35). Decisions to use medicine or surgery to shape a child based on a parent's social, cultural, or aesthetic preferences – especially those that limit the child's ability to make significant choices central to his or her identity -- would be given more attention (Ouellette 2009, p. 18).

Enhancement: Cultural complicity with unjust norms

Sometimes a supposed enhancement becomes complicit in and reinforces unjust norms. Complicity exists "when one endorses, promotes, or unduly benefits from norms and practices that are morally suspect" (Little 1998, p. 170). If we want to map out the terrain for the future regulative procedures, it is necessary that we move from the field of parents' preferences about the characteristics of their children ("temptation to tyranny") toward a higher level of abstraction, where relations among regulatory institution and users of enhancement will become visible. This relation is a "tyranny of expertise," which, according to Carl Elliot, is the monopolization of personal moral compasses (Elliot 2007, p. 44). The danger of this "tyranny" is reflected in the fact that, instead of looking inward to an internal moral compass, we are beginning to look outward to figures who derive their moral authority from a special kind of training.

To gain a better comprehending of Elliot's approach to enhancement, it is necessary to look at his critique of bioethics as a new profession, the characteristic of which is to penetrate into bureaucratic structures (Elliot 2007, p. 45). But many bioethicists insist that they are not moral experts and that they claim no special authority.

From the perspective of Wright Mills' *Sociological Imagination* and *The Power Elite*, what bioethicists fail to understand is that the real issue is not what skills and knowledge they claim to have. It is the position of authority that they have been given, usually by virtue of their place in a particular bureaucracy.

If an ethicist occupies an important position in a hospital, pharmaceutical company, professional body, or regulatory organization such that their ethical judgments carry more weight than those of other people -- people who do not have the same training and bureaucratic status -- they already have a kind of expertise and social authority, no matter what their claim (Ibid.).

Such bioethicists do not recognize their own social role as professionals.[8] They hide behind the statement that they do not possess a certain power of moral expertise, yet they happily occupy the expert's chair on the television news, regulatory body, presidential commissions, and the like.

Experts serve a useful social purpose. Many bioethicists have struggled for recognition because they believe that expertise is the route to social change. But when a particular group becomes genuinely established as experts (as socially acknowledged professions), their expertise becomes important, not because of their credentials and skills, but because of their links to the dominant structure, such as industry, government, and or a professional body (Elliot 2007, p. 46). Having that in mind, Elliot asks the question whether we really want a professional class of bioethics experts. Some people, whether because of ideological trends or other reasons, clearly do. But bioethics experts bring with them a particular kind of danger (Ibid).

First of all, the danger concerns questions of individual autonomy and social justice. It is a matter of moral conformity and the loss of individual sovereignty and personal integrity. It is also a matter of serving the dominant power structure rather than serving those who are subject to that power. Another kind of danger comes from the potential (mis)use of biotechnology for purposes that surpass the original scope of indications, which, on the grounds of such bioethical expertise, could be the enhancement of certain types of social behavior. But the final danger here is that bioethicists will set up an invisible

---

[8] See for example the old and well-known division of the horizontal and vertical role of professionals as described in K. Nadir 1969. "Technical Experts in Developing Countries," (in: Nader, C. and Zahlan, A.B. eds. 1969. *Science and Technology in Developing Countries*, Cambridge: Cambridge University Press, 1969, p. 462). Nadir emphasizes that "the role of professionals is not just the role of researchers, but also includes the role of administrators, technical advisers, teachers, public representatives, technological innovators and developers seeing through the main functional sectors of society. The role must correspond to the horizontal dimension – for scientific ends, as well as in vertical aspect – for the achievement of socials goals (positioning science in society). Professionals could, through different social functions, make their own activities more visible. Such activities are important for creativity and vital benefits, and are especially important for the stimulation of scientific activities to achieve social progress. In short, even if experts are not fully engaged in scientific work, but act only as administrators, managers or bureaucrats more generally, they should, in light of their educational background, still strive to display high standards of ethical reasoning in the public sphere.

barrier between you and your own moral life. Unless you pay the consultation fee, access will be denied (Ibid).

Conclusion

Having in mind the epistemological clinch and the ideological usage of the objective range and result of biomedical technologies, I recommend the constant analysis of the epistemological basis of moral premises.

Whatever one thinks about the moral obligations of professionals and those who seek their services in the quest for enhancement, it is important to acknowledge that when professionals give in to patients' pleas for enhancement, unjust norms may be strengthened, no matter how honorable and compassionate one's intentions may be (Murray 2007, p. 512).

But how then could we solve the problem of losing personal moral orientation? One of the possible solutions could be described in A. Buchanan's explanation.[9] He says that the meaning of such moral orienteering is a process by which individuals come to have and sustain such beliefs as social: "They learn them, and they learn to disregard evidence that conflicts with them, through the operation of various social practices and institutions" (2007, p. 289). While Elliot underlines the danger arising from the pact between bioethicists and bureaucratic structures, Buchanan analyzes bioethics as an epistemological institution, which is partially dependent on the range and type of the bioethicists' social role.

That perspective raises the question: are bioethicists (themselves) an influential institution, or do institutions influence them? How well bioethicists perform their role in the division of epistemic labor will depend upon the epistemic feature of the institutions within which they function (Buchanan 2007, p. 294).

---

9   See L. A. Eckenwiller and F. G. Cohn 2007. *The Ethics of Bioethics: Mapping the Moral Landscape*, Baltimore: The Johns Hopkins University Press, p. 288-297.

References

Agar, N. 2004. *Liberal Eugenics – In Defence of Human Enhancement*, Oxford: Blackwell Publishing.

Bogdanović, M. 2010. Vreme nade i rizika, tržišno zasnovana genetika. *Sociologija* 52: 49-77.

Bostrom, N., and Roache R. 2008. Ethical issues in human enhancement. In: Ryberg, J., Petersen, T. and Wolf, C. eds. 2008. *New Waves in Applied Ethics*, Palgrave: Macmillan. Online at http://www.nickbostrom.com/ethics/human-enhancement.pdf.

Buchanan, A. 2007. Social moral epistemology and the role of bioethicists. In *The Ethics of Bioethics: Mapping The Moral Landscape*, ed. A. L. Eckenwiler A and F. G. Cohn, 288-97. Baltimore: Johns Hopkins University Press.

Cohen, P. 2002. This little piggy had none. *New Scientist* 173: 7.

Deegan Cook, R. 1995. *The Gene Wars: Science, Politics and the Human Genome*. New York and London: Norton and Company.

Elliott, C. 2007. The Tyranny of Expertise. In *The Ethics of Bioethics: Mapping The Moral Landscape*, ed. A. L. Eckenwiler A and F. G. Cohn, 43-77. Baltimore: Johns Hopkins University Press.

_____. 1998. What's wrong with enhancement technologies? *CHIPS Public Lecture*. Center for Bioethics. University of Minnesota, February 26.

Eckenwiler A. Lisa, Cohn G. Felicia, 2007, *The Ethics of Bioethics: Mapping The Moral Landscape*, Baltimore: The Johns Hopkins Univesity Press, p. 43-47.

Foucault, M. 1994. *The Birth of the Clinic: An Archaeology of Medical Perception*. New York: Vintage Books.

Frankel, S. M. 2003. Inheritable genetic modification and a brave new world: Did Huxley have it wrong? *The Hastings Center Report* 33: 2.

Fukuyama, F. 2002. *Our Posthuman Future: Consequences of the Biotechnology Revolution*. New York: Straus and Giroux.

Harris, J. 2007. *Enhancing Evolution-The Ethical Case for Making Better People*
Princeton: Princeton University Press.

Kass, R. L. 1996. Can nature serve as a moral guide? *The Hastings Center Report* 26: 21-24.

_____. 2000. The moral meaning of genetic technology. *Human Life Review* 26: 76-87.

_____. 2007. Defending human dignity. *Social Science Journals* 124: 57.

Little, M.O. 1998. Cosmetic surgery, suspect norms, and the ethics of complicity. In *Enhancing Human Traits: Ethical and Social Implications*, ed. E. Parens, 162–75. Washington, DC: Georgetown University Press.

McKibben, B. 2003. *Enough: Staying Human in an Engineered Age*. New York: Times Books.

Mills, W.C. 1956. *The Power Elite*. New York: Oxford University Press.

Mitrović, V. 2010. Argumenti *za* i *protiv* 'poboljšanja' ljudskih bića genetskom intervencijom. *Sociologija* 52: 75-96. [??, br. 1, Mart 2010, Filozofski fakultet, ISI, Beograd, DOI: 10.2298/SOC1001075M, str. 75-96.

_____. 2012. Mit o moralnom poboljšanju: povratak u budućnost? *Filozofija i društvo* 23: 111-23. Institut za filozofiju i društvenu teoriju, DOI:10.2298/FID1202111M, str. 111-123.]

Murray, H. T. 2007. Enhancement. In *The Oxford Handbook of Bioethics*, ed. B. Steinbock, Bonnie, 491-516. Oxford: Oxford University Press.

Ouellette, A. 2009. Eyes wide open: Surgery to westernize the eyes of an Asian child. *The Hastings Center Report* 39: 15.

Parens, E. 1998. Special Supplement: Is Better Always Good? The Enhancement Project. *The Hastings Center Report* 28: S1-17. (Accessed on jstor-3527981.)

Persson, I., and Savulescu, J. 2011. Unfit for the future? Human nature, scientific progress, and the need for moral enhancement. In: Savulescu, J. ter Meulen, R.and Kahane, G. eds. 2011. *Enhancing Human Capacities*, Chichester: Blackwell Publishing Ltd., p. 632-51.

Potter, V. R., and Potter, L. 1995. Global bioethics: Converting sustainable development to global survival. *Medicine & Global Survival* 2: p. 185-91.

The President's Council on Bioethics 2003. *Beyond Therapy: Biotechnology and the Pursuit of Happiness*. Online at http://bioethics.georgetown.edu/pcbe/reports/beyondtherapy/index.html.

Savulescu, J. 2009. Genetic interventions and the ethics of enhancement of human being. In: Steinbock, B. ed. 2009. *The Oxford Handbook of Bioethics*, Oxford: Oxford University Press, p. 516-536.

Spohrer, J. 2002. Nano-, bio-, info-, cogno-, socio-convergence to improve human performance: Opportunities and challenges. In: Bainbridge, W.S. and Roco, M. eds. 2002. *Converging Technologies for Improving of Human Performance: Nanotechnology, Biotechnology, Information technology and Cognitive Science*, Arlington, VA: National Science Foundation, p. 101-17.

List of authors

Brenda Almond is Emeritus Professor of Moral and Social Philosophy and an Associate of the Institute of Applied Ethics at the University of Hull in the UK. She has published widely in the field of philosophy, especially moral philosophy and was co-founder of the Journal of Applied Philosophy. Her books include *The Philosophical Quest*; *Exploring Ethics: a traveller's tale*; and *The Fragmenting Family* (2008), a book which challenges the social constructivist ideology of the family. She has served on the Human Fertilisation and Embryology Authority and on the Human Genetics Commission in the UK and is an elected foreign member of the Austrian Academy of Sciences.

Finn Arler. MA (Philosophy, Aarhus University), Ph.d. (Aarhus University), Dr.scient. (Faculty of Science and Technology, Aalborg University). Associate professor in Human Ecology and Sustainability at Department of Planning, and head of Centre for Applied Ethics, Aalborg University. His main interests include ethics, politics, science and planning in relation to sustainability, nature and the environment, particularly in areas like biodiversity, landscape, energy, greenhouse effect, justice and equity, democracy, and economics. Has published a large number of articles, and written or edited several books, including: *Kulturlig økologi* (1992), *Omkring dømmekraften. Essays om videnskab, etik og natur* (ph.d.-thesis 1992), *Miljø og etik* (1997), *Cross-Cultural Protection of Nature and the Environment* (1997), *Humanøkologi. Miljø, teknologi og samfund* (2002 and 2006), *Biodiversitet. Videnskab Kultur Etik, vol. I-II* (doctoral dissertation 2009), and *Bæredygtighed. Værdier, regler og metoder* (forthcoming).

Anne Gerdes is an Associate Professor at University of Southern Denmark, Department of Design and Communication, where she teaches courses on ICT-ethics and value based design. She is a member of the steering committee of ETHICOMP and leader of the Danish Research Network on IT-ethics. Her research interests include ethical issues in relation to AI, cyborg technology, embodied technology, privacy and national security, online radicalization and persuasive technology.

Thessa Jensen, ph.d., associate professor, Interactive Digital Media, Institute for Communication and Psychology, Aalborg University. My research area at the time being is social media, mainly focussing on fan fiction. The ethics involved, possibilities for interaction, creativity, and co-creation of products and services on the internet.

Tito Magri is Professor of Philosophy at Sapienza University, Rome. He has done work in political philosophy, in ethics and rational choice, and in action theory.

Michael Kühler currently works as Visiting Professor for Practical Philosophy in Bern, Switzerland, and as Senior Research Fellow at the Centre for Advanced Study in Bioethics at the University of Münster, Germany. His areas of specialization include ethics, metaethics, political philosophy, and the philosophy of love. He has recently published a monograph on the relationship between "ought" and "can" (Sollen ohne Können?, Münster: mentis, 2013) and co-edited a special issue of Ethical Theory and Moral Practice (Private Autonomy, Public Paternalism?, forthcoming) as well as the volume Autonomy and the Self, Dordrecht: Springer, 2013.

Terje Mesel, PhD, is associate professor in ethics at the institute of philosophy, religion and history at Agder University, and senior researcher at Sørlandet Hospital, Kristiansand, Norway. Mesel has published several books and articles within the fields of professional ethics and medical ethics. Earlier this year he co-edited the book "Makt og avmakt. Etiske perspektiver på feltet psykisk helse"(2013). By winter 2014 he will publish a monograph with the title "When things go wrong. Stories of guilt, shame and responsibility in health care".

Veselin Mitrović is a research associate of the Department of Sociology, Faculty of Philosophy, at the University of Belgrade. He is working in the project of the Serbian Ministry of Education and Science, "The Challenges of the new social integration: Concepts and Agents". Within the framework of this project he is examining the "Artificial reproduction technologies and the Social and Procreative Altruism in Serbia." Mitrović is inter alia author of *The Stride of Bioethics, New Bio-Technologies and Social Aspects of the 'Enhancement' of the Healthy* (2012) and *Jazz as a sociocultural improvisation – The qualitative research of the social mobility* (2012), both in Serbian.

Lennart Nørreklit is Doctor in philosophy and professor emeritus. Creator of actor and reality construction theories and pragmatic constructivism as well as ethical philosophy on love and reasons to live. Contribution in methodology, including concept analysis and -construction, logic as well as the usage of dialogue in methodology. Founder of philosophy studies at Aalborg University. The philosophical inspiration of the international interdisciplinary research group on actor reality construction.

Hannes Nykänen is adjunct professor of philosophy at Åbo Akademi University and university researcher at University of Helsinki. He is the author of *The 'I', the 'You' and the Soul. An Ethics of Conscience*, Öppningar och labyrinter, *Samvetet och det dolda*, "Conscience and Collective Pressure" and "Heidegger's Conscience".

Mogens Pahuus, prof. emeritus, Institute of Learning and Philosophy, Aalborg University. He has written about philosophical anthropology, ethics, aesthetics and existential questions in literature.

Ole Preben Riis, professor in sociology of religion at University of Agder, Norway, appointed to PhD-school of Religion, Values and Society. Has studied social values, philosophy of science and humanities, methodology and sociology of religion. Recent publications: A Sociology of Religious Emotion (2010) with Woodhead, Lancaster. Latest: Åbne Vinduer (2012).

Patrik Kjærsdam Telléus (1974), Ph.D., assistant professor in Applied Philosophy at Aalborg University. In his Ph.D. thesis, he explored the idea of conceptual deliberation as central to the understanding and praxis of applied ethics. Patrik's research focuses on Wittgenstein and Ordinary Language Philosophy, and applies this philosophical position to areas within e.g. bioethics and medical ethics, as well as questions concerning university pedagogy.

Jörg Zeller, assoc. prof., Institute of Learning and Philosophy, at Aalborg University. He has written about philosophy of language and science, semiotics, ethics, and philosophical method. The last few years the focus of his research is on the logic of practice and the construction of reality.